In Recovery

The Making of
Mental Health Policy

IN RECOVERY
THE MAKING OF
MENTAL HEALTH POLICY

NORA JACOBSON

VANDERBILT UNIVERSITY PRESS

NASHVILLE

Published by Vanderbilt University Press
First Edition 2004

This book is printed on acid-free paper.
Manufactured in the United States of America
Designed by Dariel Mayer

Library of Congress Cataloging-in-Publication Data

Jacobson, Nora, 1964–
In recovery : the making of mental health policy /
      Nora Jacobson.—1st ed.
      p. ; cm.
Includes bibliographical references and index.
ISBN 0-8265-1454-5 (cloth : alk. paper)
ISBN 0-8265-1455-3 (pbk. : alk. paper)
      1. Community mental health services—Wisconsin. 2. Medical
policy—Wisconsin. [DNLM: 1. Community Mental Health
Services—organization & administration—Wisconsin. 2. Health
Policy—Wisconsin. 3. Mental Disorders—rehabilitation—Wisconsin.
WM 30.6 J17r 2004]
I. Title.
RA790.65.W6J33 2004
362.2'2'09775—dc22   2003025103

CONTENTS

Acknowledgments

I can't decide whether the need to write acknowledgments arises at the worst possible time or at the best. It follows weeks devoted to revision—perhaps the most discouraging period in authorship, when the writer faces the growing certainty that the whole book is trite and stupid and therefore is not feeling grateful for much. On the other hand, writing acknowledgments interrupts that isolated disgruntlement, forcing recognition of the generosity of others.

For suggesting that I focus my postdoctoral research on some element of the Wisconsin system redesign, I want to recognize Joy Perkins Newmann, the director of the Mental Health Services Research Training Program at the University of Wisconsin while I was a fellow there. My two fellowship years (the first two years of research on this project) were supported by the National Institute of Mental Health, NIMH grant #5T32MH14641, and by Vivian Littlefield, dean of the university's School of Nursing.

For their help in developing the analytic framework that structured my approach to much of the material in this book, I thank the members of the Bowers Data Analysis Group at the School of Nursing during the period 1997–2001: Barb Bowers, Soon-Yi Baik, Chris Baker, Mary Canales, Chantal Caron, Sarah Esmond, Barb Lutz, Sally Norton, and Brenda Ryther. I also thank Kristy Ashleman and Patti Herman, members of a smaller research group of which I was also a part. All of them, particularly Barb Bowers, have given me the tools to think like an interpretive researcher.

For reading all or parts of the manuscript and making many helpful suggestions, I am grateful to Jason Altenberg, Kristy Ashleman, Amber Ault, Chris Baker, Paula Goering, Salinda Horgan, Dolly Jacobson, and Jennifer Poole. The two anonymous reviewers who vetted the manuscript for Vanderbilt University Press provided thoughtful criticism that allowed me to deepen and strengthen my analysis. In a short exchange at a public event, Ken Schlosser pushed me to consider several issues that I otherwise might have ignored.

For valuing this project and allowing me the time to do this work, I am exceedingly grateful to Paula Goering, director of the Health Systems Research and Consulting Unit at the Centre for Addiction and Mental Health. Elizabeth Ben-Ishai, a summer student on the unit, gave me much-needed assistance with many details.

For their continuing support and their humor, I recognize my parents, Dolly and Harvey Jacobson.

For the custom quilt pictured on the cover of this book, I thank Shira Spector of Red Velvet Cake in Toronto.

For directing me to Michael Ames and Vanderbilt University Press, I am grateful to Robert Zussman. For understanding what I was trying to do (when no other publisher did) and accepting the manuscript, I thank Michael Ames. For their work on the production of the book, I want to recognize Dariel Mayer, George Roupe, and Anne Bower.

Finally, and most of all, for their hard work and commitment and their willingness to share it all with me, I must acknowledge the members of the State of Wisconsin's Recovery and Consumer-Family Involvement Workgroup and the Recovery Implementation Task Force. They remain anonymous here, but I thank each of them for their contributions.

INTRODUCTION

A RESEARCH MEMOIR

The dinosaur, a stylized stegosaurus, made a grand entrance onto the stage of the Great Hall in the University of Wisconsin's Memorial Union. Fashioned from dense blocks of jigsaw-cut blue foam, it measured perhaps fifteen feet from tail to nose.

It was late one morning in May 1999, the first day of a two-day workshop called "The Next Step: Recovery," which had brought together Wisconsin mental health service recipients and providers to engage four questions: What is recovery? How might the system change to embrace recovery? How might you change to embrace recovery in your own life? What might recovery look like/feel like in your life/work? Together, the workshop attendees had spent several hours listening to speakers, talking in small groups, and taking part in wide-ranging open-microphone discussions about the implications of recovery for personal and social transformation.

Now, the Bones to Bridges Collective, the group that had created the dinosaur, took the stage for its unveiling. The blue dinosaur represented the old mental health system, members of the collective told the audience, whose extinction we are here to hasten. The collective invited people to write down their grievances against that system—the indignities endured, the harms suffered—and then to come up on stage to attach them to the dinosaur's body. Soon, small scraps of white paper obscured the blue.

The dinosaur stood for the rest of the day and overnight and throughout the next morning. On the second afternoon, after more presentations and discussions, the collective came back onstage. As music played and the audience watched, members of the collective moved together in a rehearsed choreography to shift a few jigsaw pieces and prop up several sheets of painted plywood. Then they retreated. The spiny arc of the dinosaur's back had become the span of a bridge, a path into the transformed future.

The word *recovery* occurs frequently both in ordinary conversation and in professional discourse. People speak of having recovered from a severe cold or cancer or of needing to recover from the stress of a trying week at work. Objects of value are recovered from shipwrecks. Nations recover from periods of economic downturn, communities from the physical devastation wrought by a tornado or flood. Problem drinkers describe themselves as in recovery when they become abstinent. Damaged minds are said to heal through the recovery of memories of childhood abuse. The language of recovery, then, refers both to processes of restoration and to acts of reclamation.

Beginning in the early 1990s, recovery became a stated goal of service providers and policy makers in public mental health systems across the United States. The movement to develop "recovery-oriented" service systems coincided with a fiscal imperative to apply managed care models to publicly funded services and with a social imperative to involve mental health consumers,[1] the users of services, in the development of programming and policy. Traditionally, recovery from mental illness has been thought to signify symptom abatement or return to a premorbid state, but as consumer activists, mental health professionals, and state-level policymakers have promoted recovery as a new paradigm in mental health, it has become apparent that recovery has many meanings. For some consumers, recovery refers to a phenomenology of learning to live well despite the continuing symptoms of mental illness. For others, it is explicitly political, a word that describes the attempt to wrest authority away from the state and psychiatrists and place it in the hands of "empowered" consumers. For many mental health professionals, recovery represents a rationalized approach to service provision, one that synthesizes the best practices of several extant service models. Others look upon it as a pernicious promise of "false hope." For policy makers who are also the purchasers of (managed) care, recovery has financial implications: it may either increase costs—by expanding the definition of "medical necessity"—or control costs by justifying the termination of services once individuals have achieved certain functional goals.

This book is about the making of definitions. It is an examination of the contexts in which meanings are produced and of the material consequences of meaning. The exemplar at the center of the book is the meaning of recovery from mental illness and its role as a philosophical framework for the development of mental health policy. In the chapters to come, I will examine the many definitions of recovery, the contexts in which those definitions have been made, and their different implications for individuals, for mental health organizations and systems, and for society. While I pay closest attention to the definitions, contexts, and implications of recovery in Wisconsin, my subject of opportunity and a state with a reputation as something of an innovator in mental health services, recent attention to recovery in the U.S. public mental health system as a whole (e.g., President's New Freedom Commission on Mental Health 2003) and internationally makes this analysis broadly relevant as well.

In September 1997, I moved to Madison, Wisconsin, to begin a postdoctoral fellowship in the University of Wisconsin's Mental Health Services Research Training Program. At that time, the state was planning a major redesign of its public mental health system and, in the spirit of the "Wisconsin Idea"—or making the work of the University relevant to the community—the postdoctoral program director made clear the expectation that my research somehow be linked to this reform effort. I was given a copy of the recently released final report of the state's Blue Ribbon Commission on Mental Health (Blue Ribbon Commission 1997) and sent off to think about how I might make a contribution.

The commission's report laid out a broad plan for restructuring the system, including recommendations for adopting a capitated managed care model, expanding prevention and early intervention services, improving accountability by emphasizing consumer outcomes, and eradicating stigma and discrimination against persons served by the system.

At the center of the redesign plan was the recommendation that Wisconsin build "a recovery-oriented mental health system." In the report, "recovery" was variously described as "the successful integration of a mental disorder into a consumer's life . . . , [the ability] to let go of what was and rebuild new dreams, that is, to accept the realities of illness while focusing on LIFE" (iii) and as a "deeply personal, unique process of changing one's attitudes, values, feelings, goals, skills, and/or roles. It is a way of living a satisfying, hopeful, and contributing life even with limitations caused by illness. Recovery involves the development of new meaning and purpose in one's life as one grows beyond the catastrophic effects of mental illness" (Anthony 1993, quoted in Blue Ribbon Commission 1997, 13–14). A "recovery-oriented system," the document explained, is one that "reaches beyond the critical issues of assuring personal safety and managing symptoms and focuses on the rebuilding of full, productive lives despite a mental disorder. . . . In a recovery-oriented system, mental health consumers rebuild meaningful lives while decreasing their dependence on the system" (Blue Ribbon Commission, 14). The discussion of recovery concluded with a list of "basic recovery-oriented principles"—such as "recovery is possible," "just start anywhere," and "one must be empowered in order to empower others"—to guide in the planning of services for the new system.

The state's redesign plan provided great scope for mental health services research. I might have chosen to work on a traditional health services research topic—to study the effectiveness of different prevention strategies, for example, or to help design an instrument to assess consumer outcomes—but I found those choices less than compelling. Instead, it was the notion of recovery that intrigued me. In particular, I was struck by the multiplicity of expectations and assumptions that seemed to be embedded in the concept. That multiplicity, and the sloganeering style in which it was described, left me wondering what recovery would look like for individuals and how it would be realized in practice and in system policy.

I decided to do a study that would examine recovery. My approach, based on the theoretical tradition of symbolic interactionism (Mead 1982 [1909]; Mead 1982 [1913]; Blumer 1969; Strauss 1993; Charon 1995) and the methodological traditions of grounded theory (Glaser and Strauss 1967; Strauss 1987) and dimensional analysis (Schatzman 1991; Caron and Bowers 2000), construed recovery as a concept under construction, one being formed by multiple negotiations over meaning. That is, I began by assuming that recovery was not one thing, one reality, but many, and that what it was—and thus its implications—would change as the perspective shifted.

This was a fine social constructionist project, certainly, but I also was committed by my postdoctoral fellowship (and by a sense of obligation) to do something useful. As I spent some time going to meetings the state was holding to discuss various aspects of the proposed redesign, it became apparent to me that my own lack of certainty about recovery was not an idiosyncratic anomaly. That is, almost everyone seemed perplexed about this concept they were meant to make the centerpiece of their new system. While some people admitted to not understanding recovery, others were quite confident in their own definitions but didn't realize that these meanings were not universally endorsed. Sorting out these understandings—and linking them with specific practice and policy strategies—would in itself, I realized, be a useful contribution, a fulfillment of the "Wisconsin Idea."

The study I designed had four parts: a review of the literature on recovery; a survey of what other states were doing to implement "recovery-oriented" systems; participant observation with the workgroup charged with developing Wisconsin's recovery policy; and individual interviews with some of the workgroup members. I hoped through these different endeavors to frame and answer three kinds of questions:

- **QUESTIONS ABOUT DEFINITION**
  Who is defining recovery? What are their definitions? What social and historical factors are reflected in these definitions? Are some definitions privileged over others? How do definitions change as circumstances shift? How are the proposed strategies for implementing recovery linked to these definitions?

- **QUESTIONS ABOUT PROCESS**
  Where do negotiations over recovery take place? Who is involved? Through what processes is the meaning of recovery negotiated? What other processes go into shaping recovery implementation?

- **QUESTIONS ABOUT CONSEQUENCES**
  What does a "recovery-oriented" mental health system look
  like? How is it different from the current system? Who
  benefits from these differences? Who loses? In what ways
  is recovery compatible with other system changes? In what
  ways is it incompatible? How will success or failure be
  evaluated? By whom? What are the implications of recovery
  for the people most involved in the public system, including
  consumers, family members, providers, and policymakers?

Of course, the preceding description is a gloss, an oversimplification
that collapses months of hard work. Recovery and I have had a reciprocal relationship, as my interests have shaped it and its contingencies
have shaped my interests. Because this is a book about meaning-
making and because, as you will see, I have become one of the makers
of the meaning of recovery, this book also is in part a research memoir,
the story of that reciprocity.

Like many interpretive social scientists, I write "memos" throughout
the research process. Memos serve many purposes: a safe page on which
to wrestle with the vicissitudes of a developing project; a record of turning places and choices made; an intellectual diary; a first draft. When I
started the research that was to culminate in this book, I began keeping
memos in four categories—personal, methodological, observational, and
analytical. Personal memos were accounts of my own assumptions, difficulties, and reactions as they related to the work. In the methodological
memos, I tracked decisions about how to approach the research, including
the questions I wanted to be sure to ask. Observational memos described
the conversations, meetings, documents, etc. to which I was attending.
In the analytical memos, I tried to take it all to the next level, to develop
some sort of synthesis.

So in personal memos I began by exploring my own responses to the
idea of recovery from severe mental illness and looking at the roots of
those responses in my own experience. When I first read the Blue Ribbon
Commission's report, I was struck by the assumptions and values that
were embedded in its discussion of recovery. Recovery was portrayed as a
cross between the American Dream and the apotheosis of New Age self-
actualization: "a productive and fulfilling life" as manifested in a home,

a family, friendship, love, meaningful work, personal growth, and higher purpose. My own life certainly didn't measure up. Was it at all tenable to think that the public mental health system should be responsible for all that? I was also irritated by the hortatory vagueness of the language, which led me to question the extent to which recovery was anything more than hype.

Early on, then, my overriding feeling was one of skepticism. I wasn't sure that recovery was anything other than a repackaging of pleas for greater humanism in the mental health system. (This reaction was certainly one I heard often among faculty associates in my postdoctoral program, many of whom had been involved in public mental health systems as providers or researchers for decades.) It seemed illogical to expect the public mental health system to transform itself so completely as to promote its own obsolescence. I was also skeptical of some recovery claims: it seemed unlikely to me that individuals who had suffered with severe illness and its effects for years could emerge unscathed, as some recovery advocates seemed to be suggesting. As my understanding of the complexity and multiple meanings of recovery grew, however, I saw that this kind of response could always be disputed by resorting to another set of definitions. For example, skepticism about complete recovery assumed something of a medical model, whereas if one defined the problem as political, consciousness raising and liberation did in fact mean complete recovery. In this way, I found an affinity with recovery, a way into the idea, as I recognized in it an endorsement of one of the tenets of social constructionism: that things become real because we define them as being so.

As I had more interaction with people around the issue of recovery, I noted some of their assumptions about me—in particular, the assumption that I was a mental health consumer—and looked at my discomfort with these assumptions. During my months of conversations with people about recovery, it was quite common for me to be asked if I was a consumer. In many ways, it was a natural question, for at this point many of the researchers working in the area of recovery did in fact identify themselves as consumers. I also recognized in the question, however, a technique for assessing me, a way of probing for my likely assumptions and allegiances. It took a while before I learned how to answer. I didn't want to be perceived as portraying myself as a model of mental health, as distancing myself from consumers, but neither did I want to claim an experiential status I did not hold. At first I'd fumble about, saying things about certainly having experienced depressive episodes in my life, but not identifying as a mental health consumer per se. One man I talked to then gave me the "right" answer when, after my clumsy reply to his question, he said, "Oh, so you've never been diagnosed with a major mental illness." Some months later, at a recovery conference at which everyone was introducing themselves as either a consumer or a professional and I kept saying, "Uh, researcher," or "Um, sociologist," I learned an even better response when a consumer looked me up and down and said, "How about 'Not yet diagnosed'?"

The personal memos also contained accounts of my struggle to balance my role as an observer with my felt obligation to participate, to make myself useful. I wrestled with the expectation that I perform as an "expert" on and as an "advocate" for recovery. There also were important things that these memos didn't record, but probably should have—most notably, my own recovery from an episode of serious physical illness, which occurred only a few months into the research.

The methodological memos stand as a roadmap of project development, an account of framing the research and then figuring out how to approach it. I began in the "blooming, buzzing confusion" of a new idea. I wanted to understand recovery, but didn't have a plan for how to do it. I started by collecting recovery documents and meeting the players, by immersing myself in the recovery world. I made commitments to work on certain projects. At the same time, I was learning grounded theory and dimensional analysis. I was learning how to have colleagues, fresh eyes when one's own work has grown stale and oppressive.

What kept tripping me up was the question of focus. Was I interested in studying recovery as an individual process pertaining to mental illness or recovery as a focus of policy development? Recovery as a lens through which to examine the mental health system? Recovery as a historically located ideology? I was interested in all of that. I visualized recovery as a kaleidoscope, offering an endless variety of light, color, and shape that shifted in response to the position of the hand and the eye. The selection of a position seemed momentous, for that choice would determine what pattern I would see.

It always kept coming back to meaning. With much help, I developed a methodological framework that allowed me to focus on the meaning of recovery. The framework was derived from two sources: dimensional analysis—an approach that helps the analyst to look at the dimensions of a concept, integrating how perspective, context, and conditions shape the concept, and how the concept itself has consequences (Schatzman 1991; Caron and Bowers 2000); and the social construction of public problems approach—which looks at how public problems are not simple reflections of putative conditions, but the result of claims-making processes by interested individuals and groups (Berger and Luckman 1966; Blumer 1971; Gusfield 1981; Spector and Kitsuse 1987; Hilgartner and Bosk 1988).

I focused on understanding recovery as a concept that implicitly contains both an understanding of a problem and a solution to the problem. I posed the following questions: From what perspectives is recovery being conceptualized? What does recovery look like from each of these perspectives? What is the nature of the problems implied by these notions of recovery? Where are the problems located? What are the contextual factors that affect the problems? Where does recovery locate the problems? Who has responsibility (authority, credibility) for fixing the problems? What are the consequences of the problems and their solutions? Under what conditions do problems/solutions change? How do different understandings of problems/solutions affect one another?

Asking and tracking the answers to these questions quickly resulted in an overwhelmingly complex web of data. The methodological memos recorded many more iterations of focus/approach/question development that allowed me to manage these data, to make some order out of the chaos, to shape intelligible products.

Of the four stacks of memos spread out on the floor by my desk right now, the pile of observational memos is highest. These memos describe what I saw and heard at meetings, in informal conversations and formal interviews, and while reading books and articles. In them, I pieced together a survey of the landscape, a view shaped by my own concerns and choices—the "sensitizing categories" implied by my methodological framework. I recorded the jargon of mental health and state policymaking in verbatim statements and approximated paraphrases. I described interactions among interested parties. I noted where tensions seem to be developing—for example, between different conceptualizations of recovery, between the State of Wisconsin and its counties, between authority and responsibility. Practically, the observational memos were a storage facility, a memory bank, a place to mark ephemera that seem to be significant, but that I had not yet analyzed and thus could not understand. They were imperfect work products, limited, as I've noted, by my choices of what to attend to, and also by my stamina. (In the beginning, I would spend almost as much time writing up field notes as I had at the actual event.)

Finally, there are the analytical memos. Here, I used my data (documents, field notes, interview transcripts) and my methodological framework to identify and dimensionalize the elements of "what 'all' is involved" (Schatzman 1991, 310) in recovery. These memos examined the multiple, and sometimes conflicting, definitions of recovery: its internal dimensions—process and endpoint; adaptation and integration; empowerment; collaboration; choice; hope—and its external contexts and conditions—the mental health system as it currently exists and in its proposed forms; consumers and their traditional and ideal roles; different theories about how to make change. I looked at the many perspectives from which these definitions were emanating—personal narrative; social movement; system rationalization and reform. I explored the broader implications of recovery for the mental health system—new definitions of expertise; revised roles for providers and agencies; different kinds of services—and for society as a whole—just who is it that has to recover?

For example, in July and August of 1998 I wrote a long analytical memo that attempted to summarize everything I thought I knew. I laid out what I saw as the origins of recovery as a social movement and a model for service provision, followed by its emergence as a focus for system reform in the context of the cost-containment and accountability framework of managed care. I identified some of the consequences of turning recovery into a framework for system reform: the development of particular implementation strategies; specific goals on the part of activists, service providers, and policymakers; and the promotion of new meanings of recovery. I looked at how strategies, goals, and meanings shifted and were re-sorted according to whether they were portrayed from the point of view of social movement, service model, or system reform. (Chapters 3 and 6 in this volume are more seasoned versions of some of this material.)

The real job of analysis—the work of fighting for clarity and making difficult compromises—takes place in the transformation from memos to words written for an audience. It is in this step that the secure and private working categories (personal, methodological, observational, analytical) break down, and meaning is made in their synthesis into a public whole.

By the spring of 1998, in preparation for the first meeting of the state's Recovery Workgroup, I had written three reports about the recovery landscape—an annotated bibliography of recovery literature and resources (Jacobson 1998a), a summary of what mental health bureaucrats in a dozen states had told me about the programs and policies they were implementing under the recovery rubric (Jacobson 1998b), and an exploration of the strategies that states, organizations, and individuals were using to promote recovery (Jacobson 1998c). Two papers also came out of this early stage of the research. The first, cowritten with Laurie Curtis (a recovery educator hired to work as a consultant to the Recovery Workgroup), was based on those "landscape" reports and looked at the various practice and policy strategies that states were using as they implemented the recovery model (Jacobson and Curtis 2000). The second, my contribution to the burgeoning literature on consumers' firsthand accounts of recovery, was an analysis of consumers' written narratives in which I identified four processes that together constituted the experience of recovery (Jacobson 2001).

None of these products answered, nor even posed, the bigger questions I had about recovery, however. I began to attempt that work later on, around the spring of 2000, when I was contracted to develop a conceptual model of recovery (Jacobson 2000; Jacobson and Greenley 2001) for use in some of the state's recovery implementation projects. (I describe the development of that conceptual model, and my eventual ambivalence toward it, later in this book.) I made a second attempt with a paper that looked closely at the state's Recovery Workgroup, asking, in particular, how the group managed to develop a single set of policy recommendations when the individual members had such divergent understandings of the meaning of recovery (Jacobson 2003). (Chapter 4 is an expanded and revised version of material from that paper.) In the months and years it has taken to bring this book to publication, I have also grown more interested in the microprocesses of recovery implementation. My most recent work (Jacobson et al. 2003; Jacobson and Altenberg, in process) examines the question of how recovery's big ideas can be played out in organizations the size of individual mental health service agencies.

Recovery is a subject that has become increasingly salient for mental health consumers, providers, and policymakers in many locales. My goal in this book is to use Wisconsin's experience to grapple with some of the questions that come with the commitment to develop recovery-oriented mental health systems. Toward that end, in the next six chapters I present a descriptive analysis of recovery—complexes of meaning that I label "recovery-as."

In the symbolic interactionist tradition, phenomena are not inherently meaningful, but are made so through social interaction. Any object—be it a physical item or an idea—gathers meaning as social entities (individuals, organizations, societies) respond both to it and to the ways others have responded. Meaning is accomplished through interactive processes of gesture and interpretation, which are manifested in language (and other systems of signification) and action. New objects often require more gesture and interpretation than do older objects, whose meanings may be more firmly established. All meaning-making takes place in a context created by other meanings, a history of other gestures and interpretations. The meaning of an object has consequences as well—for social entities and their gestures and interpretations, and for the object itself.

In this book I write about recovery as an object of meaning-making, examining the gestures and interpretations that have surrounded it, the contexts in which these responses have occurred, and the consequences of its meaning both for different social entities and for new meanings. First, I look at three older meanings of *recovery:* recovery-as-evidence, recovery-as-experience, and recovery-as-ideology. Next, I turn to a more recent meaning, recovery-as-policy, tracing the ways in which this meaning was constructed in Wisconsin during a period of system reform. Finally, I offer my thoughts and speculations on recovery-as-politics, the meaning of recovery that is emerging as more and more organizations and systems embrace recovery-as-policy.

The context for recovery-as-evidence was constituted by the first one hundred years of mental health services in the United States, from the building of state hospitals in the mid-nineteenth century to the new scientific psychiatry of the mid-twentieth. *Recovery* was given meaning in the interactions between doctors, hospital superintendents, legislators and other agents of government, patients, their families, and the public. The gestures and responses of these entities included statistics, legislation, etiological theories, therapies like moral treatment or medication, the founding of different kinds of institutions, and choices about seeking treatment. In the interaction among these gestures and interpretations, recovery emerged as a duality, "real" versus "practical" recovery, and the likelihood of its occurrence was attributed to characteristics of individual patients—their socioeconomic status or the severity or duration of their symptoms—as well as to the settings and modes of their treatment. In turn, these meanings had consequences for the disposition of particular patients, for the kinds of institutions and treatments that received financial support and professional attention, and for attitudes toward mental illness.

Recovery-as-experience was made meaningful as the voices of those who had been diagnosed and treated, from celebrated ex-patient Clifford Beers to the more anonymous mental health consumers of the present day, became part of the conversation. It emerged as a significant force for change in the context of the social and political unrest of the 1970s, when groups of individuals who had "survived" the mental health system joined together in emulation of other recent social movements to make personal and public claims for the fact and impact of their oppression. The gestures and responses that gave meaning to recovery-as-experience included the narratives or stories of individuals, the organizations that were founded on the basis of commonalities identified in these narratives, the new definitions of and explanations for "mental illness," the political demonstrations that demanded change and reparation, and the alternative sources for and types of help devised. The meaning of recovery-as-experience included notions of trajectory over time, of struggle and eventual triumph, of change against a conventional wisdom of stasis, of a quest for the self. In these themes, recovery-as-experience was consistent with the zeitgeist of the emerging "culture of recovery" (Rapping 1996)—movements like AA and its spin-offs that dealt with individual healing through personal transformation (Kaminer 1992; Eastland 1995). Unlike the culture of recovery associated with

AA, however, recovery-as-experience drew an equivalence between the individual and the collective, developing an explicitly political analysis. In this way, it had more in common with the disability rights movement, which focused on the need for societal transformation (Anspach 1979; Zola 1982; DeJong 1983; Oliver 1990).

In the years following the Second World War, as the technology of outcome assessment came into its own, research showed surprisingly good long-term outcomes for many people who had been diagnosed with severe mental illness, challenging the century-old assumption of inevitable deterioration. This finding, in combination with a recognition of the weaknesses of many of the community-based services started after deinstitutionalization, led to new calls for the rationalization of mental health services. Recovery-as-ideology emerged in the context of this move toward rationalization, drawing on recovery-as-experience and recovery-as-evidence to rally support for specific approaches and service delivery models. The gestures and interpretations that gave meaning to recovery-as-ideology included research studies of patient outcomes, published manifestos by prominent service providers, and a new emphasis on "best practices" in psychiatry and mental health services, all of which made recovery a prominent theme in professional discourse. Very soon, the consequence was a movement toward recovery-as-ideology as the philosophical basis for system reform—the meaning of recovery-as-policy.

Beginning in the Reagan '80s, changes in the financial arrangements between the federal government and the states led to less money being available for publicly funded systems of mental health services. In the 1990s, the managed care juggernaut that followed the Clinton administration's failure to institute significant health care reform consumed the private system, and soon began to seem inevitable in public systems as well. It was in this context that many states began gearing up for another cycle of mental health reform. Recovery-as-policy emerged as representative bodies—commissions and task forces—were brought into being to plan for the next era of change. It was given meaning through the interactions between the system stakeholders (consumers, providers, family members, administrators, government representatives) who served on these bodies and by the plethora of vision statements, reports, white papers, and implementation strategies they devised. The development of recovery-as-policy proved to be a story of negotiation: accommodations over divergent meanings and struggles to balance concepts like collaboration and hope with practices of cost containment and accountability. The consequences of recovery-as-policy have included new programs of training and education, structured reviews of system and organizational policy and procedure, and increased attention to consumers as active participants in the provision of services and the making of policy.

The implementation of recovery-as-policy in a time of economic downturn and against a background of traditional views about evidence, experience, and ideology set the context for the development of recovery-as-politics—the conundrums and conflicts that arose as planning met reality. The politics of recovery have raised questions about expertise and the participatory roles of consumers in recovery-oriented systems, about accountability and measurement, about the issues of collaboration and risk that follow the implementation of recovery in practice, about the congruence between recovery and elements of coercion that continue to exist in most mental health systems, about the reach of the mental health system and how society will commit its financial resources, and about the commodification of recovery. At stake is a choice between recovery as a real challenge to the extant power structures and recovery as a framework for reform—a kind of tinkering around the edges. The outcome of this choice, and thus consequences of recovery-as-politics, cannot yet be known.

Chapter 1 sets the stage for this unfolding story of "recovery-as" by providing background on the history of mental health services in the state of Wisconsin since the mid-nineteenth century, placing this history against the backdrop of the four major mental health reform movements that swept through the United States during that time (Morrissey and Goldman 1986). The chapter examines Wisconsin's sometimes unique approaches to these reforms and describes the circumstances surrounding the redesign project that itself became the context for the state's commitment to developing a "recovery-oriented" mental health system. Chapters 2 and 3 look at historical constructions of recovery in the mental health literature. Chapter 2 recounts this history in four episodes that correspond to the four mental health reform movements introduced earlier. In Chapter 3, I trace the "modern" history of recovery, looking in particular at the social phenomena that laid the groundwork for the emergence of recovery as an organizing principle for mental health practice (recovery-as-ideology). Chapter 4 focuses on how Wisconsin's Recovery Workgroup set about specifying the operationalization of the concept in its recommendations for a "recovery-oriented" mental health system (recovery-as-policy). More generally, this chapter addresses the processes of policy development, with special attention to the divergent definitions of recovery held by various Workgroup members and how those definitions played out in the final policy recommendations. Chapter 5 describes the first efforts made to implement the Workgroup's recommendations, exploring how ideas about meaning and change were negotiated in projects to develop specific recovery promotion products. Finally, Chapter 6 updates the state of recovery implementation in Wisconsin and beyond, examining some of the problematic implications of recovery policy in action (recovery-as-politics). I tell a more personal story—a memoir of my reciprocal relationship with recovery and with this work—in several short essays called "Interstices" that are scattered between these chapters.

1

ON WISCONSIN

With his signature on an executive order dated May 13, 1996, Wisconsin governor Tommy Thompson established the Blue Ribbon Commission on Mental Health, a body to be made up of "representatives from government, the mental health professions, the public and private sector and individuals who have an interest in the future direction of mental health care in Wisconsin." Citing a need to "closely examine the present mental health care delivery system and how said system should evolve into the twenty-first century," the Governor's order called upon these representatives "to explore redesigning [Wisconsin's] mental health care delivery system to ensure that persons in need of tax supported mental health services are provided with access to appropriate, high quality and cost effective services that promote health and wellness, improvement and recovery, and quality of life." The Commission was to undertake a review of the state's treatment and support services, its organizational arrangements, and its financing mechanisms, and, within a year, make recommendations that would restructure them into a coordinated system with an emphasis on prevention, stigma reduction, consumer outcomes, treatment effectiveness, efficiency, and accountability (Wisconsin Office of the Governor 1996).

Embedded in the short text of this executive order, and in the form of the body it called into being, are clues to the distinctive history of Wisconsin's mental health system and to the assumptions and values that would shape the process and the products of the redesign project. The purpose of this chapter is to set the context for that project—in particular for plans to develop a "recovery-oriented" system in Wisconsin—by examining the history of the state's efforts to provide mental health services for its citizens.

A Brief Introduction to the Badger State

In 1848, Wisconsin became the thirtieth state, with the capital at Madison. The U.S. census taken in 1850 found that Wisconsin had a population of just over 300,000 people. Its inhabitants included Native Americans, French Canadians, migrants from other U.S. states and territories, and immigrants from the British Isles. Most residents worked as farmers and loggers. Others mined lead. (Living and working underground, as they did, these men were tagged "Badgers," an appellation that lives on in the nickname for the University of Wisconsin's beloved sports teams.)

The second half of the nineteenth century was a period of industrialization, urbanization, and heavy European, particularly German, immigration to Wisconsin. These immigrants settled in the cities and towns of the southeastern part of the state, along Lake Michigan and close to the major regional center of Chicago, and worked in factories that manufactured engines and industrial machinery. By the late 1800s they had made Milwaukee the most populous city in the state and the home of one of the highest concentrations of foreign-born residents in America. At the turn of the century, the census showed a total Wisconsin population of over two million people, more than a quarter of whom were immigrants.

Madison, located in the rich farmlands of the south central region, continued as the seat of government. With the establishment and subsequent growth of the University of Wisconsin, it became the intellectual center as well. The idea for the University originated in the late eighteenth century, when the ordinance that established the old Northwest Territory mandated that the region provide public education. When Wisconsin achieved statehood, the University of Wisconsin was founded on the basis of land grants made by the federal government, with the understanding that the proceeds of such lands were to support the university in perpetuity (Thwaites 1900). Built on a hill overlooking the city of Madison and its lakes, a straight line from the site of the state capitol building, the university opened its doors in 1849.

Wisconsin's historical reputation rests largely on the state's status as a leader in the progressive movement of the early twentieth century and on the unique relationship that developed between the university and state government in service of progressive ideas and policies. Historians have hotly debated the definition of progressivism (Buenker 1998). Daniel T. Rodgers (1982) locates its meaning in "three distinct clusters of ideas": "the rhetoric of antimonopolism"; "an emphasis on social bonds and the social nature of human beings"; and "the language of social efficiency" (123). In Wisconsin, these ideas were expressed as "the development of the efficiency of the individual and the safeguarding of his opportunity, the jealous guarding of the governmental machinery from the invasion of the corrupting force and might of concentrated wealth, the shackling of monopoly, and the regulating of contract conditions by special administrative agencies of the people" (McCarthy 1912, 16). Progressive-era president Theodore Roosevelt called Wisconsin "a laboratory for wise experimental legislation aiming to secure the social and political betterment of the people as a whole" (Roosevelt quoted in McCarthy 1912, vii). Among these legislative innovations were the country's first workman's compensation law, which passed the Wisconsin state legislature in 1911; income tax legislation; laws regulating the railroads; and some of the earliest conservation laws in the United States (Buenker 1998).

Two forces contributed to the development of Wisconsin-style progressivism. The first was an activist, socialist-minded labor movement, centered in the factories and working-class German neighborhoods of Milwaukee. The second was a partnership between government and the university at Madison, a partnership grounded in a belief in rational reform and the utility of expertise (a "leadership of the 'competent' " [Buenker 1998, 591]). The practice of this belief came to be known as the "Wisconsin Idea," and it was manifested in the advisory relationships that developed between certain university professors and sectors of the state government (relationships so close that for a time the University of Wisconsin was nationally renowned for being "the University that runs a state" [Buenker 1998, ix]).

Although there were tensions between these two forces—Milwaukee's brand of reform was politicized and populist, Madison's intellectual and elitist—they shared a demand for clean government, a belief in the promotion of the general welfare, and a call for social policy to emerge out of collaborations between government, the private sector, and citizen coalitions:

> Wisconsinites in many walks of life united into groups of like-minded persons. They debated, resisted, moderated, and shaped the course of change, each seeking to impose an individual brand of order and system upon a seemingly inchoate process. Whatever their individual goals, the proponents of change pursued them through organized, purposeful intervention in public life. . . . [T]hey began to form coalitions with other activist groups and with agencies of government, often seeking intervention by state government to secure changes in a wide variety of areas. . . . [C]ollectively, they formed a tide of unprecedented demands upon state government in number, scope, and variety. (Buenker 1998, 358–59)

(Of course, the state was larger than Milwaukee and Madison. Much of progressive policy addressed the needs of the industrial and agricultural south. Beginning in the early twentieth century, the vast area to the north—"Wisconsin's Appalachia," the "Cutover" of denuded forest—arguably was left behind.)

Development of the "Wisconsin Plan" (1850–1900)

Public attention to what today would be called the "human services" began early in Wisconsin's statehood. Wisconsin opened a school for the blind in 1849, a state prison in 1850, and a school for deaf children in 1854. Each institution was governed by a board of trustees and was funded by direct appropriations from the state legislature. Each served the entire state. Accountability took the form of required annual reports to the governor (Odegard and Keith 1940).

Calls to build a state-supported institution for individuals suffering from mental illness—a "lunatic asylum," in the language of the day—were made around the time of statehood but, in part because the federal government declined to make a financial contribution, did not come to fruition. In 1854 the state passed legislation enabling the building of such a facility; a site on Lake Mendota, near Madison, was selected, but political squabbling over the award of the construction contract, along with other problems, stifled the effort (Robison 1980). In 1857 new enabling legislation was passed and construction began. The facility (Mendota State Hospital)—under administrative conditions similar to those of other Wisconsin institutions, i.e., a board of trustees, an annual report to the governor—finally opened in 1860.

In the mid-nineteenth century, throughout North America as in Wisconsin, care for the "insane" was a haphazard patchwork. A small number of private hospitals served the wealthy. A few states had built public hospitals. The vast majority of mentally ill persons, however, were either kept at home or were incarcerated in the county jails and alms-houses that were the refuge of the criminal, the old, and the indigent (Grob 1994b).

Across the United States, the movement to build state hospitals resulted from the confluence of two streams of reform. The first is most often associated with activist Dorothea Dix, who, beginning in the 1840s, lobbied extensively at both the state and federal levels for more humane treatment of the insane, a new attitude that was to be demonstrated by a governmental commitment to purpose-built facilities in which mentally ill persons would be free of the abuses common in jails and poorhouses (Deutsch 1949). The second was a therapeutic philosophy called moral treatment. Developed in France and England in the late eighteenth century, moral treatment was based on an understanding of mental illness as a physical or functional defect of the brain caused by adverse environmental conditions (Caplan 1969). Because the brain maintained its flexibility, for a time, mental illness could be treated—and cured—by a change to a more salutary environment: in particular, by a sojourn in a modern hospital where the patient, attended by an authoritative and benevolent physician, might partake of the benefits of a healthy diet, fresh air and exercise, worthy occupation, high expectations, and removal from the malignant influence of the family and home surroundings (Deutsch 1949; Dain 1964; Caplan 1969; Grob 1994a). Not incidentally, as Andrew Scull (1979) has argued, the linkage of moral treatment and the building of public hospitals served to provide both scope and setting for promoting the nascent profession of psychiatry.

An endorsement of moral treatment was implicit in the rhetoric of those who lobbied for Wisconsin's first state hospital, for whom the statistics of "cure" became powerful political tools. As historian Dale W. Robison (1980) has noted, belief in the effectiveness of moral treatment allowed the argument for building a state hospital to be given an economic emphasis: "early and correct treatment of the mentally ill would transform a non-productive charity case into a self-supporting individual who would no longer be a burden to the state" (34–35). In order to be effective, however, it was necessary to begin moral treatment early in the natural history of the disorder. Thus in Wisconsin (as in other locales) the state hospital was to give admission preference to new cases of acute mental illness (Robison 1980; Grob 1994a). The chronically mentally ill, the "incurables," were to be left in existing local facilities: in jails if they were violent or in poorhouses if they were not (Odegard and Keith 1940).

Very soon the new state hospital was crowded beyond its intended capacity. Historians have attributed the phenomenon of overcrowding in this period—which was not unique to Wisconsin—to a number of factors, including population growth due to increased rates of immigration, a higher incidence of mental illness induced by the rigors of the Civil War (Robison 1980), and the failure of moral treatment as a therapeutic modality (Morrissey and Goldman 1986). Practically, overcrowding meant that the state hospital increasingly was devoted to the custodial care of incurables. The confluence of a vulnerable patient population, poorly trained and paid staff, and substandard physical conditions led to repeated investigations of wrongdoing and abuse. State officials responded by enabling the building of a second state hospital (Winnebago State Hospital) at Oshkosh, in the northeastern part of the state and, as many other states were doing at the time (Grob 1994b), by forming a new board to assume oversight of all Wisconsin institutions (Robison 1980).

The 1871 legislation authorizing the state Board of Charities and Reform specified that the new body was to be devoted "to the end that the administration of public charity and correction may be conducted upon sound principles of economy, justice and humanity and that the relations existing between the state, its dependent and criminal classes may become better understood" (quoted in Odegard and Keith 1940, 2). Board members were charged with oversight of all public institutions in the state, including the hospitals, jails, county poorhouses, and special schools (e.g., the state school for the deaf). Their duties encompassed visitation, inspection, and research, with an emphasis on issues of sanitation, separation of hardened criminals, provision of useful employment for inmates, and "the degree of humanitarian treatment afforded the insane" (Odegard and Keith 1940, 4). They were to make recommendations to the state, but had no power to require reform. Institutions retained their individual boards of trustees, which continued to be responsible for all administrative and financial matters.

Wisconsin followed the state-hospital-based model of care for the mentally ill—that is, the use of one or more centralized hospitals for the care and treatment of persons throughout the state—through the 1870s. These hospitals mixed chronic and acute cases in their patient populations. They were run by politically appointed psychiatrists/superintendents, who oversaw day-to-day operations, and by boards of trustees. Funding came directly from the state legislature—a situation that created a strong financial incentive for counties to transfer their "incurables" from local facilities to the state hospitals (Morrissey and Goldman 1986; Grob 1994a).

Beginning in the early 1880s, however, the state began to diverge from this arrangement. In 1881 government officials created the state Board of Supervision of Wisconsin Charitable, Reformatory and Penal Institutions, an appointed body whose charge was to oversee the finances of all state institutions. The boards of trustees of individual institutions were abolished and their administrative and budgetary authority turned over to the state Board of Supervision. The Board of Supervision and the Board of Charities and Reform were meant to work in concert, the former concerned with reducing monetary waste and corruption, the latter with ensuring humanitarian treatment for all inmates in state institutions (Odegard and Keith 1940). Not surprisingly, though, in practice the relationship between the two boards was fraught with territorial tensions. Ten years after the founding of the Board of Supervision, both boards were abolished and a new body—the state Board of Control of Wisconsin Reformatory, Charitable and Penal Institutions—was formed in order to "secure the just, humane and economical administration of the laws concerning the charitable, curative, reformatory and penal institutions of the state" (quoted in Odegard and Keith 1940, 6).

It was during the period of coexistence of the two boards—the

1880s—that Wisconsin developed the scheme of joint state/county responsibility that became known as the Wisconsin Plan. The Board of Charities' access to the practices of the state hospitals and county jails and poorhouses showed the humanitarian failures of the state-hospital-based model, while the Board of Supervision's access to their books showed its financial weaknesses. Although members of the Board of Charities had originally joined with the state's psychiatrist/superintendents in supporting a plan to build separate large state hospitals to house acute and chronic cases (as other states were doing at the time, see Grob 1983), by 1881 both boards promoted and won legislative passage of the County Care Act. Under this legislation, counties were empowered to levy taxes for the building of local asylums for incurables—small self-supporting farms where inmates would live and work the land. These county asylums would be governed by individual boards of trustees appointed by county boards of supervisors. Daily administrative duties would fall to a nonmedical superintendent who would live with and supervise the work of asylum inmates. Funding for the support of inmates would come from the state, on a per capita basis. In return, counties would be expected to make a per capita contribution toward the support of county residents who were being cared for in one of the state hospitals (Levine and Weiss 1967; Robison 1980). This system of shared responsibility was facilitated by the relative strength of county government and the relative weakness of state government and by a Wisconsin state government tradition of devolving administrative responsibility to local authorities (Stein 1989; Buenker 1998).

The Wisconsin Plan rested on several premises. The first was a belief in a qualitative distinction between acute and chronic mental illness. Before admission to a county asylum, all cases were to be assessed (either by a judge or a committee of two physicians). Those deemed "acute" would be sent to the state hospital for treatment. Those deemed "chronic," or determined after a period of time in the state hospital to be "incurable," were to be sent to the asylums in their counties of residence for long-term custodial care (Robison 1980). (Although the law promised to safeguard individuals from hasty determinations of chronicity, historians agree that under conditions of severe overcrowding in the state hospitals this requirement was often overridden [Deutsch 1949; Farrow 1973; Robison 1980].) The second premise was that the small, "home-like" environment of the asylum, located in the community, close to families and friends and providing opportunities for wholesome occupation, would have a therapeutic effect on its inmates (Robison 1980; Ebert and Trattner 1990). The third premise was that shared state/county responsibility would provide a balance of financial incentives and oversight that would make for both cost-effectiveness and resistance to corruption (Robison 1980).

Contemporary opponents of the Wisconsin Plan made different arguments. Psychiatrists objected to the "demedicalization" of chronic mental illness, pointing out that placement in a county asylum meant the end of all medical intervention (Robison 1980) and, implicitly, a shift to lay control of a particular patient population—a move that effectively limited the authority and reach of the profession. Other critics disputed that oversight of county asylums would be sufficient to ensure that they operated humanely. Rather, they warned, greedy county supervisors would push superintendents to make their asylums sources of profit for the county (Levine and Weiss 1967; Robison 1980). Finally, supporters of the state-hospital model argued that the dual system would work to the detriment of hospitals by allowing asylums to "cream" the most compliant and docile patients, leaving in hospital care only those who were violent or extremely ill (Levine and Weiss 1967; Robison 1980). Although variants of the Wisconsin Plan eventually were adopted in other locales, in general the system remained highly controversial outside the state (Grob 1983).

Modern historians and social scientists have attempted to assess the successes and failures of the early days of Wisconsin's state/county model (Levine and Weiss 1967; Ebert and Trattner 1990). They find that the county asylums were successful in meeting their goal of providing humane custodial care, but that discharge—except by death or elopement (that is, running away)—was rare. Inmates did not make ties to their communities. Many individuals may have been labeled "incurable" with little evidence. The asylums probably provided economic savings for the state, but as contemporary critics suspected, county officials may have succumbed to the temptation to make them profit centers. Retrospectively, the critique of the county asylum has become a critique of the idea of chronicity: "it was economics which defined chronicity and it was economics which defined its 'treatment' " (Levine and Weiss 1967, 35).

However, when historians have assessed per capita expenditures, selected as a proxy indicator for quality of care, nineteenth-century Wisconsin consistently rates high among the states (Grob 1983).

An exception to the strict demarcation between state care for acute cases and county care for chronic cases developed in Milwaukee County. As early as 1878, several years before the County Care Act, the state passed legislation allowing counties that had exceeded their patient quotas at the state hospitals to build their own hospitals (Robison 1980). Effectively, this legislation addressed the situation of populous Milwaukee County. From the late 1870s on, therefore, the county devised a mental health system that paralleled the state/county system, with its own hospital as well as a number of small asylums (Robison 1980; Wood 1989).

MENTAL HEALTH SERVICES INTO THE TWENTIETH CENTURY (1900–1950)

By the turn of the twentieth century, disillusionment with the lack of good outcomes for patients in state hospitals had coalesced into a backlash against the "cult of curability"—the idea that moral treatment as practiced in institutions could cure mental illness (Deutsch 1949). The psychiatric profession sought to become more "scientific," to rationalize its approach to the treatment of mental illness, and in so doing began to sever its association as an institution-based specialty (Caplan 1969). A new mental health reform movement, mental hygiene, led by both a former psychiatric patient, Clifford Beers, and representatives of the new scientific psychiatry, sought to broaden the context in which mental illness was understood and addressed as a medical and social condition, seeking, in harmony with the progressivism of the time, its "eradication [through] . . . a fusion of scientific knowledge and administrative action" (Grob 1983, 144). Together, these trends led to a turn away from state institutions and toward the development of new facilities—the psychopathic hospital and ward, the psychiatric dispensary, and the child guidance clinic (Sicherman 1980; Morrissey and Goldman 1986).

Mental health services in Wisconsin showed some effects of these national trends. Soon after it was founded, Beers's National Committee for Mental Hygiene undertook a survey of conditions in Wisconsin institutions. The Board of Control acted on several of the committee's resulting recommendations (Dain 1980). The state opened a forensic hospital (Central State Hospital at Waupun) in 1914. That facility, in turn, led to the development of the Psychiatric Field Service. Envisioned as "a tool of real value in facilitating a more enlightened conduct of institutions" (Odegard and Keith 1940, 31), the field service team conducted psychiatric examinations of all new inmates and parole applicants, looking for underlying physical or psychiatric problems—or perhaps seeking to use science to discover a cure for crime (Odegard and Keith 1940). In 1913 the Psychiatric Institute, a research and teaching facility, opened at Mendota. By the early 1920s, it had been moved to the University of Wisconsin (Odegard and Keith 1940). In 1918, the Madison veterans' hospital opened a psychiatric unit (Odegard and Keith 1940). In addition, programs for training psychiatric nurses were instituted in the state, and social work entered the psychiatric field with the development of posts for "after care agents" (who did postdischarge follow-up in the community) at some state hospitals (Farrow 1973; Robison 1980). More general progressive-era legislation also had some peripheral effect on mental health services: a 1905 civil service law reduced the political nature of superintendents' jobs at state institutions, and the progressives' focus on social improvement through the application of science led to passage of a law allowing sterilization of citizens deemed "mentally defective," including some persons diagnosed with mental illnesses (Robison 1980).

The Wisconsin Plan remained in place. In the late 1800s there were two state hospitals (Mendota and Winnebago), a county hospital in Milwaukee, and twenty-one county asylums. By the 1930s, there was also a forensic hospital (Waupun) and more than three dozen county asylums (Odegard and Keith 1940). Together, these state and county institutions housed some twelve thousand individuals (Odegard and Keith 1940). In the early 1900s, the Association of Trustees and Superintendents of the County Asylums was founded to promote the administrative interests of county asylums, institutions some thought were being ignored by the state Board of Control (Robison 1980). The new organization signaled the growing degree of county control over the asylums, and a waning of state oversight (Grob 1983). The state Board of Control itself underwent change in the early twentieth century, merging into the growing apparatus of state government; by the late 1930s, its functions had been assumed by a newly developed Division of Mental Hygiene within the state Department of Public Welfare (Odegard and Keith 1940).

TRANSITION TO COMMUNITY TREATMENT (1950–1970)

Historians attribute the American movement toward community-based care after the Second World War to several factors. First was the war experience itself, which had demonstrated the effectiveness of nonhospital treatment for mental disorders in soldiers. Second were shifts in psychiatric theory and treatment orientation, including the mental-hygiene-influenced emphasis on social problems as an etiological factor in mental illness. Third was the introduction of new therapies, primarily drugs like Thorazine for the control of psychosis. Finally, with passage of the National Mental Health Act of 1946, there was an increased federal role in mental health, specifically in promoting the development of community-based mental health services (Morrissey and Goldman 1986; Grob 1991).

The 1946 act, which also established the National Institute of Mental Health (NIMH)—an agency that was to have a central role in the planning and implementation of U.S. mental health policy (Grob 1991; Rochefort 1993)—provided matching grants to the states to open outpatient mental health clinics on a demonstration basis. In Wisconsin, these funds helped to establish a number of services—including posthospitalization follow-up, vocational rehabilitation, social services, and family care—which operated out of a number of community-based agencies and clinics (Wisconsin Department of Public Welfare 1958).

A snapshot of the state at this time—circa 1950s—shows community-based services as one aspect of a developing assemblage of services, an assemblage that also includes the three state hospitals, psychiatric wards in the general hospitals, thirty-six county institutions, and Milwaukee County's semiautonomous system (Wisconsin Department of Public Welfare 1952; Wisconsin Department of Public Welfare 1958). There is some loosening in the rigid distinction between acute and chronic treatment in state and county facilities. A report of the state's Department of Public Welfare draws a distinction between "diagnostic and treatment hospitals," which provide "remedial services" and "custodial type institutions," which offer only "continuing care," but declines to equate the one with state hospitals and the other with county institutions (Wisconsin Department of Public Welfare 1952). The state hospital at Winnebago, for example, has established social service and outpatient departments, allowing it to follow patients after periods of hospitalization and extending its reach into local communities (Farrow 1973). The county asylums, on the other hand, have added some treatment services to their custodial care (Levine and Weiss 1967).

The late 1950s and early 1960s were an extremely active period for mental health policy planning at the federal level (Grob 1991; Rochefort 1993; Grob 1994b). In 1955, with the guidance of the NIMH, Congress passed the Mental Health Study Act, legislation that provided for a large-scale federal study of mental health throughout the nation. Conducted by the Joint Commission on Mental Illness and Health, a group made up largely of American Psychiatric Association–affiliated psychiatrists and academic behavioral and social scientists, the study examined state-level policies and services, the state of theoretical and practical knowledge about mental illness, and public attitudes toward persons suffering from mental illness. In its 1961 report *Action for Mental Health* the joint commission recommended increased spending for research and training, a concerted effort to provide public information about mental illness, and more federal money for mental health services. The report also made specific policy recommendations, calling for a reduction in the number of state-hospital beds (though specifically not the elimination of all state-hospital services) and an increase in the number of community mental health clinics, with particular attention to improved coordination of services between inpatient and outpatient facilities. *Action for Mental Health* served as the basis for the 1963 Community Mental Health Centers Act, although in its final form the act ignored many of the joint commission's recommendations, instead emphasizing the development of an exclusively community-based mental health care system and increasing the federal role in mental health services provision while reducing the role of state government (Grob 1991).

Wisconsin was in tune with the times. In 1959 the state legislature passed the Wisconsin Community Mental Health Act. The act provided state funds for the continuing operation of community-based clinics and established a number of advisory committees, which included representatives of community, county, and state interests, to do system planning and co-ordination. In 1961, some eighteen community-based clinics offering treatment, maintenance, prevention, and consultation services were receiving state monies. By 1962, there were twenty-one such clinics. Passage of the 1963 Community Mental Health Centers Act provided federal money for clinic development and operation.

The statewide planning activities associated with the shift to community-based services raised questions about the role of the county institutions and state hospitals. Increasingly, these institutions were seen as anachronistic and problematic in terms of patient population, location, financing arrangements, and lack of coordination with other treatment services. The state's mental health advisory committees called for all county facilities to move from providing residential treatment to offering outpatient services. The state hospitals were to reduce their number of in-patient beds and become tertiary care centers providing the specialized services that would not be part of the newly constituted array of county services (Wisconsin Department of Health and Social Services 1972).

At the same time, planners sought to reduce the complexity of county administration of mental health services. While county mental institutions, community-based services, and services for drug and alcohol abusers and mentally retarded individuals currently were run by separate local boards and funded separately—resulting in a "non-system" of care (Stein 1989), the mental health advisory committees called for a more streamlined structure that would allow for the blending of funding streams and better integration of services (Stein and Ganser 1983).

SECTION 51.42

Codification of these changes appeared in Section 51.42 of the Wisconsin statutes, which passed the state legislature in 1971:

> The purpose and intent of this section is to enable and encourage
> counties to develop a comprehensive range of services offering
> continuity of care; to utilize and expand existing governmental,
> voluntary, and community resources for provision of services
> to prevent or ameliorate mental disabilities . . . ; to provide
> for the integration of administration of those services and

facilities . . . through the establishment of a unified governing and policy-making board of directors; and to authorize state consultative services, review and establishment of standards and grants-in-aid for such program of services and facilities.

Section 51.42 created a new structure—the unified county board—to "plan, develop, integrate, and evaluate a comprehensive range of services for the . . . disability groups for which they are responsible." These "51.42 boards" would be formed either by single counties or by small consortia of counties (and Indian tribes) that agreed to work together. Each board would be composed of county supervisors, citizen representatives, and administrative staff and would be obligated to implement some mechanism for receiving public comment. It was expected that the "comprehensive range of services" under board jurisdiction would include evaluation, diagnosis, treatment (both inpatient and outpatient), aftercare, emergency care, supportive services, prevention, and information for county residents with mental illnesses, substance abuse problems, or developmental disabilities. The legislation allowed counties either to provide these services themselves or to contract with other provider agencies to do so.

Funds for these services would come from multiple sources, including federal medical assistance money (Medicaid), state money to counties (to be allocated on the basis of a funding formula), and local matching funds (from county tax levies). In addition, the state would provide special funds for capacity-building around specific projects or mandates (Stein and Ganser 1983). The money to support people living in the community, on the other hand, would come largely from federally based systems of cash assistance—Supplemental Security Income for the Aged, the Disabled, and the Blind (SSI) and Social Security Disability Insurance (SSDI)—supplemented by local money in the form of welfare payments (Morrissey and Goldman 1986). Before receiving funding for services, all boards would be required to write a yearly plan for submission to and approval by the state. Additionally, all county-run services would be subject to oversight and regulation by the state, and the state would provide technical assistance and advice to the counties (Stein and Ganser 1983; Greenley 1985).

A key feature of Section 51.42 was a built-in incentive for counties to expand provision of community-based services and reduce their use of inpatient services. While counties would receive funding for community-based services, they would be required to pay on a per capita basis for their use of state inpatient facilities. Thus, money used for inpatient care would no longer be available to fund community-based services. Conversely, money "saved" by reducing hospitalization rates could be used to strengthen community-based services (Stein and Ganser 1983; Goodrick 1989).

The deinstitutionalization aim of this financial incentive was reinforced by structural change. Over the course of the early to mid-1970s, the state hospitals were converted to tertiary care centers, and the county institutions were transformed into nursing homes.[1] In addition, changes to Wisconsin's civil commitment law—language that required "treatment in the least restrictive environment possible"—made it more difficult to commit individuals to inpatient care involuntarily (Wisconsin Department of Health and Social Services 1994).

With Section 51.42, Wisconsin policy makers made a conscious decision to maintain the state's system of joint state/county responsibility. This decision amounted to an endorsement of tradition, of Wisconsin's uniqueness among the states. It also had tangible consequences for the future of Wisconsin's public mental health service system. Despite state oversight, the development of multiple systems of care resulted in a wide range in the type and quality of services available in different parts of the state. In the mid-1980s, for example, the percentage of their mental health budgets counties spent for inpatient care ranged from 13 percent to 73 percent (Stein 1989). Meanwhile, the oversight and regulatory role of the state made for tensions and some ill will between the counties and the state, particularly in times of economic downturn and cost cutting (Greenley 1985). These tensions and the disparities in the quality of county services were magnified by historically based regional fault lines: the rivalry between working-class Milwaukee and elitist Madison and the resentment of the perennially resource-poor north toward the wealthy south.

THE ERA OF COMMUNITY SUPPORT

The critical view of the shift away from large state institutions sees it as a phenomenon driven not by therapeutic innovations or humanitarian motives but primarily by economic interests. As Andrew Scull (1977) has written, deinstitutionalization was "a reflection of more extensive and deep-seated changes in the social organization of advanced capitalist societies. . . . [I]t reflects the structural pressures to curtail sharply the costly system of segregative control once welfare payments, providing a subsistence existence for elements of the surplus population, make available a viable alternative to management in an institution" (Scull 1977, 152). The unhappy fate of many of the people discharged from state hospitals may be taken as evidence for the truth of this point of view. Although SSI and welfare provided monetary support for a life in the community, such support was meager. Many long-term "ex-patients" found themselves living squalid, hand-to-mouth existences, without adequate shelter and without access to treatment and social support services. This lack of available help was in large part due to the failure of federally supported community mental health centers to plan and provide services for persons with severe and persistent mental illness—that is, to provide services for the very population that was being discharged from the state hospitals. Instead, community mental health centers had come to focus on the "worried well," providing short-term psychotherapy and mental hygiene programs like child guidance (Grob 1991).

In their examination of cycles of reform in U.S. public mental health services, Morrissey and Goldman (1986) point to the community support movement as a "fourth cycle" in that history. They describe this movement as "the development of crisis-care services, psychosocial rehabilitation services, supportive living and working arrangements, medical and mental health care, and case management for the chronically mentally ill" (26) and characterize it as a response to the "premature" closure of thousands of inpatient beds and the lack of sufficient support services in the community.

Wisconsin's contribution to the national community support movement was the Program of Assertive Community Treatment (PACT), which within several years of its founding became a model for service provision across the country. As recounted in James Greenley's history of PACT (1995), the program began in the early 1970s, when the Mendota Mental Health Institute (one of Wisconsin's state psychiatric hospitals) moved a team of inpatient workers (including psychiatrists, psychiatric nurses, aides, a social worker, an activity therapist, and a clerk) into a house in downtown Madison, intending to provide services in such a way as to allow their patients to "become *integrated into the community*" (Stein and Test quoted in Greenley 1995, 85, emphasis in the original) and to avoid rehospitalization. Toward this end, in addition to providing traditional psychopharmacologic treatment, team members

> taught and assisted in daily living activities such as laundry upkeep, shopping, cooking, using a restaurant, grooming, budgeting, and use of transportation. . . . Patients were given sustained and intensive assistance in finding a job or sheltered workshop placement. . . . Furthermore, patients were aided in the constructive use of leisure time and development of effective socialization skills by staff prodding and support of their involvement in relevant community recreational and social activities. (Greenley 1995, 85)

Program staff also spent a great deal of time helping clients to apply for and, once received, manage their income support benefits (Estroff 1981).

Early on, PACT sought to distance clients from their families, who were seen as barriers to the clients' assuming greater independence (and also, given the psychiatric ideology of the time, as sources of pathology). Later, that goal changed and PACT tried to work more closely with families (Greenley 1995). This change was at least in part a result of the family movement, a movement that had its origins in concerns and frustrations of families in the wake of deinstitutionalization. One of the most influential of the family organizations, the Alliance for the Mentally Ill (now NAMI, formerly the National Alliance for the Mentally Ill) was founded in 1979 by a group of Madison parents of adult children with severe and persistent mental illness (Wisconsin Department of Health and Social Services 1994; Department of Health and Human Services 1999).

Because PACT was in part a research effort, the program was, from the beginning, continually being evaluated and modified. A "historical review" of PACT published in 1990 (Thompson, Griffith, and Leaf 1990), described these modifications as a series of "phases" in which the program underwent changes in goals and processes, moving from a focus on proving the feasibility of releasing long-term hospital patients to the community to finding ways to prevent clients from ever being hospitalized, and from maintaining particular clients outside the hospital to developing a comprehensive "system of care" for all chronically mentally ill persons in the community.

Sue Estroff's *Making It Crazy* (1981) is an ethnography of PACT in Madison in the mid- to late-1970s. Estroff did participant observation with PACT staff and clients over a period of many months, attending staff meetings and doing interviews with staff and clients, taking part in program activities, and "hanging out" with clients in the coffee shops, bars, rented rooms, and shared apartments where they spent their time. "Making it crazy" refers to the ways in which PACT clients both resisted and strategically embraced the "fusion of illness with identity" (244) and how the program's approach, in concert with government regulations pertaining to income support, worked to "confirm the client's belief in and acceptance of his or her disability and chronicity" (242).

Despite the warning implied in Estroff's analysis and later criticism that accused PACT of fostering dependence and pessimism and simply replicating "the hospital in the community" (e.g., Ahern and Fisher 1999; Nelson, Lord, and Ochocka 2001), the program became hugely influential, both in Wisconsin and nationally. Within the state, PACT became the model for a special advisory committee charged with looking at county service needs. Legislation based on the committee's recommendations, which passed the state legislature in 1983, required that all counties develop PACT-like community support programs (CSPs) and provided state funding and technical assistance for such development efforts (Greenley 1985; Goodrick 1989). In 1989, the state wrote and promulgated a set of statewide CSP operating standards, to be implemented by the counties with oversight by the state. At the same time, Wisconsin's CSP programs were made eligible for reimbursement by the medical assistance program (Wisconsin Department of Health and Social Services 1994). On the national level, the NIMH named Dane County (home of Madison and PACT) as a national model and training center, ensuring that PACT philosophies and practices would be disseminated throughout the country (Morrissey and Goldman 1986; Thompson, Griffith, and Leaf 1990). In the 1980s, Dane County's mental health system received national recognition from both NAMI and Public Citizen, the consumer advocacy organization founded by Ralph Nader (Wisconsin Department of Health and Social Services 1994).

A snapshot of Wisconsin's public mental health services system in the early 1990s finds that it is serving between 80,000 and 95,000 people each year at a cost of between $200 and $250 million, not including income support payments (Wisconsin Department of Health and Family Services 1996b). In 1995, the county share of these expenses reaches over $77 million (Blue Ribbon Commission on Mental Health 1997). The county-based system of care encompasses services for some seventy-two counties and eleven tribes and is operated by sixty-three county boards. (There are four multicounty boards that together serve thirteen counties). Across the state, there are 812 outpatient clinics and 64 community support programs. The two state hospitals (the forensic hospital at Waupun was closed in the restructuring of the 1970s) have available a total of ninety-seven beds for nonforensic adult patients (Blue Ribbon Commission on Mental Health 1997). Interestingly, in its financial and regulatory aspects, the relationship between the State of Wisconsin and its counties has come to parallel the relationship between the federal government and the states, with all of the attendant strains and tensions.

THE ROAD TO MANAGED CARE

In 1977, President Jimmy Carter established the national Commission on Mental Health to review the country's current mental health treatment needs and make recommendations for organizing services to better meet those needs. Congress passed the Mental Health Systems Act, legislation resulting from those recommendations, in 1980. The act provided money for the planning and implementation of an integrated network of community-based services for persons with severe and persistent mental illness (Grob 1994b). Soon afterward, however, with the election of Ronald Reagan in 1980 and passage of the Omnibus Budget Reconciliation Act of 1981, the Mental Health Systems Act was repealed.

In its stead, the Reagan administration instituted a program of mental health block grants to the states. Block grants, distinct from the categorical funding that the federal government had been providing to the states for more than twenty years, were consistent with Reagan's conservative

philosophy in several ways: they eliminated federal involvement in service provision, provided a means for reducing the overall federal costs
for social services, and fit well into a rhetoric of improving government
efficiency (Rochefort 1993). Under the block grant program, the federal
government ceased to have an active role in planning and funding specific
services; instead, the federal government would provide only general
technical assistance to states in doing their own planning (Morrissey and
Goldman 1986). The monies available for mental health—and, soon,
for federal income support programs like SSI and SSDI—declined, and
state and local governments were forced either to make up the difference
or to work within the constraints of reduced funding (Rochefort 1993;
Grob 1994b).

In the early 1990s, following the failure of the first Clinton administration's effort at health care reform (Johnson and Broder 1996), managed
care—broadly defined as a combination of financing mechanisms like
capitation and risk sharing and oversight mechanisms like gatekeeping
and utilization review—emerged as a strategic response to calls for continued cost containment and greater accountability in the nation's health
care system. Soon there were calls to extend the managed care model to
states' publicly funded systems of mental health service provision (Rochefort 1993; Mechanic 1998). Managed care, its proponents argued,
held the promise of improving patient outcomes and increasing system
efficiency because it would institute a strategy of structural controls and
incentives that would encourage providers to offer services that were both
"evidence-based" and bound by the criterion of "medical necessity."

This call for rationalization in health service provision was mirrored
by similar attention to the practices of government-funded income
support and social services in general, culminating in the enactment of
Clinton's 1992 campaign promise to "end welfare as we know it." True to
its history of innovation in public policy, Wisconsin became one of the
first states to implement welfare reform. Beginning in the early 1990s,
under Republican governor Tommy Thompson, the state initiated several
policies that sought to reduce the work disincentives built into current
welfare rules. In 1995 it started a two-county demonstration program
that provided temporary cash assistance, job training, and job placement
services along with subsidies for child care, health care, and transportation, in return for a recipient commitment to finding paid employment

and a strict time limit on cash support. In September of 1997, with Wisconsin Works (W2) a version of this program was implemented statewide (Street 1997).

The stated philosophy underlying W2 included eight principles (quoted in Nightingale and Mikelson 2000, 2):

- Work not Welfare
- Personal Responsibility
- Strong Families
- Value of Work
- Independence and Self-Sufficiency
- Community Support
- Minimal Necessary Services
- Managed Competition for Delivering Services

Together, these principles described an approach to welfare that sought to promote the production of self-sufficient nuclear families sustained by a combination of paid work (or "work activity") and the benevolence of private community ties and to reduce the role played by government both as a source of income support and as a provider of job training and job placement services. For service recipients, the principles stressed the value of independence. For service providers, the principles emphasized the utility of market competition and accountability mechanisms in improving performance. (The philosophical shift was mirrored by a change in bureaucratic nomenclature: the state's Department of Welfare was renamed the Department of Workforce Development.)

Managed health care was an integral part of W2. Although Wisconsin, unlike some states, did make a commitment to continuing to subsidize health care for W2 participants (at least for a period of time), under the terms of a federal waiver from the Health Care Financing Administration, that care shifted from being provided under the traditional Medicaid fee-for-service arrangement to managed care, with many W2 participants enrolled in local HMOs.

Plans for welfare reform and Medicaid managed care, in addition to a major restructuring of the state's long-term care system and federal intentions to link the provision of mental health block grant money to "performance contracting," were in the foreground when, in 1995, Wisconsin's Department of Health and Social Services convened an internal work group to examine the possibility of developing a managed care system for the delivery of mental health services.[2] In addition to addressing the state's fiscal concerns, managed care was to be the solution to three problems: the fragmented care and lack of access caused by the different requirements of the multiple funding streams supporting mental health services in the state; the perceived lack of county, family, and consumer involvement in policy making and planning for the current system; and the need for various divisions within the state Department of Health and Social Services to share a common vision and to work together to develop new strategies for providing services (Wisconsin Department of Health and Family Services 1996a).

The document produced, called *Designing Managed Care Models for Persons with Mental Illness and Substance Abuse—A Concept Paper* (Wisconsin Department of Health and Family Services 1996a), laid out a set of "desired goals and objectives" for bringing a managed care model to the state's mental health system. Among these were plans to blend federal, state, and local funding streams to provide greater flexibility (though no new monies would be added to the system); to develop a capitated model that would transfer all risk to "qualified vendors"; to use outcome measures and utilization review to build greater accountability into the system; to institute "best practices" in the care and treatment of mental illness across the state; and to provide "a single point of responsibility" that would coordinate individualized programs of comprehensive care, including "physical health services, mental health treatment, substance abuse treatment, and treatment with rehabilitative, social and support services, and long term care" (5). Toward these ends, the work group sketched five options for structuring managed care. These options differed in how they defined the relationships between the four major players (the state, the counties, HMOs, and service providers) and in whether they created new administrative entities, but all reflected a commitment to a risk-based, capitated model that used managed care principles and pooled funds to provide a "holistic" system of high quality services. The work group proposed that managed care be phased in: first implemented in demonstration projects in several pilot counties and then rolled out across the state.

In its vision statement and operating framework, the work group endorsed a number of philosophical principles and values: that "the participation of clients/customers and their families is critical in the design and implementation" of a new system; that "counties need to be significantly involved" in the planning and implementation process; and that the goal of the system should be the promotion of "health and wellness, improvement and recovery, quality of life, and self sufficiency." Additionally, the work group called upon Wisconsin policy makers to make an effort to disseminate the results of their planning and implementation efforts nationally in order "to assist other states to implement state-of-the-art managed care models" (2–3).

The department's internal work group attempted to fulfill its own participatory goals by seeking reaction to the managed care proposal from a wide range of stakeholder groups, including other departments of state government, the counties, and organizations of consumers, families, and providers. The magnitude of the structural alterations being considered, however, along with the power dynamics between the state and the counties, made it unlikely that change would occur based solely on this one group's proposal. Instead, advocates for change from both within and outside the department began to agitate for system reform to be taken up in a more visible, high-level, representative fashion.

THE BLUE RIBBON COMMISSION ON MENTAL HEALTH

The visible, high-level, representative mechanism devised was the governor's Blue Ribbon Commission on Mental Health. In the May 1996 executive order described at the beginning of this chapter, governor Tommy Thompson appointed a forty-member commission composed of individuals representing several different regions of the state and many stakeholder groups, including the legislative, judicial, and executive branches of state government; officials of the counties and tribes; providers working in the public and private systems; insurers and managed care executives; consumers of mental health services; family members of individuals with mental illness; and mental health advocates. The commission's charge was broader than simply picking up where the internal work group had left off. Instead, the commission was asked to take a comprehensive look at the state's current mental health system, assessing what worked well and what was broken; to consider the new knowledge base that was being developed in the treatment of psychiatric disorders; and to focus on issues of prevention, early intervention, and stigma reduction. These issues were to be reviewed with an eye toward two major structural factors: maintenance of the Wisconsin Plan of joint state/county responsibility and an eventual shift to "an environment that emphasizes managed care, client outcomes, and performance contracting" (Blue Ribbon Commission on Mental Health 1997, i).

After meeting as a large group and in issue-focused subcommittees for nearly a year, the commission issued a final report that laid out a broad plan for redesigning the system, including recommendations for changing its financing and organizational mechanisms (essentially by adopting some form of capitated managed care model as suggested by the Department's 1996 concept paper), for expanding prevention and early intervention services, for improving accountability by emphasizing consumer outcomes, and for eradicating stigma and discrimination against persons served by the system (Blue Ribbon Commission on Mental Health 1997). The commission's recommendations aimed to retain the system of joint state/county responsibility and accommodate the new managed care "environment" by proposing to allow existing county-based service delivery organizations to bid to become the managed care entities for their counties.

The philosophical cornerstone of the commission's recommendations was the adoption of "the concept of recovery, that is, the successful integration of a mental disorder into a consumer's life, as the key tenet of the redesigned mental health system." In such a system, " mental health consumers rebuild meaningful lives while decreasing their dependence on the system. They participate in services that enable them to recover rather than become long-term users of the mental health system" (Blue Ribbon Commission 1997, iii).

The commission's recommendations were grounded in a set of assumptions that together led to a self-proclaimed "paradigm shift" in the resulting model for the provision of mental health services. These assumptions encompassed emerging notions about the nature of mental illness and the public roles of people diagnosed with psychiatric disorders, about the most effective ways to plan and deliver services, and about the proper limits of state responsibility in providing for its citizens. In its final report, the commission summarized the corollary implications of these assumptions: "The field should promote consumer-directed, family-supporting, outcome-oriented, cost-effective service systems characterized by expectations of recovery, community integration, and an affirmative desire to fund only 'best practice' services; should engage consumer and family members throughout the workforce; and should fund consumer- and family-operated services" (Blue Ribbon Commission 1997, 10).

The commission's report sketched a plan for moving toward implementation of such a service system. The first step would be a series of demonstration projects, pilot sites (counties or tribes selected through a competitive process) that would operationalize both the structural and philosophical changes described in the report. Later, the changes would be implemented statewide. To provide further guidance in the implementation process (for the demonstration projects and beyond), the commission delineated a collection of successor advisory bodies. These included the Blue Ribbon Commission Implementation Advisory Committee (BRC-IAC), a high-level stakeholder group that would oversee the entire process of planning for the redesign, and the County Planning Partners group, whose membership would be drawn from the Wisconsin counties and tribes that were interested in planning for the demonstration projects.

In one of its first actions, the BRC-IAC directed the formation of a series of work groups. These work groups were charged with adding detailed implementation recommendations to the broad guidelines contained in the commission's report. Each work group was devoted to a specific substantive area. Groups drawn from the membership of the county planning partners focused on the fiscal (e.g., capitation and risk-sharing strategies) and benefits design (e.g., enrollment procedures and service co-ordination) issues involved in the shift to managed care. Other work groups were formed to look at enabling legislation, consumer outcomes and evaluation planning, management information systems and reporting, prevention and early intervention, and recovery.

THE RECOVERY WORKGROUP

Like the Blue Ribbon Commission, the Recovery Workgroup (whose efforts to develop specific policy recommendations are the subject of Chapter 4) was intended to be a mechanism for the promotion of coalition building and the efficient sharing of expertise. In determining its makeup, then, staff of the State's Bureau of Community Mental Health (who acted for the BRC-IAC in providing organizational and administrative support to the various work groups) sought to promote, above all else, the criterion of representativeness. That is, their aim was to achieve a diversity of members whose affiliations encompassed a number of parameters, such as geography, racial/ethnic minority status (including membership in an Indian tribe), and status as a consumer of mental health services. The logic underlying the representativeness criterion reflected both a concern with fairness and a desire to increase the Workgroup's eventual effectiveness. As one Workgroup cochair explained to me, the more groups involved in the planning process, the greater the "buy-in" and the better the chance for wide acceptance.

At any one time, the Recovery Workgroup had some thirty members. Although the individual membership of the Workgroup fluctuated, overall there was stability in the constituencies represented, including

- consumers—people with histories of using either public or private mental health services in the state of Wisconsin;
- providers—clinicians or program administrators (most of whom also had clinical backgrounds) working in Wisconsin's public mental health system;
- parents—parents of children diagnosed with serious emotional disturbances who were being served by the public system and parents of adults with histories of severe and persistent mental illness who had been involved with the state's public and/or private systems over a period of years;
- advocates—people who were either employed by or volunteered with local nongovernmental mental health advocacy groups; and
- bureaucrats—individuals employed by the state's Bureau of Community Mental Health.

Individual members often defied rigid demarcations between groups. Consumers were employed as providers or as bureaucrats. Parents were active in advocacy groups. Many advocates had worked in the state system. Workgroup members with multiple affiliations usually claimed a primary affiliation with one group, however. Individuals who had personal experience with the mental health system, for example, invariably made that experience the basis of their self-identification.

Such personal experience provided substance and context to the Workgroup's deliberations and lent authenticity and legitimacy to the its recommendations. Consumer members in particular were perceived to possess an expertise based on their experiences in the system. This expertise was expressed in the form of personal anecdotes, which were often used to illustrate a point or to make an argument. Consumers' expertise usually trumped that of providers and other "professionals." In part, this was because consumers were seen as closer to the experience of recovery and thus as natural authorities. The Workgroup's commitment to the primacy of consumers' personal experience also served a strategic function when it presented its recommendations: because of the high proportion of consumer membership in the Workgroup, objections to or disagreements with its products could be dismissed as the residua of "stigma," a charge that probably quelled much external criticism.

Both the BRC-IAC and other work groups looked to the Recovery Workgroup to provide information about recovery in a form that could be useful to fulfilling their own goals. At times, other work groups sought to use the Recovery Workgroup to validate their work products. The very existence of the Recovery Workgroup, with its broad representation of consumers and family members, was used to legitimize the core philosophical shifts being promoted in the system redesign. For example, as a living exemplar of the idea that consumers should be involved in the policy-making process, the Workgroup answered arguments that implied that such a goal was unrealistic.

AN IDEA OF WISCONSIN

It is true that Wisconsinites seldom agreed about what, exactly, the Wisconsin Idea was; but they were, and

seemingly remain, adamantly convinced of its existence, its
uniqueness, and its importance. (Buenker 1998, 610)

In Wisconsin, national trends and cycles in the development of mental
health services were manifested in ways that reflected the state's own social
and historical context. Progressivism left a lasting impact, particularly in
the methods used to investigate and address social problems. Thus, when
faced with dilemmas common to every state in the nation, Wisconsin
developed unique solutions including the system of joint state/county
responsibility for the provision of mental health services, Section 51.42,
and PACT. Each solution demonstrated some version of the Wisconsin
ideas of collaboration and the application of expertise to the public ben-
efit. All were sources of local pride but also targets of criticism.

One of the most striking elements of these solutions was the way in
which they mixed economic and humanitarian motives. The Wisconsin
Plan emerged at a time when the existing state-hospital system was
perceived as both cost-ineffective and inhumane. Section 51.42 sought
to remedy financial and quality problems in the services available across
the state. PACT, a programmatic reaction to the failures of the deinstitutionalization movement, tried to effect both more cost-efficient use of
professional resources and better outcomes for its clients. As broader social
circumstances changed, however, either the economic or the humanitarian aspects of these interventions, or both, would become inadequate,
and new reform efforts would begin.

Wisconsin's mental health redesign effort of the mid-1990s may be
understood in part as a response to the economic shortfalls of the Section
51.42 system and the humanitarian criticism of PACT-like community
support programs. In trying to address these problems, the state used
mechanisms that represented modern reworkings of the tools and procedures developed early in the twentieth century. The appointment of
the Blue Ribbon Commission was an exercise in coalition building, an
attempt to achieve comprehensive representation and to promote the investment of different interest groups in the redesign process and product.
The selection of representatives to serve on the issue-oriented work groups
reflected new conceptions of what constituted expertise, but the idea of
"the leadership of the competent"—the promise of expertise—remained
a core principle. The state asked the Blue Ribbon Commission and the

work groups to immerse themselves in the past and the present, to integrate what already existed (the state/county system) with what was new
(managed care, recovery) in order to develop a reform plan that joined
economic and humanitarian solutions in ways that respected the assumptions and values—both new and historical—that defined Wisconsin.

Interstice 1

MY OWN PRIVATE WISCONSIN

Nostalgia used to be a psychiatric diagnosis (Boym 2001). Because I don't live there anymore, I fear that my portrayal of Wisconsin may be tainted with the retrospective glow of homesickness. Perhaps I should supplement this attempt at a formal history with a more personal one.

I went to Wisconsin for my postdoctoral fellowship because when given a choice, I preferred its long winters and treatment of football as the unofficial state religion to the humid summers and tolerance for public smoking of Winston-Salem, North Carolina, where I had also been offered a fellowship. My preference didn't prevent me from missing gritty Baltimore (where I had gone to graduate school), however. In the first months, I couldn't get over the strangeness of a place where everything was clean and new and everyone seemed to look alike—tall, fair, and big-boned (especially in their winter padding, Wisconsinites take up a lot of space)—but I soon learned to appreciate the ease of living in a place where people were both competent and friendly.

My father attended the University of Wisconsin at Madison in the years just after the Second World War, when any nonresident student who maintained a B average received generous tuition grants. I grew up hearing stories about the fairness and decency of the state, its progressive history exemplified by this attempt to promote a social good like student diversity through meritocratic means. There were also tales about walking across the frozen lakes during the snowy, beautiful winters and about the Rathskellar in the student union—the first in the nation to serve beer. (In Madison, local legend has it that the beer trucks were driving up before the ink had dried on the Twenty-First Amendment.)

Such admiration and affection for "the UW" run deep in the state. A friend who was interviewing Wisconsin veterans for a study of cancer treatment at the Madison VA hospital met a man who told her he planned to donate his body to the university's medical school. His motivation for doing so, she learned, was his belief that the gift would result in a posthumous granting of alumnus status.

Although Madison has a reputation for being different—an oasis of liberalism (or foolishness, depending on your point of view) in the conservative Midwest, I think it typifies the Midwest because so many people there are reacting to the more narrow-minded places they have left. The form and content of their rebellions reveal the character of the region.

I miss the sky, the prairie (daily being consumed for new subdivisions), running in the Arboretum, the University's Union Terrace overlooking Lake Mendota, central time, big pancake breakfasts, frozen custard.

The winter before I left, when I already knew I was going to go, I hit and killed a deer while driving on a snowy, twilit back road in the center of the state. To my everlasting gratitude, this incident was treated as an everyday occurrence, with some levity, rather than as a tragic manifestation of murderous carelessness.

2

Four Scenes from the History of Recovery

In this chapter I examine the idea of recovery as it has been constructed by some of the key documents produced during the prominent mental health reform movements of the past: moral treatment, mental hygiene and the new scientific psychiatry of the early twentieth century, and deinstitutionalization and community treatment (Morrissey and Goldman 1986). As suggested by the title, my examination is episodic, cross-sectional rather than longitudinal, selective rather than comprehensive. I am guided by familiar questions: What is recovery? Who can recover? Recovery from (of ?) what? Who has the authority to define recovery? By using these questions to fragment historical ideas about recovery into some of their component parts, I hope to provide context and a comparative background to the "modern" history of recovery, the topic of Chapter 3.

Moral Treatment, Recovery, and the "Cult of Curability"

By the late eighteenth century, ideas about the cause of mental illness were in flux. While many laypeople believed that mental illness was a manifestation of spirit possession or a punishment for a lack of virtue, most practicing alienists (psychiatrists) understood mental illness as a form of brain disorder or defect, one that might have physical or environmental causes. Treatments were either medical (focused on the body, like bloodletting or warm baths) or psychological (focused on the mind, which was believed to reside in the brain and thus to have an effect on its form and function). Interventions directed at the mind sought to alter the thoughts and behaviors of persons believed to be mentally ill. This moral treatment (the contemporary name for psychological treatment) was developed in asylums in England and France and had moved to the United States by the early part of the nineteenth century (Deutsch 1949; Dain 1964; Caplan 1969; Scull 1979).

In his *Description of the Retreat* (1813), Samuel Tuke, grandson of the founder of the Quaker-run York Retreat (the model for many of the state hospitals built in the United States), laid out the foundational principles and practices that characterized the English version of moral treatment. The York Retreat Quakers understood mental illness as a condition that distorted the normal feelings and behaviors of afflicted individuals. Underneath the distortion, however, even the most symptomatic patients kept a degree of control, and most importantly, retained the "desire of esteem" (Tuke 1813, 157). Moral treatment as practiced at the retreat thus aimed to increase a patient's control over behavior by capitalizing on his or her need to be liked and admired. Retreat doctors and attendants demonstrated kindness and firmness in their interactions with patients, rewarding good behavior and either ignoring or, on rare occasions, applying "coercion" (usually isolation) to correct bad behavior. Equally, the retreat believed in promoting the "general comfort" of its patients, all of whom were Quakers able to pay the retreat's weekly fees. In its daily routine, the retreat provided simple food and opportunities for exercise, socializing, and useful occupation. In its physical architecture, the retreat supplied ample space, light, and air. Together, these psychological, social, and environmental interventions seemed to be quite successful. Statistics kept by retreat administrators indicated an overall recovery rate of close to 50 percent.

As I explained in Chapter 1, in the United States moral treatment was intimately linked to the movement to promote the building of state mental hospitals. The touted effectiveness of moral treatment served as a justification for the outlay of public funds.[1] That is, state legislators were promised that their investment in new institutions would pay for itself as these hospitals, built to the specifications of experts in moral treatment, returned citizens to productivity. The theory and practice of moral treatment, and the optimism it engendered, thus were embedded in the bricks and mortar of the state hospitals constructed throughout the United States in the 1800s.

Historians of moral treatment in America have interpreted the word *recovery* as a synonym for cure. Documents produced at the time certainly support this interpretation. For example, the 1863 Report of the Worcester State Hospital (quoted in Caplan 1969, 84), in which the hospital superintendent recounted the fate of the institution's patients, described people who had been discharged recovered as "restored to health." More specifically, their symptoms had been relieved—"exciteability calmed," "pains assuaged," "delusions controlled"—and the individuals had left the hospital to be "given . . . back to their homes and the world, to usefulness and the common enjoyment of their families, society, and to the usual responsibilities of citizenship."

Samuel Tuke himself, however, drew distinctions between recovery and cure. First, in part because both the causes and biological mechanisms of mental illness remained obscure, he claimed ignorance about "what degree of sanity is generally thought sufficient to warrant the application of the term, *'cured'.*" Instead, he chose the word *recovered,* which "applied only where the patient is fully competent to fulfill his common duties, or is restored to the state he was in, previously to the attack" (Tuke 1813, 216). Second, Tuke differentiated between cure and recovery in terms of agency. That is, he believed that the term *cure* should be applied only when improvement had come about through some direct action on the part of retreat staff. Because the retreat could "profess to do little more than assist Nature, in the performance of her own cure, the term *recovered* is adopted in preference to that of *cured*" (216–17).

During the era of moral treatment, recovery was perceived to be dependent on qualities of the individual patient. There was a long list of descriptive terms that could be applied to persons afflicted: acute/chronic; new case/old case; pacific/violent; normally intelligent/feeble-minded; rich/poor; educated/ignorant; native born/foreign. In each instance, those patients meeting the description of the first term in a pairing were believed to be more amenable to moral treatment, more likely to recover. Similarly, recovery potential was a quality more or less inherent in different symptom groupings. Those patients who demonstrated rapidly cycling extremes of mania and melancholia were more likely to be discharged recovered than were those suffering paranoid delusions, hallucinations resulting in violence, or dementia.

Extrinsically, recovery depended on systemic qualities of timing and accessibility. Writing in 1844, Pliny Earle, then superintendent of the Bloomingdale Asylum, claimed, "[I]t appears to be satisfactorily proved that, of cases in which there is no eccentricity or constitutional weakness of intellect, and where the proper remedial measures are adopted in the early stages of the disorder, no fewer than eighty of every hundred are cured" (quoted in Deutsch 1949, 152). The likelihood that state hospitals could effect recovery thus was seen as proportional to their ability to provide early treatment, which in turn depended on the availability of space for new cases and on public awareness of the importance of seeking professional treatment soon after the symptoms of mental illness first appeared.

The central fact about recovery was its status as a notable event: discharge from the institution. The politicization of recovery that occurred in the nineteenth century resulted from the use of discharge as a proxy for recovery and its deployment as evidence for the effectiveness of treatment. Historians have named this politicization the "cult of curability." According to Albert Deutsch, the cult's main argument was stark: "all the insane, or nearly all, could be cured in institutions; none, except a very few, could be cured outside" (Deutsch 1949, 187). It was in service of this proposition, and the money and professional power that would flow from its realization, that the statistics of recovery became the overriding preoccupation of hospital[2] superintendents in the nineteenth century.

Readings of the primary sources show that it was common for superintendents to report yearly cure rates of over 90 percent. Young and ambitious superintendents sometimes claimed to have pushed that proportion to 100 percent. Such optimistic statistics increased the likelihood of continued, and even expanded, public funding to state hospitals. For individual superintendents, reports of stellar results led to fame and prestige within the newly organized professional associations of alienists that were starting to define the discipline of psychiatry. It is likely that publicity about such high success rates also attracted more physicians to the specialty, despite its lack of scientific grounding.

But the statistical escalation had a dark side, as well. Public expectations began to outstrip even the most optimistic reported cure rates.

A drop of a percentage point or two from year to year would be taken as a sign of superintendent incompetence and might become grounds for dismissal or be used as ammunition for reducing the public monies allotted to the institution. At the same time, the patient population in state hospitals increasingly was composed of individuals whose characteristics were more likely to be consistent with the lesser of the pairings in the descriptive terms listed earlier. That is, more chronic cases, more immigrants, more poor people, and more uneducated people were being admitted to hospitals. Moral treatment had never made claims about its effectiveness with patients like these, and in fact it was failing.

It was in this context that in the late 1880s, Pliny Earle, once one of the most vocal proponents of the cult of curability, undertook a series of studies on "the curability of insanity" (Earle 1972 [1887]). Earle's method was to deconstruct the statistics of recovery and in so doing to argue for "other methods for the custody and care of a large part of the insane than that of collecting them in expensive and unwieldy curative institutions" (Earle 1972 [1887], 3).

Earle's exegesis of decades of reported recovery rates found that superintendents commonly used a number of tricks to inflate these rates. For example, rates often were reported by *case*, rather than by person. In this way, "[a] man may recover several times; and not only so, but, after several recoveries, he may still die insane" (9). A second trick was to manipulate rates by limiting which cases could be counted in the denominator: sometimes, the denominator might be composed only of "new" cases (that is, acute patients admitted within the last year, who were known to be more likely to recover) or even of discharged cases. In the former instance, the percentages were obscuring the fate of patients who had not recovered within a year and then were shifted to the "incurable" category, where they were not counted in the statistics. In the latter, the rates became little more than tautologies, reporting recoveries among only those patients who had been discharged, when discharge was in effect the operational definition of recovery. Taking these deceptions into account, Earle's recalculations suggested that recovery rates were more likely to be in the range of 20 to 30 percent, and certainly no more than 40 to 50 percent.[3]

Although it is his statistical work that often is held out as having deflated the cult of curability, Earle also raised interesting conceptual issues about the very nature and meaning of recovery. He noted, first, the subjectivity of its definition, taking as his examples the commonplaces of an increase or decrease in recovery rates following a change in hospital administration (where the change had been of too short a duration to have made any substantive difference) and of family and friends believing an individual to be fully recovered when he had reverted to his customary behavior, no matter how bizarre or dysfunctional such behavior might appear to physicians. He explored how recovery had become intertwined with the politics of advancement for his profession, pointing out that, in effect, alienists had claimed for mental illness higher recovery rates than for any physical ailment treated by other specialties. While hospital superintendents were eager to take credit when their patients recovered, Earle decried the tendency of his colleagues to look outside themselves when patients did not recover—for example, their eagerness to blame the family for not seeking treatment soon enough. Finally, he argued, the achievement of a recovery was always conditional on an unlikely confluence of ideal circumstances, most of which were out of any physician's or institution's control: "that by the performance of an impossibility, you may arrive at a probability or a possibility" (44).

Earle thought that any recovery, even a short-term one in a pattern of cyclical illness, was preferable to no recovery, and thus he continued to advocate public support of state mental hospitals. However, he also believed that the incidence of insanity was increasing ("as civilization has advanced"), and that an accumulation of chronic patients—"incurables" like "epileptics, paralytics, [and] imbeciles" (91)—soon would come to fill hospital wards. Legislators and citizens, he warned, should not expect that money poured into expensive institutions would improve the recovery rates in this patient population. Thus by the late nineteenth century the optimism that had followed the adoption of moral treatment had degenerated into pessimism.

A PUBLIC RECOVERY: THE STORY OF CLIFFORD BEERS

As a young man living and working in the business world of New York City in the early years of the twentieth century, Clifford Beers went mad. He moved back to his family home in New Haven, Connecticut, where he slowly grew worse. Over the next several years, he was hospitalized almost continuously in three different institutions, both public and private. In these hospitals, Beers received treatment, such as it was—sedating drugs, a wholesome diet, encouragement to pursue certain activities and to abandon others. Mostly, however, he was contained: prevented, first, from doing harm to himself and then, later, to others. After several years, Beers recovered and wrote a book about his experience. He then embarked on a carefully plotted mission to reform mental health care in the United States.

In that book, *A Mind That Found Itself* (1960 [1908]), and in the standard biographical work on Beers, *Clifford W. Beers: Advocate for the Insane,* by historian Norman Dain (1980), the particulars of Beers's life are reported this way: Beers grew up in a family of five sons. He attended school in New Haven and eventually was admitted to Yale. One of the Beers brothers had been diagnosed with epilepsy, and during his college years Clifford Beers was very much involved in helping to care for him. After the brother died (of what seems likely to have been a brain tumor), Beers became preoccupied with the thought that he too was destined to develop epilepsy. He never spoke to anyone about this fear, but grew depressed and withdrawn. After he could no longer work, he returned to New Haven, where his family treated him as an invalid. One day, shortly after having been served lunch in bed, when his conviction that he would soon suffer an epileptic seizure became overwhelming, Beers attempted suicide by dropping feet first from the second story window of his bedroom.

Beers did not die but received physical injuries serious enough that he was hospitalized for a number of weeks. During this period of hospitalization, he became convinced that his actions had brought dishonor to his family and to Yale and that he soon would be prosecuted for the attempt to take his own life, and for other vague, imaginary crimes. Again, Beers told no one about his thoughts, but instead took refuge in silence, refusing to speak. After his discharge from the hospital he went home, but his family soon realized that his condition was more serious than just several broken bones, and he was taken to a private hospital for treatment.

In the hospital, Beers continued to believe that authorities of the state were amassing evidence against him for an eventual prosecution. He grew to distrust everyone, his doctors and family included. As the financial burden of his care began to overwhelm his family, he was transferred to a state hospital. There, his fears and depression continued, and he made elaborate plans to commit suicide, plans that were thwarted by his belief that he was under constant surveillance.

One day Beers decided to test whether the man who came to visit him was in fact his brother, as the visitor claimed, or a clever imposter seconded by the police to gather more evidence against him, as Beers believed. Enlisting the help of a fellow patient who had town privileges, Beers sent a letter to his brother at the New Haven address listed by the post office. In it, he told his brother that were he to come to the hospital with the letter, Beers would know it was he and not an imposter. When the brother did show up, letter in hand, Beers experienced a revelation. His mind cleared, and he no longer believed that he was being persecuted: "Untruth became truth. A large part of what was once my old world was again mine. To me, at least, my mind seemed to have found itself, for the gigantic web of false beliefs in which it had been all but hopelessly enmeshed I now immediately recognized as a snare of delusions" (Beers 1960 [1908], 85).

Seemingly from one moment to the next, Beers shifted from depression and silence to elation and extreme volubility, both oral and written. Just as quickly, he became convinced that he had much to teach the world about mental illness and its proper care and treatment. He believed that he was destined to lead a crusade for the reform of mental hospitals. As he was not to be discharged immediately, despite his miraculous reversal of fortune, Beers determined to collect as much information as he could about the inhumanity of the facility where he was a patient.

Although in his own writing Beers presented the events of the next year, during which he was once again transferred to a private hospital, as entirely volitional, part of his work of information gathering, it seems clear that at least some of his behavior was out of control. He began writing hundreds of pages of letters to friends, family, and politicians, describing his plans and the heights he would achieve. He grew argumentative and combative with hospital staff—holding a particular animus against one of the junior doctors who was his primary physician. His outrageous behavior, whether intentional or not, provoked staff to demote him from the privileged wards in which he had been living quietly to wards designed for violent and unruly patients. There he experienced isolation, restraints, and beatings administered by ignorant and angry attendants.

Not suddenly, but slowly, Beers emerged from this phase. He grew calmer in his interactions with staff, and privileges were returned to him. After several months in much less restrictive custody, he was discharged to the care of his family.

Beers retained his desire to lead a mental health reform movement. He determined that the best strategy to start such a movement was to write an exposé of conditions in mental hospitals, an autobiographical account of his own experience—the journey into and out of madness, with particular emphasis on the ways in which hospital personnel had demeaned and humiliated him.

For the next several years Beers divided his time between writing and attempting to resume his career in business. Eventually he was rehired by his old firm and given a kind of traveling salesman position, which gave him much time to write during idle hours in hotels. As his book took shape, Beers drew on his Yale connections, and upon his own initiative, and sent the manuscript to figures prominent in business and medical circles, hoping to enlist them to his cause. In this way he drew the attention of William James, who became an adamant personal and professional supporter, and of psychiatrist Adolf Meyer of Johns Hopkins, who along with Beers became cofounder of the organization that was to be called the National Committee for Mental Hygiene.

Beers had lofty ideas about mental health reform, but his agenda was somewhat nonspecific. In general he believed that the work of reform should be focused on drawing attention to the plight of people suffering from mental illness and on improving conditions in hospitals. What was most tangible in Beers's plan was his desire to publicize his own story. By contrast, Meyer, known as the father of modern American psychiatry, came to reform with a fully developed theoretical model and scientifically justified rationale for certain points of intervention: his "psychobiology" conceptualized mental illness as a behavioral disorder, the end result of a causal chain of environmental, hereditary, physical, constitutional, and personality factors. Mental illness began as a skewed response to external stimuli that became a bad "habit" and then took on qualities of fixed dysfunction over time (Sicherman 1980). Psychiatry thus needed to intervene early, at both the social and individual levels. Meyer agreed that Beers was useful as a spokesman for his own experience but saw Beers's part in any national organization as limited. The eminent psychiatrist believed that any reform movement should focus on psychiatrists and should have a psychiatrist at its head; laypeople could be part of the cause but only in supporting roles.

The National Committee for Mental Hygiene was officially founded in 1909. Its charter called for the organization to work toward protecting the mentally ill and raising standards of care through careful study and information dissemination, through lobbying to increase federal funding of mental health care, and through the formation of state chapters. After several years of fundraising and other organizational activity, a physician was hired to head the committee, and Beers was named secretary (a paid position that he badly needed, after long having worked for the movement without a salary while depending on his family for financial support).

Norman Dain describes the next twenty-five years of the committee's existence as an unrelenting turmoil of external and internal politics. Beers became a master fundraiser, using his book (which went through many editions) and countless public retellings of his story to court the rich and powerful. He and Meyer were constantly at odds over the direction the organization should take. As Beers worked furiously to develop alliances with supporters and board members who would take his side, Meyer was doing the same, using Beers's history of mental illness as a weapon against him. Eventually, Meyer severed his association with the committee, but in its direction and emphases it was clear that he had won. More and more, the committee focused on areas like child guidance and preventively oriented social psychiatry.

Beers continued to work with the organization until he retired. Although he took some part in planning the committee's activities (and continued to be heavily involved in its internal politics), the bulk of his time was taken, as always, with telling his story. He still used the story to raise funds for the committee, but increasingly promotion of the organization and the cause were blending into promotion of the man. (In later editions of his book, much of the text was taken up with reprints of testimonials to Beers and his courage.) The irony, and the tragedy, of Beers's later life were that although the mental hygiene movement in general, and the National Committee in particular, had long ago stopped reflecting his vision, he could not separate himself because they nevertheless had come to represent his identity.

By the time he retired in 1939 Beers had become severely depressed, withdrawn, and somewhat delusional. Once more, he was admitted to a mental hospital. He died in the hospital in 1943.

A Mind That Found Itself portrayed Beers's recovery as utter, complete. The book suggested that his lengthy hospitalization and the years of depression that preceded it were an isolated episode. When he left the hospital, he was cured, never again to suffer the torments of mental illness. His value as a spokesman for the cause of mental hygiene rested on this premise. That is, his legitimacy depended both on his having had the experiences he described and on having left them behind forever: were the latter ever to seem uncertain, the truth of the former also would be called into question. If the poster child for mental hygiene were still experiencing mental illness, what worth could the movement claim?

As biographer Dain depicts his life, however, Beers was never a model of mental stability. His activity on behalf of the National Committee often became frantic. (He couldn't keep a secretary because his working habits—staying away from the office for days and then working eighteen to twenty hours at a stretch—were so erratic.) Yearly trips to summer in Maine allowed him a physical rest but also seem to have been timed to coincide with recurrent depressive episodes. Dain suggests that his extreme devotion to the cause and the melding of Beers the man and mental hygiene the movement were in part manifestations of Beers's fears about his own mental health: "In his mind, if the organization should go under, he might lose his standing as a recovered mental patient and be exposed as a fraud" (329).

While Beers's National Committee colleagues publicly endorsed the version of the story that had Beers fully recovered, in private they often spoke to him, and about him, in ways that revealed their belief in the "fragility" of his mental state. In the years of their power struggle over the committee, Meyer made overt references to Beers's instability, suggesting that were Beers to have a leadership role in the organization it would become a public relations disaster for the committee and a psychiatric disaster for Beers.

When one reads *A Mind That Found Itself*, it becomes clear that

Beers believed that his recovery occurred not during the period when he gradually worked his way back from violence and restraints but at the instant when "untruth became truth." That is, he identified his recovery as taking place at the moment when he transitioned from depression to mania. Beers had good reason for doing so: depression was painful for him, while he seems to have quite enjoyed the period of manic activity. More importantly, it was at the point of transformation and in the hectic months that followed that Beers was inspired to take up mental health reform and began to make the expansive plans that he actually acted upon after leaving the hospital. Were he to understand this inspiration and commitment as part of his illness, his life's work might have come to seem pathological.

Beers's account of life before his hospitalization (his early years as a somewhat reticent boy, the confusion and fear attendant upon his brother's illness) demonstrated an intellectual adherence to Meyer's model of mental illness as the result of an accumulation of multiple factors over time. His language, however, suggested quite a different emotional understanding. Beers described his illness as something sudden that came upon him from the outside: "an Army of unreason, composed of the cunning and treacherous thoughts of an unfair foe, [which] attacked my bewildered consciousness with cruel persistency, and would have destroyed me" (1). While the movement to which Beers devoted his life stressed the need to develop and disseminate scientific methods of treatment, Beers attributed his own recovery not to any treatment (and he implies that no action taken by any doctor could have helped) but to "a triumphant Reason [which] finally interposed a superior strategy that saved me from my unnatural self" (1).

Once he became famous, that belief in reason as an inborn quality necessary for recovery was reflected in many of his dealings with and attitudes toward others struggling with mental illness. After his book was published, Beers received many letters from discharged mental patients who were trying to put their lives back together. At times, these correspondents asked him for help. Beers's responses tended to emphasize the need for each individual to pull himself back up by his bootstraps, as he himself claimed to have done. In the 1930s, when groups of ex-patients began joining together in the first incarnations of the self-help movement,[4] Beers was antagonistic, seeing such a movement as a threat to his mental hygiene organization. Perhaps most shocking was his response to the mental illness that plagued his own family. In time, each of Beers's surviving three brothers was to experience bouts of severe depression, paranoia, and psychosis. Two eventually killed themselves, and the other, like Beers, died in a mental hospital. After receiving condolences over the death of one brother, Beers wrote back to his correspondent, opining that it was unlikely that the brother "would ever have recovered because he was making no effort to do so, and if he had recovered it is doubtful that he, with his make-up, would have stayed well. [He] had many fine traits and abilities, but he lacked persistency and ability to interest himself in any one thing for very long at a time" (quoted in Dain, 257).

For almost three-quarters of a century, *A Mind That Found Itself* remained the paradigmatic public account of recovery from mental illness. (As late as 1984, a woman writing about her own experiences with schizophrenia said it was the only account she had ever been able to find [Lovejoy 1984].) Beers portrayed his recovery as a version of the American Dream (Porter 1987): a man is struck low but by marshaling "reason" and "persistency" is able to triumph. Coming as it did in the midst of the pessimism that followed the deflation of the cult of curability, Beers's story was a revelation. Mental illness could be cured; it could be overcome.

Upon deeper examination, however, Beers's recovery was more ambiguous. Despite his many achievements, he remained, arguably, quite symptomatic. (Dain seems to suggest that the symptoms of his continuing mental illness, particularly the energy of his manic periods, were inextricably linked to his success.) For Beers and his copromoters of the mental hygiene movement, Beers's recovery was a publicly constructed phenomenon, a political necessity, without which the movement might be threatened. In private, though, his recovery was something conditional, open to question.

THE NEW SCIENTIFIC PSYCHIATRY: DEMENTIA PRAECOX AND THE PROBLEMATICS OF RECOVERY

In the late 1800s and early 1900s, adherents of the new scientific psychiatry, many of them physicians trained in the German-speaking countries of Europe, sought to boost the effectiveness and prestige

of the specialty by developing psychiatric nosologies based on ac-
cumulations of empirical evidence. One entity described during this
period was the group of disorders subsumed under the name dementia
praecox (now known as schizophrenia). Dementia praecox was characterized by severe abnormalities of both thought and behavior and most
often struck young people. The clinical importance of the disorder rested
both on its severity and on the fact that many of the chronic patients
living in hospitals were believed to suffer from it.

The classic descriptions of dementia praecox, which were to dominate
psychiatric thought for most of the next century, were written by Emil
Kraepelin (1919 [1896]) and Eugen Bleuler (1950 [1911]). Kraepelin's
account delineated the signs and symptoms associated with the disorder
and for the first time classified them into a number of different subtypes.
Bleuler's work, taking its foundation from Kraepelin, further explored
the biological and psychological origins of the disorder and named it
schizophrenia.

Kraepelin described the disease as one of inevitable deterioration,
resulting in "profound" and "terminal" dementia. He based his description on a number of cases and case series, and his work is replete with
detailed accounts of the unhappy lives and deaths of these patients. Bleuler
noted the great variation to be found among individuals diagnosed with
the disorder, but he, too, emphasized its downward course. Despite the
foundational assumption of deterioration, however, the notion of recovery
is persistent in the work of both men.

In choosing the patients whose characteristics would come to determine the features of this diagnostic category, Kraepelin made a conscious
decision to include "only such cases as had led to profound dementia or
to distinctly marked and permanent phenomena of decreased function"
(90). "'Recovered' cases were not taken into account," he wrote, "because
of the uncertainty of their significance" (89). Dementia praecox thus
was defined as resulting in deterioration not because every diagnosed
individual deteriorated, but because individuals who recovered made no
sense to the man who understood that deterioration was inevitable.[5]

Despite his "uncertainty" surrounding its "significance," Kraepelin
devoted many pages in his classic text to describing the dimensions and
degrees of recovery. Patients might show improvement in aspects such as
mood, behavior, and symptoms. They might demonstrate an increased

ability to work or an increased understanding of the "significance of the morbid phenomena" (190) ("insight," in modern parlance). Patients could be categorized along a range of outcomes: from the expected ("not able to manage without special care" [184]) to the seemingly impossible ("completely well" [183]) and all points in between—from "essential improvement of the condition but without the complete disappearance of all morbid phenomena" to "quiet" "orderly" and "in a position to earn their own living again without difficulty" (183).

Evidence of recovery presented Kraepelin and his followers with a conundrum: if dementia praecox was, by definition, a disease of poor outcome, how could one account for the cases that had demonstrably good outcomes? One solution was to revise the diagnosis: an individual who recovered after being diagnosed with dementia praecox had probably been misdiagnosed initially and was in truth suffering some other, less grave disorder. A second response was to discount all apparent recoveries, even those many decades long, as temporary "remissions" that would be followed by relapse. (The distinction between relapse and a new episode of the same disorder—a phenomenon well known in diseases of the body—was hotly debated.)

Perhaps the most nuanced answer was to parse the meaning of recovery. Both Kraepelin and Bleuler were careful to distinguish it from cure. A true cure, according to Bleuler, would necessarily constitute a *restutio ad integrum*, a complete return to normal. What one saw with dementia praecox patients, however, was more aptly described by the phrase "recovery with defect," a circumstance in which "all the more striking morbid phenomena may disappear, while the less important changes of the psychic personality remain, which for the discharging of the duties of life may have no importance, but are perceptible to the careful observer" (Kraepelin 1919 [1896], 186). (The most careful observer, of course, was the psychiatrist. Bleuler wrote, "I have never released a schizophrenic in whom I could not still see distinct signs of the disease" [Bleuler 1950 (1911), 256].) Bleuler also described a somewhat lower-order version of this phenomenon: "healing with scarring"—the occurrence of individuals who seemed healthy, but only by dint of having "lowered the level of aspiration with regard to their accomplishments and claims on the world" (Bleuler 1950 [1911], 263).

The idea of recovery thus was formally bifurcated into two notions that had been implicit since Tuke wrote about it in the early nineteenth century: "real" recovery, or cure, and "practical," or "social," recovery. While the former was clearly superior, it was also rare—an assertion that maintained the foundational principle of inevitable deterioration along with its attendant pessimism. Practical recovery—"recovery with defect" or "healing with scarring"—once recognized as a matter of definition, seemed quite a common occurrence, but the dominance of the idea of deterioration meant that it would be years before it attained much purchase among mental health professionals.

THE SCIENTIFIC PURSUIT OF RECOVERY

The plethora of psychiatric medications developed in the years after the Second World War turned the discipline toward the practice of testing these therapeutics through clinical trials and other, less formal, means. Advances in the theory and technology of neuroscience led researchers to seek a more complete understanding of the biology of mental illness. Social psychiatry, influenced by the mental hygiene movement, used large descriptive studies to comprehend the course of mental illness, with an eye toward finding those points at which individual or social intervention might act as primary, secondary, or tertiary prevention. Following deinstitutionalization, programs of community-based treatment sought to improve the daily functioning of clients suffering from severe and persistent mental illness. In the context of these new endeavors, recovery, particularly recovery from severe mental illnesses like schizophrenia, became salient as a measurable result, a multidimensional outcome.

Conceptualizations of recovery in the 1960s and 1970s were largely utilitarian, practical for developing assessment scales or clinical models. Articles in psychiatric journals operationalized recovery as improvement in symptoms and then sought to find patterns in the ways people recovered (e.g., Saenger 1970; Donlon and Blacker 1973; Carr 1983). Two such patterns received particular attention. The "dimensional," or "continuum," model conceptualized recovery as "changes in symptomatology . . . [that occur] on a severity continuum for each discrete symptom or symptom cluster" (Carr 1983, 96). In this model, disease entities were disaggregated into symptom domains (e.g., psychosis, depression, anxiety), and recovery was a function of improvement measured in one or more domains. The "categorical" model, on the other hand, described recovery as "a sequence of discrete, reliably identifiable stages which are qualitatively distinct and mutually exclusive" (Carr 1983, 104). These stages were presented differently by different authors, but generally consisted of categories like disintegration, symptom reduction, function resumption, and reconstitution (Carr 1983).

Both the dimensional and the categorical models of recovery emphasized pathology. That is, recovery was conceptualized as a function or domain of illness, not of wellness. In the dimensional model, recovery was synonymous with the diminution of symptoms but not necessarily the assertion of strengths, while in the categorical model it was constructed as simply another stage in the course of the disease. (Some categorical adherents developed their models by studying the process of disintegration caused by mental illness and then simply reversing the stages! [e.g., Donlon and Blacker 1973].)

Beginning in the 1980s, such highly clinical, disease-oriented conceptualizations of recovery were supplemented by more phenomenological accounts (e.g., Breier and Strauss 1984; Ratey, Sands, and O'Driscoll 1986; Davidson and Strauss 1992). These models of recovery were based not on etic, externally imposed markers like measures of symptoms, but on emic reports of lived experience.[6] They too described dimensions or stages, but their categorical content focused less on the degree of observed pathology and more on assessments of sense of self and involvement in social relationships. Their salient phenomena were processes like "convalescence" and "rebuilding" (Breier and Strauss 1984) or "reintegration and organization of bodily experience" and "movement toward other people" (Ratey, Sands, and O'Driscoll 1986), processes that described not just the ebb and flow of symptoms but the nature of being in the world.

The conceptualizations of recovery seen in these two types of models represent a reworking of the bifurcation in the meaning of the term that had been apparent since moral treatment: the competing notions of "real" versus "practical" recovery. Clinical models of dimensions and stages looked to recovery as a quality of pathology, defining it as a "real" event characterized by the presence or absence of certain objective disease indicators. Their specificity made these models very useful for assessing the impact of very targeted and controlled interventions, like medication trials. Phenomenological models, on the other hand, eschewed objective ways of knowing. Instead, they constructed recovery as a process of growth and change that could only be accessed subjectively. The subjective and processual nature of recovery meant that it was highly dependent on context: recovery was to be found in the "practical" interplay among the disease, the individual, the treatment, and the social milieu. For community treatment programs, where the goals of intervention included integration into the worlds of family, work, and the community and thus were just as contextual, these models were well suited to evaluating success.

150 YEARS OF RECOVERY

In the moral treatment era, epistemological lacunae led observers to make a distinction between physiological restoration, which could not be known, and social restoration, which could. A second line of demarcation was drawn by agency: cure was what doctors did to patients; recovery was what happened to patients with the help of nature alone. Individual characteristics of patients and systemic factors linked to access were seen either to help or to hinder the achievement of improvement. Recovery was operationalized as an event, discharge.

Clifford Beers's illness and recovery were the defining events of the man and, through him, of a movement. The public nature of this recovery, and the political purposes it was drafted to serve, distorted it. Beers's recovery became fixed, a diorama behind museum glass, the exhibit labeled "a mind that found itself." As the curator of his own life, a position he held on sufferance, Beers voiced a narration of complete recovery. The apparent reality of his life, however, was that this recovery was never fixed but always in flux.

Dementia praecox, a diagnostic entity defined by the impossibility of recovery, confounded the men who classified it. "Recovery with defect" and "healing with scarring" were categories designed to reduce their cognitive dissonance. The conceptual distinction between "real" recovery and "practical" recovery was a solution that maintained the principle but accounted for the evidence. Psychiatric conceptualizations of recovery developed in the mid- to late twentieth century extended the "real"/"practical" distinction, locating the former in clinically observed patterns of symptomatology and the latter in phenomenologies of lived experience. Both types of models proved useful for purposes of judging the success or failure of treatment.

Throughout these historical episodes, we see cycles of optimism and pessimism about the likelihood of recovery from mental illness. As Joseph Morrissey and Howard Goldman (1986) have written, each major mental health reform movement has started "with the promise that early treatment in the new setting would prevent the personal and societal problems associated with long-term mental disability" (785). This promise, this optimism, serves to promote the new approach just as the new approach serves to promote optimism. As "changing and unanticipated circumstances" (785) reveal the weaknesses of new approaches, however, pessimism sets in.

A second common theme has been the bifurcation of recovery into two notions: the denotation of "cure" (or "real" recovery) and the connotation of "practical" recovery, which, while falling short of cure on most spoken or unspoken scales of comparison, represents some form of improvement. While "real" recovery has been modeled on the phenomenon of recovery from physical illness, and thus has been recognized by objective measures of diminution in clinical signs and symptoms, "practical" recovery has always been more subjective. Because of this subjectivity, there have been changes in its meaning, in what counts as evidence for recovery. In the days when treatment for mental illness consisted of institutionalization, practical recovery was defined by discharge. As treatment for mental illness moved into the community and gained more and more responsibility for the lives and functioning of its patients, practical recovery grew to encompass domains like work, social interaction, self-esteem, and happiness. In this way, expectations for recovery are structured by the capacity and reach of the model of mental health services that is current at the time.

Also extant in each episode is the idea that some people are more likely to recover than others. The propensity for recovery is linked to the ascribed or achieved characteristics of individuals, to disease category or severity, and to social circumstance, such as the availability of treatment in a given locale. Implicitly, this variation in ability to recover creates a hierarchy among sufferers, with those believed more likely to recover seen as more deserving of treatment. The notion of recovery may contain the blueprint for a rough sort of triage.

In each episode, recovery was an idea with public implications, one that served a number of public functions: accountability, education, propaganda. That is, recovery was used as evidence for the effectiveness of different approaches, for different audiences, with different purposes. Legislators and other funding bodies heard about recovery in order to justify expenditures and to persuade them to increase the monies allotted to the service system of the era. Families and the general public were instructed in the possibility of recovery in order to educate them about the proper disposition of persons with mental illness (seek treatment early and often) and with the goal of enlisting them as advocates in the greater cause of resource allocation. The promise of recovery served to promote professions (psychiatry, social work), movements (mental hygiene, community treatment), and specific treatments or therapeutic modalities (moral treatment, psychotropic medications). These public uses of recovery depended on the expression of optimism, an expression that may or may not have accommodated the subtleties of the "real"/"practical" distinction.

Finally, in each of these episodes, the authority to define recovery, and to identify recovery in individuals, rested with professionals. Hospital superintendents decided who could be discharged and when. Clifford Beers sought out the most influential psychiatrist of the day to validate his story and (perhaps to his everlasting regret) to be the cofounder of his movement. Psychiatric classifications and models included expert criteria or guidelines to be used for ascertaining the presence or absence of recovery. Even the phenomenological models of the 1980s, which sought to give voice to the lived experience of mental illness, were interpreted by and written in the language of experts.[7]

Interstice 2
Recovering

What happened:[1]

By late January 1998, my first winter in Wisconsin, I had been in pain for years. Lower back pain. Pelvic pain. Painful and messy periods endured only by taking so much ibuprofen that my ears buzzed, creating a protective field of enervation. Some time earlier, I had pursued the matter medically only so far as to rule out ovarian cancer. (I was writing my dissertation at the time and wanted to find out if finishing was to be my last, brave act. Perhaps we could hold the final defense in the hospital, committee members gathered around my deathbed?)

In the insidious manner of chronic pain, it got worse. I couldn't sleep. Riding the city bus over speed bumps or potholes hurt like hell. One, then two weeks a month gastrointestinal distress made my daily runs a misery of pit stops and time-outs to assume a clammy fetal position by the side of the road. A new burning, shooting pain joined the nausea and cramps and regular aches and throbs between my waist and thighs.

The perverse thing was, while on one level I knew how much pain I was in, I couldn't put things together to see how it was affecting my life. I thought I was having a hard time adjusting to a new place. I thought I was depressed. I thought I couldn't sleep or concentrate on my work because I was really depressed.

Finally, it all reached a crisis. One afternoon, the pain began to intensify, to focus itself. By the middle of the night, after hours of pacing and squirming to try to find a comfortable position, I called the clinic where I had recently selected a primary care provider. I thought I had a kidney stone, but the doctor on call told me it sounded more like a pulled muscle and to phone back in the morning. (Apparently I had neglected to use the key word, agony.) Hours fourteen and fifteen passed in a nightmare of pain and nausea and vomiting. Then a quieting of the pain and, by early morning, its cessation. I slept for several hours.

The medical student who took my history at the clinic missed what were, I later learned, some of the textbook signs of kidney stone attack. My urine was swarming with white cells but contained only a few red. The doctor diagnosed a probable kidney infection and sent me off with a prescription for a sulfa drug and the instruction to drink a lot of water. "We used to automatically hospitalize people for a kidney infection so they could be hooked up to intravenous antibiotics," she told me cheerfully, "but we've found they do just as well at home."

A week later I was admitted to the hospital from the urgent care clinic. I had a fever, had lost a lot of weight, and was so weak I could hardly walk. I felt like weeping with gratitude when the doctor on duty told me she wanted me to be hospitalized ("people who look as sick as you do are usually in the hospital"), but on the wheelchair ride to my room on a general medical floor, I caught glimpses of my fellow patients—querulous, sallow, chronically ill with diabetes, heart disease, COPD or emphysema—and thought that I was really too healthy to be there.

The first night, a CT scan showed bilateral kidney stones, the larger one perched at the end of the left ureter, almost ready to drop into the bladder—my nemesis from the night of pain the week before. My urine indicated unchecked infection. My temperature continued to rise. The scan also found growths on one ovary and a series of blood tests turned up all sorts of abnormal counts and shapes.

I was to spend four days in the hospital, but almost right away I started fighting to go home because I was afraid they were going to kill me. My various test results meant I was now being looked after by an attending physician and several residents in internal medicine, a medical student, two different radiologists (one pursing the kidney and the other the ovary), a nephrologist (the hospital's "stone man") and his fellows, and a hematologist and his fellows. I saw a different nurse every shift. No one person (save perhaps the medical student, rumpled Francis) seemed to be responsible for me, and no one was talking to anyone else. My liquid input and output were being monitored and my urine filtered, so every time I peed I had to report it and wait for someone to come around to examine what I had produced. I had two IV-line infiltrations and an allergic reaction to one of the antibiotics. After the first day my white blood-cell count suddenly dropped way below normal. I was put on neutropenia restrictions: a big red sign tacked to my door warned that I was to have no plants or raw food, and that visitors and medical personnel were to wash their hands and wear masks inside. Everyone had a different theory of what was going on—an adverse reaction to the drugs, an obscure tropical disease acquired in my travels, HIV, sepsis caused by an uncontrolled kidney infection. I wasn't getting anything to eat except juice and Jell-O. I couldn't read or sleep. The attending physician mistook me for another patient with the same name and began insisting that he had seen the results of tests I'd never had. An orderly who wheeled me back from the radiology department left me by the nurses' station on my floor and, masked for my own protection and drowsy from the Benadryl I'd been given for the allergic reaction, I had no idea how to get back to my room.

They let me leave on a Friday afternoon, after my white cells had shown signs of rebounding and the stone had popped out. I was thinner and weaker than when I had been admitted. I had lots of pills to take and many follow-up appointments—a three-page list of discharge instructions. Nothing ever felt better than taking a shower at home and getting into my own bed.

So I found myself a semi-invalid, needing to recover. I had to gain weight in a healthy way. I had to get back my fitness—physical energy, strength, and endurance. I had to concentrate hard enough to work again. I had to learn to be assertive during the months of medical interventions[2] yet to come. I had to decide not to become too focused on the experience and my "conditions"—to avoid making an avocation of my health.

One night during my convalescence, I awoke in a cold terror of having realized my own mortality. I was sure in a way I'd never been before that I was going to die. After that, as I began to get better—as I was able to take short, then longer, walks, to leave the house for reasons other than doctors' appointments, to read and write and think for sustained periods of time—I experienced a kind of euphoria. I was alive! I was well! I suddenly had perspective. The little things really didn't bother me anymore. I felt cheerful and optimistic. This wave of uncharacteristic good feeling lasted for months, but eventually it, too, passed.

3
A Simple Yet
Powerful Vision

Historically, then, recovery was a matter of consequence, the *result* of a particular event, effort, or treatment. The character of the result might differ ("real" versus "practical" recovery), but it was clearly a matter of objective improvement, or at least of apparent normalization, in an individual's thought or behavior, word or deed, symptom or function. The public value of recovery thus rested on its status as evidence. This chapter recounts several transformations in the significance—the public value—of recovery: the shift from recovery as evidence to recovery as experience and then to recovery as ideology—"a simple yet powerful vision" (Anthony 1991, 14)—to guide in the provision of mental health services.

I locate the sources of these shifts in three phenomena. First, the publication of a series of longitudinal studies of persons with severe and persistent mental illness, particularly schizophrenia, that showed good long-term outcomes in this population. Second, psychiatric rehabilitation, an approach to service provision that emphasizes the promotion of the skills needed for day-to-day functioning among individuals who have psychiatric disabilities. Third, the consumer/survivor movement, a social movement focused on drawing attention to the marginalization of people carrying a label of mental illness and on advancing human and civil rights for those so labeled. Although the longitudinal studies, psychiatric rehabilitation, and the consumer/survivor movement are linked, both temporally and thematically, I begin by exploring them separately.

LONGITUDINAL STUDIES

The assumption of inevitable deterioration embedded in the original nosological descriptions of schizophrenia, combined with the so-called Clinician's Illusion—the tendency of practitioners to see only the sickest of any category of patients (Harding, Zubin, and Strauss 1987)—together gave mental health professionals, and through them, patients, families, and the general public a sense of pessimism about the disorder. Schizophrenia, it was thought, was akin to a death sentence, at worst, or, at best, a life sentence. As recovery has been promoted as a new paradigm in mental health services, however, a series of longitudinal studies of people diagnosed with schizophrenia has been used to promote a different impression.

In his book *Recovery from Schizophrenia*, Richard Warner (1994) reviews some eighty-five studies of long-term outcome in schizophrenia. He groups the studies by decade, beginning in the 1890s with the work of Kraepelin, and focuses on three outcomes: "complete recovery" (or "real" recovery), "social recovery" (or "practical" recovery), and hospitalization. (Warner's main argument, which I take up in Chapter 6, is that outcome is linked to the state of the economy, with more recoveries seen during periods of economic boom.) His tabulations suggest that, except during the Great Depression, recovery rates have remained fairly steady over time, hovering at around 20 to 25 percent for complete recovery and 40 to 45 percent for social recovery.

One of the studies included in Warner's review (of greatest interest, perhaps, because it implies such a juicy Freudian back story) was published in 1972 by Manfred Bleuler, son of Eugen Bleuler, whose own work had been so influential in establishing the assumption of deterioration. As chief of a psychiatric clinic in Zurich, Bleuler the younger embarked on an ambitious project: to follow some 208 of the clinic's schizophrenic patients (and their families) over a period of more than twenty years, with an emphasis on understanding the course of the illness over time (Bleuler 1978 [1972]). In contrast to the pessimism of his father, Bleuler's findings led him to be quite optimistic.[1] Rather than taking the "chronic-progressive" course often described, most of Bleuler's patients were found to be "constantly changing back and forth between states of recovery, improvement, nonimprovement, and deterioration" (Bleuler 1978 [1972], 413). Over time, the majority of patients in the study did experience significant periods of recovery or improvement,[2] leading Bleuler to conclude that some two-thirds to three-quarters of cases of schizophrenia are of the "benign" type—that is, characterized by "long-term recovery periods . . . [or] recoveries that are interrupted only by brief psychotic episodes, and the mild chronic 'end states'" (414).

The research most often cited in recent discussions of recovery is the Vermont Longitudinal Study. (Publications from this study were not included in Warner's review.) The study had its roots in the Vermont Project, which began in 1959, when 269 "chronic" patients at Vermont State Hospital, most of whom had been diagnosed with schizophrenia, were enrolled in a new rehabilitation program, then released into the community (Harding 1986; McGlashan 1988). Regular follow-ups of this cohort (see Harding and Brooks 1980; Harding et al. 1987a; Harding et al. 1987b) over three decades found that "widely heterogeneous patterns of social, occupational and psychological functioning evolved over time" (Harding et al. 1987b, 732). Taken together, these follow-up studies indicated that up to two-thirds of the original group of patients attained significant levels of recovery, showing great reductions in symptoms and an ability to live and work in the community with little or no professional support.

Despite the general consistency of all of these reports, they were not sufficient to sway the mainstream of psychiatric opinion toward a comprehensive optimism. In a literature review of long-term follow-up studies of schizophrenia (McGlashan 1988), for example, the author's first synthetic finding was that "schizophrenia is a chronic disease, frequently disabling for a lifetime" (527). (This more pessimistic outlook was often reinforced by methodological criticism of studies showing good outcome, such as the practice of dismissing their findings as the result of initial misdiagnoses [Harding, Zubin, and Strauss 1987].)

Together, however, the impact of longitudinal research was to chip away at the assumption of deterioration. The same review concluded that the extant literature suggested heterogeneity of outcome among patients diagnosed with schizophrenia, outcomes that varied "between complete recovery and continuous incapacity" (528). Although the author attributed the finding of heterogeneity to "sample characteristics and/or differences" like level of chronicity at time of study enrollment, age at illness onset, economic status, and degree of responsiveness to medication, the implication was still clear: for some people, at least, recovery from schizophrenia was a distinct possibility.

This implication was of extraordinary value. As Manfred Bleuler had noted, the assumption of inevitable deterioration "exerts its paralyzing influence on therapeutic initiative, and in its own secretive, insidious way, promotes hopelessness and resignation among doctors, nurses, families, and among the patients themselves" (Bleuler 1978 [1972], 413). The possibility of recovery found in longitudinal research provided a scientific justification for hope. Further, the lack of certainty about the mechanisms of recovery, the inability to predict which patients would recover and which would not, suggested that clinicians "must operate 'as if' improvements will happen for anyone in order to maximize the number of turn-arounds toward higher functioning" (Harding, Zubin, and Strauss 1987, 483). For those who were open to hearing it, the "as if" imperative had an important implication: in order to do the greatest good for the greatest number, services should be designed not to maintain a chronic minority, but to promote recovery for the majority.

PSYCHIATRIC REHABILITATION

In the middle part of the twentieth century, the large-scale movement of people with mental illness from the hospital to the community, and the failure of many of these individuals to make a successful transition, occasioned an increased interest among mental health professionals in finding ways to promote functioning, as well as symptom reduction (Wing and Morris 1981; Lamb 1994). Psychiatric rehabilitation, one result of this increased interest, developed with the aim of "assur[ing] that the person with a psychiatric disability can perform those physical, emotional, social, and intellectual skills needed to live, learn, and work in the community, with the least amount of support necessary from agents of the helping professions" (Anthony and Liberman 1986, 542).

Proponents of psychiatric rehabilitation claim for it a multifaceted lineage. Some point to origins in moral treatment, with its emphases on behavior and the therapeutic value of environment and wholesome activity (Wing and Morris 1981; Anthony and Liberman 1986; Lamb 1994). Others link it to the tradition of "socialization" as practiced first in hospital-based group therapy and later in community-based social

clubs for ex-patients (Grob 1983). The development of psychiatric rehabilitation also is believed to have benefited from its adoption of several
specific innovations, including the introduction and widespread use of
antipsychotic medications (Lamb 1994), government-sponsored vocational rehabilitation programs designed for physically disabled veterans
of the Second World War, and advances in the behavioral sciences that
led to new methods for skills training (Anthony and Liberman 1986).

The conceptual framework underlying psychiatric rehabilitation
construes mental illness as a multidimensional disorder with biological,
psychological, and social components. The complexity of illness expression and of individual and societal response means that the impacts of
mental illness are multidimensional as well. These impacts have four
levels: impairment, dysfunction, disability, and disadvantage (Anthony
and Liberman 1986; Anthony, Cohen, and Farkas 1990). Impairment
relates to the psychological or physiological effects of the illness itself; dysfunction addresses the individual limitations resulting from impairment;
disability the role limitations (for example, as a parent or worker) caused
by dysfunction or impairment; and disadvantage the social implications
of impairment, dysfunction, and disability.

Psychiatric rehabilitation seeks to intervene at each level of impact
(Anthony and Liberman 1986). In collaboration with psychiatry,[3] it
uses medication and other treatment modalities to reduce impairment.
It deploys skills training and support to remediate dysfunctions and disabilities in the domains of family, friendship, work, and daily living. In
addition, it addresses disadvantage by promoting "societal rehabilitation,"
or changes at the level of the organization or community that facilitate
the successful integration of people with psychiatric disabilities. Thus,
psychiatric rehabilitation has a multilevel focus: "either teaching persons
the specific skills needed to function effectively or developing the community and environmental resources needed to support or strengthen their
present levels of functioning" (Anthony and Liberman 1986, 542).

The principles that direct the practice of psychiatric rehabilitation
follow on this conceptual framework. Bachrach (1992) summarizes these
principles: the need for individualization in all aspects of practice; an
emphasis on understanding environmental factors and the interaction
between the individual and the environment; a focus on ascertaining and
exploiting existing individual strengths; a positive outlook that promotes

hope; optimism about the possibility and value of work; a concern with a broad array of life engagements (i.e., not just vocational activities); the requirement that people with mental illness be active participants in planning their rehabilitation programs; and the recognition that psychiatric rehabilitation is a process, not a single intervention.

In the first edition of their comprehensive text, Anthony, Cohen, and Farkas (1990) delineate the key processes that define the practice of psychiatric rehabilitation: assessment, planning, intervention, and monitoring or evaluation. Assessment involves determining a client's strengths and wishes, as well as the degree and effect of impairment. Planning relies on "environmental specificity," a focus on the context of the client's life and the choice of goals he or she wishes to attain. Intervention encompasses both plan implementation and ongoing support. Monitoring and evaluation seek to determine the success (or lack thereof) of the plan in promoting the client's happiness, functioning, and role status. These processes may take place in a variety of settings, including the day hospital, the clubhouse, or the rehabilitation center (Lamb 1994). Anthony, Cohen, and Farkas (1990) emphasize that a true psychiatric rehabilitation program requires three elements: an explicit rehabilitation mission, an organizational structure that promotes rehabilitation principles, and access to rehabilitation environments.

Critics of psychiatric rehabilitation have raised objections from both ends of the ideological spectrum. Based on the attitudes and practices of certain programs, some psychiatrists have charged psychiatric rehabilitation with being "anti-psychiatry" in orientation and with rejecting the biological basis of mental illness (Bachrach 1992). Others have accused programs of promoting "unrealistic expectations" in and of persons with mental illness (Bachrach 1992, 1458). Psychiatric rehabilitation has also been criticized for being overly focused on placing clients in paid employment (Bachrach 1992), for being overly directive (rather than open to consumer participation), and for being oriented toward individual (rather than societal) change (Lord et al. 1998).

The range of criticism raised against psychiatric rehabilitation reflects cultural shifts—in particular, the rise of the values and principles of the consumer/survivor movement (as I will explore in the next section), but also some change in how the approach has been conceptualized and presented. While earlier discussions tended to describe psychiatric rehabilitation as a clinical modality performed by professionals and based on professional knowledge and expertise (see, for example, Wing and Morris 1981), more recent presentations emphasize the collaborative nature of the rehabilitation process.[4] Psychiatric rehabilitation remains a professional practice, but one that claims to be grounded in valuing and promoting the autonomy of the client (Joint Commission on Accreditation of Healthcare Organizations, undated).

The historical notion of "practical" recovery resonates throughout the theory and practice of psychiatric rehabilitation. Although the approach does not ignore some of the elements that traditionally have defined "real" recovery (e.g., symptom reduction), its emphasis is on promoting social recovery by providing strategies for improving functioning in the domains of daily life, including work. By developing and disseminating a technology for the promotion of practical recovery, psychiatric rehabilitation directs attention to the idea, raising its profile as an alternative to the definition of recovery as cure.

Finally, psychiatric rehabilitation uses a key metaphor: that of physical disability. Equating mental illness ("psychiatric disability") and physical disability has several effects. It serves to explain the approach and to legitimize it in the eyes of other mental health professions and the public. It also can be used as propaganda for the possibility of improvement. The following passage from Anthony, Cohen, and Farkas (1990) explores these effects:

> Explaining psychiatric rehabilitation by using an analogy of physical rehabilitation (e.g., rehabilitating persons with spinal cord injury or cardiac disease) makes psychiatric rehabilitation more comprehensible. An analogy is more easily remembered than is a definition or a list of concepts. The image creates understanding . . . [and can be used] to inspire commitment. . . . In our society rehabilitation of persons who are physically disabled is very much valued. Can society do less for persons who are psychiatrically disabled? . . . A physical disability is considered to be less stigmatizing than is a psychiatric disability. Furthermore, the rehabilitation of persons with physical disabilities appears more credible and understandable to the

layperson. Thus, by using the analogy . . . , the field of psychiatric rehabilitation becomes more legitimate and acceptable. (59–60)

The metaphor also provides a route to attaining political leverage. That is, it allows the community of mental health advocates to ally with the physical disability movement in making rights claims and in lobbying for specific public policies.

THE CONSUMER/SURVIVOR MOVEMENT

Although as far back as the 1930s there have been documented instances when people diagnosed with mental illnesses came together for mutual support (including, for example, the groups Clifford Beers was so quick to dismiss), as a distinct social movement,[5] what today is known as the consumer/survivor movement generally is acknowledged to have begun in the early 1970s (Chamberlin 1978; Brown 1981; Everett 1994; Roschke 2000). In several cities, circa 1970–1972, small groups of people who had encountered the mental health system began to meet with one another. As individuals they talked about their experiences in the system. Together, they found commonalities in the harms that had been done to them and identified the systemic problems that had determined their experiences. Together, they developed agendas for change. Their anger, and the radical nature of their analyses, were signaled in the names they gave their organizations—in Portland, Oregon, the "Insane Liberation Front"; in New York City, the "Mental Patients' Liberation Project"; in San Francisco, the "Network against Psychiatric Assault" (Roschke 2000)—and themselves—"ex-patients"; "ex-inmates"; and "psychiatric survivors."

Theoretically, these groups drew from the new social constructionist history and sociology of mental illness and the antipsychiatry movement of the 1960s. In work of scholars and polemicists like Erving Goffman, Thomas Scheff, Michel Foucault, and Thomas Szasz, they found a conceptual model that construed mental illness not as a disease of the mind but as a method of social control deployed by agents of the oppressive state (primarily psychiatrists and the other "helping professions") against individuals whose behavior marked them as deviant. In reality, their critique had it, such "deviance" was a manifestation of marginalization contingent on factors like gender, sexual orientation, poverty, and anti-establishment ideology and action. "Diagnosis" was a means of affixing labels designating particular kinds of trouble, while "treatment" was a way to quell the trouble and to dispense punishment for conventions transgressed.

Politically, these groups fashioned themselves after other extant social movements of the era, particularly the women's movement and the civil rights movement. Like early second-wave feminists, groups of "ex-patients" and "psychiatric survivors" used consciousness raising as a mechanism first for recognizing and naming their oppression (including the internalized oppression of self-stigma and the "false consciousness" of "insight") and then for placing this oppression in a larger social context (Chamberlin 1978). Like African Americans and other racial and ethnic minorities, they sought to promote an understanding of the unfairness of discrimination based on a group characteristic (the term "mentalism" was coined as a corollary to "racism" and as a rallying call [Chamberlin 1978]) and to force society to recognize them as citizens, claimants to all the rights granted with the status, through both legislation and litigation (Brown 1981).

The movement's social change agenda came to revolve around two activities: self-help and advocacy (Chamberlin 1990; Roschke 2000; Van Tosh and del Vecchio 2000). As recounted in Judi Chamberlin's *On Our Own* (1978), many groups focused their energies on developing "user-controlled alternatives" to the traditional mental health system. Such alternatives were distinguished by three characteristics—a rejection of hierarchical relationships, no status distinction between the helper and the helped, and complete participant control—characteristics that were embodied in programs like drop-in centers, crisis retreats, and communal housing. Advocacy, on the other hand, was directed at changing the social status of persons labeled mentally ill by ending all forms of legally sanctioned discrimination (Chamberlin 1990). The work of advocacy took place on a variety of levels: individuals standing up for one another in the face of threats to liberty like involuntary commitment; demonstrations and other public events designed to raise community awareness; development and promotion of a "bill of rights" for people incarcerated in mental hospitals (a list of imperatives that sought to maintain the integrity of body and mind); and the lobbying of representatives of local and federal government about issues like the right to refuse treatment (Brown 1981; Chamberlin 1990; Roschke 2000).

Initially, money for these activities came from a variety of sources. Housing cooperatives, for example, might be funded by pooling the income support payments of each participant. Litigation might be paid for by centers devoted to public interest law. Many groups relied on volunteer labor (a practice seen as entirely consistent with the nonhierarchical aim of the organizations) and private monetary and in-kind donations. Early on, programs that received direct government support often were funded out of antipoverty or community development grants rather than mental health budgets (Chamberlin 1978).

By the 1980s, however, many of the movement's ideas and activities were catching the attention of mainstream mental health systems. Groups offering peer support and other services became eligible to seek funding from mental health authorities. With funding came bureaucratic requirements like accreditation, record keeping, and reporting. Community mental health centers and other professionally run services promoted their own versions of peer support and crisis intervention. NIMH, under the aegis of its community support program, funded conferences where service users and ex-patients could meet to talk with each other and with professionals. (These conferences, later sponsored by the Substance Abuse and Mental Health Services Administration [SAMHSA],[6] soon replaced some of the meetings the psychiatric survivor movement had been organizing for itself.) Like other organizations borne out of social movements (e.g., women's health centers), survivor-run services began to struggle against co-optation (Chamberlin 1990; Everett 2000).

One co-optation threat was the rise of the "consumer" (Chamberlin 1990; Frese 1998). Barbara Everett (1994) characterizes the distinction between consumers and survivors as the difference between a "reform agenda" (associated with the former) and a "liberation agenda" (promoted by the latter). Judi Chamberlin, who places herself in the survivor camp, describes consumers as a "reformist," "co-operative" group whose ascendancy "developed as the psychiatric establishment began to fund ex-patient self-help" (Chamberlin 1990, 333). Chamberlin argues that consumers fail to recognize the power relations inherent in the mental health system, claiming equality with "providers" (the term often used in conjunction with "consumer") when equality does not in fact exist (as evidenced by the continued use of involuntary commitment and forced medication). Consumers' failure to recognize, acknowledge, and confront this power differential ensures that it will endure. On the other side, a self-identified consumer has characterized survivors as "radical" and "extreme," particularly in their rejection of the biological basis of mental illness (Roschke 2000).

Despite these differences, the two groups have made common cause in their promotion of certain values and aims (Everett 1994). (As I have done in the title of this section, the dissension that remains is often elided in the convenient punctuation of the solidus.) The consumer/survivor movement emphasizes the importance of achieving abstractions like self-determination and autonomy, self-expression, individuality, and happiness, as well as ensuring access to tangibles like decent housing, work, and humane and competent health services. It seeks to end stigma and other forms of prejudice and discrimination against persons identified as mentally ill. It has allied itself with another social movement, the disability rights movement, in arguing for the full rights of citizenship for all people. It seeks visibility and audibility in the public sphere: to speak for itself, in its own voice (Chamberlin 1984, 1990; Deegan 1992; Everett 1994; Frese 1998; Roschke 2000).

As I have noted, power has been explicit and central in many of the values and goals of the consumer/survivor movement, particularly within the survivor faction. Psychiatric survivors' critiques of the medical model and the mental health system were grounded in their recognition of the power differential between "patients" and professionals. Individuals entered the mental health system on the basis of characteristics related to their marginalization, or lack of power in the wider society. Once in the system, the authority granted to professionals allowed them the power of diagnosis and treatment, processes that served to degrade further the ability of a patient to speak, to make choices, and to be autonomous. "Good" patients were those who acquiesced, who accepted the power of professionals and internalized it. Unequal power thus operated at a number of levels: in the interactions between psychiatrist and patient, in the cultural designation of mental illness as the explanation for certain kinds of reviled behavior, and in the laws allowing forced treatment and involuntary commitment.

The movement's corrective was to work toward a redistribution of power at each of these levels. Self-help organizations provided an alternative to the mental health system, one that, in philosophy and structure, sought to model a system based on an equal distribution of power. Such a system had no diagnostic moment, no power to restrain or to violate the integrity of the body. Individuals seeking help were understood to be the same as individuals offering help. The explanatory models of self-help focused not on individual deficits but societal inequities. Advocacy took the struggle to the macro level, using litigation and lobbying as tools to equalize power in law and policy.

A particular case of power redistribution can be seen in the notion of expertise. Historically, in mainstream mental health systems, expertise resided with the professional. Professional credentials conferred the power to name, to decide, and to act. Patients had no such power. (A very successful patient might gain a bit of it by demonstrating "insight," a kind of mimicry of professional expertise.) The consumer/survivor movement, however, promoted the idea of the patient as expert.[7] Such expertise began in the observation that it was the patient who was experiencing the problem. Thus it was the patient's experience "that is the most valid measure of whether a particular treatment is helpful or harmful" (Chamberlin 1978, 68). Beyond judging treatment effect, patient expertise was seen to encompass the ability to define the problem, to choose the nature, extent, and timing of treatment, and to decide what constituted a successful outcome. Because all of this was grounded in individual experience, it became very important for individuals to embrace that experience—to understand it, to acknowledge it, to offer testimony about it, to own it. Experience and expertise developed a reciprocal relationship: experience was legitimated by expertise; expertise was authenticated by experience.

The emphasis on individual experience figured in another phenomenon of the consumer/survivor movement: a parallel equivalence of individual and collective experience. That is, implicit in the movement was an understanding of individuals' experiences as representative not just of their own stories, but also of that of the collective. While together individual stories might make up the collective narrative, the narrative also was constitutive of the stories. This equivalence held true both for defining problems and identifying solutions. For example, the analysis of mental illness as a form of social control provided a collective-level explanation for individual experience, while the individual empowerment function of self-help was embedded in its collective nature.[8]

A final characteristic of the consumer/survivor movement was what Everett (1994) calls its drive to "create symbolic change enroute to real change" (63). Three types of symbols have been particularly important. The first is language. The consumer/survivor movement used words as part of a strategy to change minds. They appropriated terms like "insane" and "madness" for their own purposes, imbuing them with resistance to their derogatory connotation in common parlance (much as gay activists were to do with words like "queer"). They insisted on "person-first" terminology, pointing out the dehumanization involved in referring to a man or a woman as "the schizophrenic." They exposed the assumptions and complexities embedded in certain words—the ideological differences, for example, between "patients," "consumers," and "survivors." The second symbol is representation, in the sense of public image. As fighting stigma became a key goal of the consumer/survivor movement, many organizations and groups began to monitor how persons with psychiatric diagnoses are presented in the media. These groups have been vociferous in their objections when they believe such public representations are likely to promote prejudice and discrimination—for example, when news reports of violent crime emphasize that the alleged perpetrator had been treated for a psychiatric disorder or when fictional characters are portrayed as mentally ill and violent. The third symbol might also be called representation. Here, the word means presence. Consumer/survivor activists have demanded, and are receiving, places at the table where policy planning and other decision-making processes take place. Increasingly, such representation is required by the decision-making body itself. (However, the extent to which such participation remains simply symbolic—a kind of tokenism—is a source of tension.)

Although the three phenomena I have examined represented very different spheres of endeavor—research, practice, and social movement—they were similar in that each challenged the idea that a diagnosis of mental illness meant an inevitable decline. The longitudinal studies did so through the accumulation of scientific evidence; psychiatric rehabilitation through the promotion of a specific practice technology; and the consumer/survivor movement by redefining the basic nature of the problem in question. In their own ways, then, each provided hope. There were also differences and disjunctions among the three, however. The longitudinal studies looked at outcome and objective markers of improvement. Psychiatric rehabilitation focused on process and the promotion of improved role functioning in very specific contexts. The consumer/survivor movement construed hope as explicitly political, defining it largely as a matter of consciousness raising and resistance. Thus, while each of these phenomena promoted the idea that people could recover from mental illness, the word *recovery* meant different things.

In the next two sections I examine two written works that emerged from the context created by these three phenomena: a paper by Patricia Deegan that develops the concept of recovery-as-experience and one by William Anthony that suggests how recovery-as-experience might serve as the basis for recovery-as-ideology, a guide for the provision of services. I see each as having been key to making recovery—in all its many manifestations—a central idea in the current practice and policy environment.

THE LIVED EXPERIENCE OF RECOVERY

In "Recovery: The Lived Experience of Rehabilitation," author Patricia Deegan (1988) develops her argument using an extended metaphor of "poles."[9] The metaphor has several connotations: that of mapping, of specification of a point in space, and, in the notion of "polarity," of opposition or contrast. Deegan works with each of these connotations. She recounts her own story—a diagnosis of schizophrenia as a teenager, years in which life consisted only of a "numbing succession of meaningless days and nights" (13), the mysterious appearance of hope, and a slow reemergence to life (paraphrasing the poet Roethke, "the urge, the wrestle, the resurrection" [15]). Thus she maps the terrain of the process she names recovery, marking particular turning points. She is careful to contrast this process, this "lived experience" or the "self pole," with psychiatric rehabilitation, the "services and technologies that are made available to disabled persons so that they may learn to adapt to their world" (11) or the "world pole":

> It is important to understand that persons with a disability
> do not "get rehabilitated" in the sense that cars "get"
> tuned up or televisions "get repaired." Disabled persons
> are not passive recipients of rehabilitation services.
> Rather, they experience themselves as *recovering* a new
> sense of self and of purpose within and beyond the limits
> of the disability. (11, emphasis in the original)

From the self pole, the experience of recovery unfolds in nonlinear stages. It begins with a catastrophic event, followed by disbelief, rage, and denial. There are many days of despair and anguish. Then the spark of hope—"a tiny, fragile spark of hope appeared and promised that there could be something more than all this darkness" (14)—that prompts a willingness to try and a "willingness to act" (14). As individuals rebuild their lives, they do so with "an ever-deepening acceptance of [their] limitations" from which, paradoxically, "spring [their] own unique possibilities" (14–15). Recovery becomes "a way of life, an attitude, and a way of approaching the day's challenges" (15). It is not static, but fluid—"at times . . . we falter, slide back, re-group and start again" (15). Thus, recovery consists not of "an absence of pain or struggle" but instead marks "the transition from anguish to suffering," (15) where suffering connotes living with a pain that has been made meaningful and thus bearable.

From the world pole—the "polemic and technology of psychiatry, psychology, social work, and science" (14)—the experience of recovery remains ineffable. Its mystery and grace are "elusive" because they "cannot be completely described with traditional scientific, psychiatric, or psychological language" and "will not fit neatly into natural scientific paradigms" (12). "Polemic and technology" cannot "manufacture" recovery, but they can "create environments in which the recovery process can be nurtured" (15). Such environments should strive to reject the "traditional values of competition, individual achievement, independence, and self-sufficiency" that can be "oppressive" (17). Instead, they should promote fail-safe accessibility, individualization, choice, and opportunities for disabled individuals to share their "hope, strength and experience" by "becom[ing] role models for each other" (18).

The effect of Deegan's piece is to shift meaning and perspective. She clearly states that recovery does not mean cure ("real" recovery), nor, she implies, is it limited to something like "practical" recovery, an increase in social functioning as the result of some treatment or service program. Rather, recovery is a way of being in and of the world that can only be known subjectively. She compares the subjectivity of recovery from psychiatric disability with that of recovery from physical disability (she tells her own story in conjunction with that of a man who, as a teenager, suffered a paralyzing injury) and, beyond that, suggests that service providers can be effective only to the extent that they, too, have an awareness of having themselves "recovered" from their own tragedies and struggles—have an awareness of their own subjectivity. She thus detaches recovery from its traditional meaning as an objective or externally knowable state. Instead, recovery becomes an existential phenomenon.

A GUIDING VISION

In "Recovery from Mental Illness: The Guiding Vision of the Mental Health Service System in the 1990s" (1993), William Anthony takes up the world pole. He uses the existential phenomenon of recovery identified by Deegan (and others who have experienced it) to formulate a plan for how the fact and nature of this phenomenon can become a "guiding vision" for the provision of mental health services.

Anthony draws upon consumers' narratives of their recovery experiences to describe it as "a deeply personal, unique process of changing one's attitudes, values, feelings, goals, skills and/or roles . . . a way of living a satisfying, hopeful, and contributing life even with limitations caused by illness" (15). He notes that the experience of recovery has not been well researched, but he provides a summary of what is known about the phenomenon based on these narratives (18–20): Recovery exists; it is not an indication that the person was never "really" mentally ill. Recovery is not linear. The process of recovery can happen without "professional intervention," but it can be aided by the support of trusted others. It has nothing to do with the individual's beliefs about etiology. It is not synonymous with symptom relief, but it might be correlated with a reduction in the "frequency and duration" and intrusiveness of symptoms. Individuals need to recover from the "consequences" of illness (dysfunction, disability, and disadvantage) as much, or more, than they do from the illness itself (impairment).

Anthony argues that much of the dysfunction, disability, and disadvantage experienced by people diagnosed with mental illness are not caused by illness, but by the systemic and societal treatment of individuals who have received psychiatric diagnoses:

> Recovery from mental illness involves much more than recovery from the illness itself. People with mental illness have to recover from the stigma they have incorporated into their very being; from the iatrogenic effects of treatment settings; from lack of recent opportunities for self-determination; from the negative side effects of unemployment; and from crushed dreams. (15)

Recovery, Anthony argues, is promoted by two extant models of service provision: the community support system model and the psychiatric rehabilitation model. The latter, as I have described, defines and addresses the impacts of severe mental illness, while the former provides a structure for the "essential services" needed by persons with psychiatric disabilities who are living in the community—services like treatment, crisis intervention, and case management. A "recovery-oriented mental health system," then, "incorporates the critical services of a community support system organized around the rehabilitation model's description of the impact of severe mental illness—all under the umbrella of the recovery vision" (16).

As Anthony acknowledges, community support and psychiatric rehabilitation programs already exist, and function, outside the recovery "umbrella." The main shifts he proposes are those of attitude:

> Recovery-oriented system planners see the mental health system as greater than the sum of its parts. There is the possibility that efforts to affect the impact of severe mental illness positively can do more than leave the person less impaired, less dysfunctional, less disabled, and less disadvantaged. These interventions can leave a person not only with "less," but with "more"—more meaning, more purpose, more success, and more satisfaction with one's life. (16)

And then of intentional action:

> Recovery oriented mental health systems must structure their settings so that recovery "triggers" are present. . . . The

mental health system must help sow and nurture the seeds
of recovery through creative programming. . . . Helpers must
have a better understanding of the recovery concept in order
for this recovery-facilitating environment to occur. (21)

Like Deegan, Anthony draws multiple analogies between recovery from
mental illness and other human experiences. He too uses the example of
paralysis and other physical disabilities ("Recovery is what people with
disabilities do" [15]), suggesting that the knowledge of recovery gained
in these contexts is applicable to recovery from mental illness. He argues
that recovery is "a truly unifying human experience" (15). "All people," he
writes, "experience the catastrophes of life (death of a loved one, divorce,
the threat of severe physical illness, and disability)" (15). The universality
of pain and trouble means that recovery is something familiar, common,
imminently possible.

Throughout his 1993 article, Anthony looks at the ways in which
the recovery "vision" can improve the lives of people with psychiatric
disabilities by providing new opportunities for growth and meaning.
In a companion piece (Anthony 1991), published two years earlier, he
explores the value of the vision for professionals, especially mental health
services researchers. Other professions have visions that guide their work,
he argues, and such visions provide support for innovation and aid morale
building among colleagues and within disciplines. Mental health services
researchers, however, have tended to lack overall vision. He attributes this
lack to a fear of raising unfulfilled hopes. But "if we continue to work
toward and advocate that vision, then the vision is not misleading—it
is encouraging. . . . [It] begets not a false promise but a passion for what
we are doing" (13). Accumulating evidence (from consumer accounts
and research reviews) suggests that recovery from mental illness is not
"an illusory concept" (14), but a real possibility. Thus, mental health
services researchers should embrace it. Such a vision will guide them "in
developing the knowledge base so that more and more people recover
successfully from mental illness" (14). Similarly, for service providers "it
is a concept that can open our eyes to new possibilities for those we serve
and how we can go about serving them" (Anthony 1993, 22).

Many of the ideas that constitute recovery-as-experience and recovery-
as-ideology show their origins in one or more of the three background

phenomena I have examined. Deegan's work makes manifest the consumer/survivor valorization of personal experience and the imperative that those who have been diagnosed with mental illnesses must speak in their own voices. The notion of recovery draws its authenticity from the "self pole" of her narrative. She illustrates the utility of making common cause with persons with physical disabilities and points out the marginalization of all disabled persons. The mental health system she envisions includes the user-controlled alternatives promoted by the movement but also some of the services and technologies that characterize the traditional array, including psychiatric rehabilitation. Anthony, too, attempts to draw on the experience-based expertise of consumer/survivors as expressed in their own narratives. He reframes existing service models like community support and psychiatric rehabilitation as promoters of recovery-as-experience. The nature of the outcomes he seeks to promote combine the traditional outcomes of psychiatric rehabilitation (improved role functioning) with those emphasized by the consumer/survivor movement—increased self-determination and empowerment.

Both recovery-as-experience and recovery-as-ideology implicitly rely on the assumption that attitude can create reality. For Deegan, this notion is represented by her explorations of the value of hope. As she describes it, hope is mysterious and ineffable in its origins. It changes nothing but attitude. Through attitude change, however, recovery becomes a reality. Anthony applies the same idea at the level of programs and services. Professionals can facilitate recovery when they believe in the "vision" of recovery. Recovery can be promoted when the services are grounded in the principles of recovery: key among these, the belief that recovery is possible.

OTHER RECOVERIES

Although I have been sticking rather closely to what I see as the immediate lineage of the current attention to recovery in the public mental health arena, recovery has other histories as well—many of which no doubt have played a role in the development of the ideas that I have been examining in this chapter.

The "recovery movement" is a term long associated with Alcoholics Anonymous and its affiliated programs for the relatives or children of alcoholics (Kritsberg 1985; Al-Anon Family Groups 1994; Eastland 1995), as well as spin-offs that apply the twelve steps to a wide variety of dysfunctional behaviors that are conceptualized as forms of addiction (Kaminer 1992; Rapping 1996). These programs use a self-help group format with a heavily spiritual component to promote healing. Group participants, who may be addicts or individuals suffering the effects of a close relationship to an addict, learn to "work the steps"—admitting powerlessness, recognizing and surrendering to a "higher power," taking "moral inventory" of character defects, and making amends for wrongs committed. Recovery is a process of achieving and maintaining abstinence (whether from alcohol or other addictions) through continual self-monitoring and prayer. Twelve-step programs are communal in their use of the group as a mechanism for confession and self-discovery, and the last step calls for individuals to "carry this message" to others, but their emphasis is on individual transformation, decontextualized from broader social issues (Haaken 1993; Rapping 1996).

A second setting in which recovery has been salient is in feminist therapy, particularly in its analysis and treatment of eating disorders and the sequelae of trauma. While mainstream psychiatry has assessed recovery from eating disorders using objective criteria like body weight and the return of menses (e.g., Herzog et al. 1999), feminist therapists and sociologists have focused much more on the subjective experience of recovery, using first-person narrative accounts to develop models that describe recovery as a spiritual journey or as a process of empowerment leading to healthy embodiment (Brown and Jasper 1993; Peters and Fallon 1994; Garrett 1997). Similarly, feminist activists and practitioners have fought for professional and societal recognition of the reality of trauma and its role in creating psychiatric disability. They have conceptualized recovery from trauma and abuse as a combined process of individual restoration and collective restitution (Herman 1992; Alcoff and Gray 1993). Although much of this work has had a therapeutic focus, examining how individuals can be helped, its feminist roots means that there is also explicit attention to the social context of suffering and to the political nature of intervention and recovery.

Finally, as I have mentioned in passing, recovery has been—in concept if not in word—an important element of the disability rights movement. This international social movement defines disability as a wholly social problem, rejecting models that conceptualize it as a form of illness or as a "personal tragedy" (Oliver 1990). Instead, disability is a matter of societal context, a narrowness and ignorance that either intentionally or negligently excludes some portion of the population from many of the rights and privileges of full citizenship. It is society that must "recover," transforming itself so as to eliminate the literal and figurative barriers that are the cause of disability (DeJong 1993; Marks 1999; Barnes, Oliver, and Barton 2002).

The meanings of recovery that I have been examining in this chapter—recovery-as-experience, recovery-as-ideology, and their sources—show similarities to each of these three phenomena: the recovery movement and recovery-as-experience place a similar emphasis on the healing power of personal narrative. Early self-help groups for psychiatric survivors seem to have been modeled, at least in part, on AA (Van Tosh and del Vecchio 2000). Recovery-as-ideology shares with feminist therapy the dual focus on individual and environmental conditions. Many of the most vocal recovery activists have been self-identified survivors of trauma and abuse. Both psychiatric rehabilitation and the consumer/survivor movement have been explicit in making common cause with the tenets and strategies of the (physical) disability rights movement.

But there have been important divergences as well. Tensions have emerged between the ideologies of recovery from mental illness and those of the recovery movement as exemplified by AA and its descendents.[10] Extant critiques of the recovery movement and the disability rights movement also have implications for the implementation of recovery-as-policy. (I return to this point in my discussion of recovery-as-politics in Chapter 6.)

RECOVERY ENTERS THE ARENA OF MENTAL HEALTH REFORM

Anthony's "Guiding Vision" appeared at a time when public mental health service systems around the United States were in a state of flux. A dozen years of decreasing resources from federal and state coffers combined with an apparently limitless demand for services meant that many public systems were facing a fiscal crisis. Following the failure of Clinton's health care reform effort and the subsequent burgeoning of managed care in the private sector, many states, like Wisconsin, believed that reform dictated by the terms of managed care was inevitable in the public sector.

Mental health reform solutions of the past, as I have explored in the case of Wisconsin, had often joined an economic element with a philosophical one that promoted humanitarian values. To many observers, managed care "values" seemed either an oxymoron or a clever euphemism for the bottom line. In the early to mid-1990s, then, mental health reform was ripe for a new philosophy, a values framework to balance the cold economic heart of managed care.

Several states, particularly in New England,[11] fastened on the "recovery orientation" described by Anthony as a source for such values. In many cases, the links between reform and recovery were made explicit. A 1994 article by Daniel Fisher, a psychiatric survivor and psychiatrist, used an explication of the "empowerment model of recovery" as a framework for system reform recommendations (Fisher 1994). The State of Rhode Island named its managed care pilot "RIcover" and sought to embed what it called "recovery principles" like access, quality, innovation, and cost into the system design (Rhode Island Department of Mental Health, Retardation, and Hospitals, undated). Ohio sponsored a conference on recovery and used it as the foundation for beginning a series of "recovery dialogues" across the state. These dialogues, in turn, led to the development of broad recovery "themes" to guide in system reform (Beale and Lambric 1995). In other places, recovery and reform were coincident. The Massachusetts Department of Mental Health built sessions on consumer empowerment and recovery into its core curriculum for clinical staff (Massachusetts Department of Mental Health 1993). Vermont's Division of Mental Health made recovery a "programmatic priority" for adults in the mental health system and established a working group charged with finding ways to bring a recovery orientation to the state (Vermont Legislative Summer Study Committee 1996). As efforts like these received attention in the arena of mental health system planning—as they were featured in educational sessions at meetings of the National Association of State Mental Health Program Directors, for example—interest in recovery, the recovery "buzz" (Jacobson and Curtis 2000), spread.

Although Anthony's "guiding vision" had been explicit in its identification of community support and psychiatric rehabilitation services as central to the development of a recovery-oriented mental health service system, the recovery buzz did not necessarily extend to the specific service configuration Anthony had been promoting. Instead, mental health policymakers and planners construed recovery largely as a philosophical framework. Recovery became a varied collection of assumptions, principles, and goals—a set of ideas that were subject to different interpretations.

"IMPLEMENTING THE CONCEPT OF RECOVERY" IN WISCONSIN

The first public expression of Wisconsin's interpretation of these ideas came in a section of the Blue Ribbon Commission's *Final Report* (1997)—the document that also laid out the state's plan for implementing a managed care model. Notably, the four pages on recovery were the only part of the lengthy report to have a named author, Kathleen Crowley, a consumer member of the Blue Ribbon Commission and a writer who went on to provide a more expansive explication of recovery[12] in her own book (Crowley 2000).

"Implementing the Concept of Recovery," the section title, promotes recovery as a macro-level intervention. The intended target of intervention, the public mental health system, encompasses the totality of actors, processes, products, and assumptions involved in the delivery of mental health services. "The system" thus stands for everything from consumers and staff and bureaucrats and the interactions among and between them, to diagnosis, inpatient and outpatient treatment, medication, and the provision of income support benefits. The current mental health system, Crowley argues, operates with two underlying goals: "assuring personal safety and managing symptoms" (Blue Ribbon Commission on Mental Health 1997, 14). Although safety and symptom management are important (Crowley calls them "critical issues" [14]), the system's exclusive focus on these goals has had an unintended consequence—namely, turning consumers into "passive recipients rather than active participants" (13), a tendency reinforced by other structural factors, like the work disincentives associated with SSI and medical assistance. This passivity, in turn, leads to "high levels of non-compliance and poor therapeutic outcomes" (13). The end result is a system that is highly inefficient.

By contrast, recovery—which Crowley describes as "attaining a productive and fulfilling life regardless of the level of health assumed attainable" and "letting go of what was and rebuilding new dreams" (13)—focuses on the higher-level goal of "the successful integration of a mental disorder into a consumer's life" (13). A shift to making such integration the systemic goal, she posits, will lead to "a better expenditure of time and resources for both consumers and professionals" (13):

> Recovery is an everybody wins scenario. In a recovery-oriented system, mental health consumers rebuild meaningful lives while decreasing their dependence on the system. From both a therapeutic standpoint as well as an economic standpoint there should be little confusion in this regard. Rather than creating long-term users of a system that fosters dependence, individuals will receive services that will enable them to recover and *decrease* their dependence on the system. (14, emphasis in the original)

Crowley is careful to note that for many people recovery will not follow the dictionary definition of "regaining a former state of health" (13). (Like other recovery authors, she illustrates the distinctions between meanings of the word by resorting to physical disability, citing both spinal cord injury and chronic pain as examples of conditions that cannot be cured but with which people can learn to live.) Indeed, a recovery-oriented system must continue to provide the entire array of traditional mental health services, including hospitalization, outpatient treatment, medication management, and psychiatric rehabilitation. The continued necessity for a full complement of programs and services means that the efficiency gained by the system will not be a result of cost-cutting through reduced service provision but of improved outcomes.

The crux of Crowley's statement lies in her annotated list of eight "basic recovery-oriented principles" that "need to be incorporated into *all* aspects of service delivery" (14, emphasis in the original). These principles (14–16) are summarized as follows:

- Recovery is possible.
- Mental health consumers must be welcomed as partners in their care.
- A "just start anywhere" mode of consumer action must be fostered.
- A broad range of consumer-run services is promoted.

- Meaningful work/educational activities
  are valued and worked toward.
- Service providers must encourage and facilitate an increase
  in consumers' abilities to self-manage disorders.
- Use of community resources should be encouraged.
- Staff must be empowered and encouraged to
  be flexible in the delivery of services.

Together, these principles point to a preference for activity over passivity, an endorsement of the universality of recovery, and a belief that recovery is both a destination and a journey. The list emphasizes the transformative potential of hope and the empowerment function of consumer participation in making life choices, performing self-care for wellness promotion, and finding meaningful work. The principles promote the value of vision for individuals, organizations, and systems—the hypothesis that attitude will change reality. Several principles point to necessary changes in the context in which mental health treatment takes place—for example, the untapped potential of community resources and the necessity for service providers to be validated as they embrace the "vision" and attempt to work in new ways. Others promote the importance of individualization—the need to move away from standardized programs or treatment plans and instead to tailor services to the unique recovery paths of each consumer.

Crowley closes with several strong declarative statements. "Mental health consumers," she writes, "want what everybody wants . . . a home and loved ones, and to continue to grow as they age. They want their lives to have meaning. They do not want to die, never having lived" (16). The mental health system must respond to these desires by "mov[ing] beyond the focus of surviving and develop[ing] the focus of thriving" (16). The strategy for transformation is clear: the system "must adopt a recovery-oriented delivery of services. It cannot afford to do otherwise, therapeutically, economically, or societally" (16).

"Implementing the Concept of Recovery" sets out to accomplish two goals: to introduce the concept of recovery and to promote it as a guiding philosophy for system reform. Crowley attempts to meet the former, instructive, purpose by providing short definitions ("recovery is . . ."), by drawing analogies to physical disability, and by stating general principles that, through implication, point out important elements of the concept. The second goal requires both that she show how the individual process of recovery might be supported by system change and make an argument that promoting recovery, and thus specific reforms, is a worthy endeavor. Crowley uses the principles, again, to tell the reader how the system can promote recovery, but provides little in the way of evidence or illustration. She argues for the worthiness of recovery by linking it to a number of societal goods, including the promotion of happiness, the value of work, the strengthening of community ties, and most importantly, the promise of increased economic efficiency.

As propaganda, "Implementing the Concept of Recovery" is an extraordinarily interesting piece of work. It taps important streams of Wisconsin's past (the German work ethic, the progressive commitment to individual betterment through collective action) as well as the state's contemporaneous present—the perceived need for cost containment in the public mental health system and the rhetoric of self-sufficiency and community (read: nongovernmental) responsibility so emphatic in Wisconsin's welfare reform effort. The evidence for the success of this propaganda effort, however, is mixed. While many Wisconsin consumer activists, mental health advocates, and state bureaucrats were enthusiastic supporters of both the general concept of recovery and its specific expression in the Blue Ribbon Commission's report, other consumers, as well as many program administrators and front-line staff, seemed more skeptical and even somewhat perplexed, even after repeated readings of the section.

Their confusion pointed to the partial failure of the work's other purpose—to instruct. While the four-page statement provided an overview and introduction to many recovery ideas, it did not examine the connections between these ideas, nor did it provide a clear framework for showing how recovery concepts and principles could be implemented in the mental health reform effort. As I will explore at length in the next chapter, when it became necessary to specify what recovery would mean in policy, the work group charged with the task was directed to "Implementing the Concept of Recovery" with the contention that it contained all the definitional and explanatory material needed. The work group, however, could not find the direction they were seeking in the statement. In part, this was because members of the work group turned out to have many more, and often conflicting, ideas about recovery than those expressed in the Blue Ribbon Commission's report.

RECOVERY-AS-IDEOLOGY

In its earliest manifestations, the idea of recovery stood for a possible outcome of treatment or services—one that could be identified and interpreted only by expert professionals and often was marshaled to serve as evidence for the agendas being promoted by these professionals. Longitudinal research, psychiatric rehabilitation, and the consumer/survivor movement changed understandings of the frequency with which recovery occurred, amplified the range of what might count as recovery, and expanded the definition of expertise. Recovery-as-experience claimed the process as one that was owned by consumer/survivors, an existential phenomenon that in many ways would always be obscure to the "polemic and technology" of the world pole. The notion proved irresistible, however, to providers seeking to promote a newly rationalized service array by capitalizing on the authenticity inherent in recovery-as-experience. Recovery became a guiding vision for the provision of mental health services, a collection of values and assumptions that constituted recovery-as-ideology.

Webster's defines ideology as "a set of doctrines or beliefs that form the basis of a political, economic, or other system." Recovery-as-ideology attempted to make recovery the doctrine and belief of the mental health services system. At its simplest level, the ideology was based on the premise that because improvement was possible, it (rather than a safe stasis) should become the driving purpose of mental health services. But the sources from which recovery-as-ideology grew—longitudinal research, psychiatric rehabilitation, and the consumer/survivor movement, and the manifestations of their ideas in Deegan's expression of lived experience and Anthony's vision—themselves were grounded in a number of "doctrines or beliefs."

On the questions of "What is recovery?" and "Recovery from what?" for example, both longitudinal research and psychiatric rehabilitation acknowledged mental illness as a disease state and viewed recovery as some variant on the historical ideas of "real" or "practical" improvement as assessed by objective standards. Recovery might mean that an individual's symptoms disappeared and that he or she led a normal life, with no further interaction with the mental health system. Or it might mean that the same individual, although still symptomatic, led a better—happier, more functional—life, with continued support from the mental health system.

For psychiatric survivors who rejected the biological basis of mental illness, however, accepting the validity of such external assessments and definitions was anathema.[13] Rather, these groups might define recovery as a state of politicization, the recognition of and eventual liberation from multiple forms of oppression. Similarly, these sources expressed divergent views about the temporal nature of recovery. Follow-up studies, even research that was longitudinal in nature, tended to fix recovery in time as an outcome, marking it a destination. Psychiatric rehabilitation and Deegan's conception of recovery as a way of being, however, clearly emphasized the processual nature of the phenomenon—recovery as a journey with many starts and stops, more meandering than linear. Although each source might have endorsed the statement that "recovery is possible for everyone," ideas about the conditions that facilitated that possibility were quite different. Longitudinal research used statistical correlation to identify a number of factors that seemed linked to recovery potential, variables like age at onset or socioeconomic status or the availability of social support. Survivors talked about conditions like the ability to access user-controlled alternatives and the ineffable mystery of grace. Psychiatric rehabilitation posited its own service model as crucial to promoting recovery. Finally, there were differences in ideas about the consequences of recovery. While psychiatric rehabilitation and longitudinal research might have conceptualized the result of recovery as being improved functioning, regained role status, and greater happiness, Pat Deegan might have seen the result as the emergence of existential meaningfulness, and the survivor movement more broadly might have identified it as collective action for social justice.

Recovery-as-ideology was subject to immediate criticism. Anthony's vision was described as "gloss[ing] over the realities of mental illness" in a way that might "lead to denial of illness and rejection of needed treatment and rehabilitation" (Lamb 1994, 1019). Researcher Harriet Lefley (1994) wrote an article in which she raised a number of concerns, or cautions, about recovery, including the uncertainties yet surrounding the definition and measurement of the concept, the expectations that might become oppressive to individuals, the invidious distinctions that might be applied to consumers who proved unable to "attain the high ground of recovery" (21), and the possibility that "recovery" would become an excuse for reducing services. To these critics, the unevidenced notion of attitude creating reality—the enshrinement of "recovery is possible" as a key principle of system reform—seemed naïve and dangerous:

> Recovery is not the same as cure; hope is not the same as wishing it were so. We want realistic hope, not fantasy; we want science, not myth. But a personal recovery vision has a momentum of its own. So we also need science to discover whether the phenomenon of hope can control behavior and have an impact on outcome; whether self-affirmation and belief in oneself, so much a part of consumer ideology, can make the heart stronger, the brain clearer, and the spirit more intact. (Lefley 1994, 22)

As recovery entered the mental health policy arena, it carried these complexities with it. The context of system change, in particular the adoption of managed care models, brought more complications. The dark side of recovery-as-ideology, clearly, was seen to be its potential to become an excuse for severing individuals from services, a threat that seemed dangerously complementary to the cost-cutting aim that was also promoting managed care. Other issues also loomed: How could the "practical" side of recovery be supported by a mechanism driven by the idea of "medical necessity"? Who—consumers, providers, managed care organizations, or purchasers—would make the care decisions? (Who would be the authorities? The experts?) In a system that claimed to use "evidence-based" approaches to ensure quality, what would count as evidence of recovery?

An ideology may not speak to these questions, focusing instead at the level of abstract concepts and values. As recovery-as-ideology was to be transformed into recovery-as-policy, however, it became necessary for the concept to be made much more specific in its definition and implications. The process of specification, the transformation from recovery-as-ideology to recovery-as-policy as it occurred in Wisconsin, is the subject of the next two chapters.

4

SPECIFYING RECOVERY

Just as Wisconsin had formed a Blue Ribbon Commission to make recommendations for reform of the public mental health system, so too did it turn to the mechanism of the representative, expert body when it came time to move from recovery-as-ideology to recovery-as-policy, the specification task assigned to the Recovery Workgroup. In this chapter, I describe the process and product of that work group, with special attention to the divergent ways in which its members gave meaning to recovery and to how the practice and policy implications of those definitions were negotiated with several external entities. My reportage is based on fieldwork I conducted with the Workgroup, on individual interviews with Workgroup members, and on readings of Workgroup documents.[1] My analytic approach is drawn from several symbolic interactionist frameworks.[2]

I tell the story of the Workgroup's process and product using three vignettes selected to illustrate the kinds of work the group did in order to meet its specification goal. (This representational strategy allows the reader to see the Workgroup in action, but it should not be misconstrued as a comprehensive account. That is, I have made decisions about what to show and what to leave out.) The first vignette examines how group members defined recovery, a process that required reaching an accommodation among many different definitions. The second looks at how the Workgroup served a legitimizing function, particularly around issues related to plans for implementing recovery principles in practice. Finally, the third vignette traces some of the negotiations over recovery-as-policy that were made necessary by the differences in orientation between the

Workgroup and the other policy planning bodies to which it was accountable.

Each of the "doctrines and beliefs" that historically constituted recovery-as-evidence, recovery-as-experience, and recovery-as-ideology came to be voiced within the Workgroup: recovery as symptom abatement; "practical" recovery; recovery as service rationalization; recovery as politicization; recovery as existential experience. The juxtaposition of these understandings in the context of a joint endeavor (specifying recovery policy) allows for comparisons among their definitional dimensions and implications and demonstrates just how complicated recovery is.

THE WORK

When the Recovery Workgroup—composed, as I have indicated, of consumers, providers, administrators, parents, and advocates—met for the first time in June 1998, its general charge was to operationalize the vision of recovery described in the Blue Ribbon Commission's report. At the Workgroup's initial meeting, members were provided with a list of specific goals that had been set by the state's Bureau of Community Mental Health: (1) evaluate the concept of recovery as described in the Blue Ribbon Commission report and identify what the State of Wisconsin defines as recovery; (2) analyze recovery implementation strategies from other states; (3) find ways to involve consumers and family members in all levels of mental health policy and planning; and (4) define specific long- and short-term recovery implementation strategies.

In introductory statements to the Workgroup, the bureau identified several other official goals: that the Workgroup meet its deadlines, that the Workgroup function efficiently, and that the membership of the Workgroup include representatives of all of the relevant groups in the state. (In pursuit of the latter goal, one of the Workgroup's first activities was to identify which groups were not represented in its current composition.) Individual members brought many other goals to the Workgroup: to make change in the mental health system; to promote one or another specific change in the system; to ensure that the voices of their constituencies would be heard in the redesign process; and to learn about recovery for themselves.

Broadly, these goals were of two types: *substantive* goals, or those which dealt with clarifying the concept of recovery and finding ways to implement it, and *processual* goals, which were concerned with *how* the Workgroup would accomplish its substantive goals. Although the specifics of the Workgroup's substantive and processual goals shifted as time passed, substantive goals may be generalized as focused on *product* (recovery policy), while processual goals were directed at maximizing *participation*. The conflicts and negotiations that occurred within the Recovery Workgroup and between the Recovery Workgroup and other groups revolved around the difficulties of accommodating both substantive and processual goals: that is, how the final policy product could represent the participation of all the interests involved in its specification.

As the Workgroup continued to meet over the summer and fall of 1998 (usually on a monthly basis), it developed work processes that allowed it to reach such an accommodation. The first process was a highly efficient division of labor: the bureau staff and the Workgroup cochairs provided organization and structure; the members provided wide-ranging ideas. Work was accomplished in the following way: The staff and the cochairs would set tasks or goals (both overall and for each meeting). These would be presented in the meeting agenda, a written document that was usually mailed to members several days before the Workgroup meetings. At the meetings, the members would make their way through the items on the agenda, facilitated by questions or exercises set by the staff and/or cochairs. The predominant method of work was free-flowing group discussion, or brainstorming. Staff and cochairs recorded the results of these brainstorming sessions in the form of minutes (or, in the case of some exercises, notes taken during the session on large flip charts). After the meeting, the staff and cochairs would gather in a smaller group to summarize and synthesize these results, producing integrative documents that were meant to represent the main decisions made by the Workgroup. These integrative documents were distributed for member checks. At the next meeting, the Workgroup would begin its work, in another brainstorming session, with modifications and additions to the documents.

Using these work processes, the Workgroup was able to be productive while at the same time maintaining member participation. Because the major decisions were made in a small group, burnout among the larger membership was limited. (A contrast, and perhaps a cautionary tale, was offered by another work group, in which every decision about substance and process had to be reached through consideration and consensus by the entire group. That work group quickly became bogged down in detail, and its members grew frustrated.)[3] These processes also allowed the Workgroup to make progress toward its goals, even when—as I explore in the next section—the group had achieved no real consensus about certain definitional matters. That is, even when the larger membership was unable to reach agreement over issues, the subgroup composed of staff and cochairs often was able to do so. The final products represented the consensus built among this smaller group. (As such, they often showed the editorial hand of the smaller group—not all perspectives voiced in Workgroup discussions were represented in integrative documents or final products.)

The activities that made up the substantive, as opposed to processual, work of the Workgroup were aimed, as directed by the bureau's list of objectives, at clarifying the meaning of recovery and finding ways to implement it. Quite soon, the Workgroup developed dual goals: a short-term goal of developing recommendations for embedding recovery principles in the upcoming managed care demonstrations and a longer-term goal of bringing a recovery orientation to the state's entire public mental health system. Thus, the Workgroup's substantive efforts were directed at specifying recovery policy both for the managed care demonstrations and for the state.

Specification entailed four kinds of work: defining, legitimizing, strategizing, and persuading. Definition delineated the shape and borders of the concept of recovery. Definitional tasks included cataloging recovery values and principles; identifying barriers to recovery; proposing solutions to those barriers; gathering information about recovery; "building context" about the system redesign; identifying needs of the population served by the system; drawing connections between principles and values, needs, and solutions; envisioning change; elaborating suggestions; and drafting recommendations. Legitimization authenticated definitions of recovery and validated specific policies or programs as truly representative of recovery. Specific tasks included checking with the group, listening to personal experience, and vetting the products of other work groups. Strategizing was advance work done to ensure that the Workgroup's operationalizations of recovery would be palatable to the groups whose approval was necessary for implementation. Strategizing tasks included anticipating snags, managing specificity, making use of existing resources, assigning accountability, planning presentations, and submitting to review. Persuasion, closely linked to strategizing, occurred when the Workgroup's recovery recommendations met real or anticipated resistance. Its tasks included hearing criticism, addressing concerns, crafting responses, restrategizing, refining definitions, and prioritizing recommendations.

Each kind of work was done both within the Recovery Workgroup and between the Workgroup and the other redesign entities with which it came into contact. All four kinds of work were done throughout the specification process, but definition and legitimization were more apparent at the beginning, while strategizing and persuading became more visible near the end.

Defining

In its charge from the bureau, the Workgroup had been told that the Blue Ribbon Commission report's statement about recovery (described in Chapter 3) was *the* definition of the concept and its time was to be spent operationalizing the letter and spirit of this definition. As the group worked toward developing policy recommendations, however, it became apparent that the report's definition did not reflect every member's ideas about recovery and was insufficient as a basis for operationalization. The Workgroup often became immersed in discussions that were, at bottom, attempts to devise a more specific and applicable definition.

The following exchange evokes the manner in which the meaning of recovery was debated within the Workgroup. It occurred in November 1998, when the Workgroup was midway through its lifespan. The group was reviewing a draft of the recommendations for the managed care demonstration sites when a family member raised a question: "If everything is based on recovery," she asked, "is there room for people who are just standing still, people who are not making progress, are not getting better?" The Workgroup's responses to this query focused not only on its main point (about the potential for a recovery-oriented system to become oppressive to consumers who are not meeting its expectations)

but also on the definition of recovery implied in the question. While the
questioner seemed to assume that recovery meant movement, progress,
and getting better, other members challenged these assumptions:

> "Who says they haven't made progress?"
> "It's not fair to blame people for their circumstances—
> like work disincentives and program failures.
> It's important not to give up on them."
> "The system has to find ways of individualizing, bringing hope
> to consumers. It can't say, 'Some people never get better.' "
> "But, yes, as with some physical illnesses, there
> are people who don't want to get better because
> the incentives are all for staying sick."
> "Recovery is about being, not becoming."
> "It's a question of balancing maintenance—a positive good on its
> own—with the idea that we can move beyond maintenance."
> "For some people, medication refusal can be a form of recovery
> because it means the person is acting on his own volition."
> "Just staying out of the hospital should be considered recovery."
> "All consumers want to get well; persons with
> mental illness are not manipulative."

As this exchange shows, much about recovery was in question. The
definitional dimensions arising in this discussion included questions such
as the following: What is the problem that recovery is meant to address?
(What are people recovering from?) Is it disease? A lack of self-determination? System failures? The failures of society? Who is responsible for
recovery? The individual? The system? Who is responsible when recovery
doesn't happen? How is recovery to be assessed? By external (objective)
standards? Internal (subjective) states of being? Just how much must be
achieved to count as recovery? What is the nature of consumers? Are they
manipulative? Are they simply responding to their environments? Are
they sick or do they just lack autonomy? What is the nature of the current system? Does a recovery-oriented system run the risk of becoming
oppressive in its expectations of consumers?

In order to specify recovery policy, the Workgroup implicitly first
had to identify the problems that recovery was meant to address and
then propose ameliorative solutions. Definitional discussions revealed

differences within the Workgroup over the issues of problems and solutions. These differences may be described along three axes: problem level, solution approach, and philosophy of change.

Members of the Workgroup located the problem that recovery was meant to solve at one (or more) of three levels: the individual, the mental health system, or the society. At the individual level, the problem was identified as "mental illness," a condition adhering to persons, generally understood to be caused by some combination of biology and social response and resulting in impaired function and limited autonomy. (No one in the Workgroup argued for an entirely biological view of mental illness, although several members seemed to advocate an entirely social definition. Most members fell somewhere in the middle, as evidenced by statements like "the problem is one-third brain chemistry and two-thirds a world that marginalizes difference.") At the level of the system, the problem was identified as either systemic inefficiencies or inequities (insufficient funds, lack of access to services) or incompetence and cruelty (a misunderstanding of the true causes and meaning of mental illness, abuse by institutions or providers). At the societal level, the problem was conceptualized as the pervasive stigmatization of persons labelled as mentally ill. This stigma was understood to operate both at the personal level (isolation, self-loathing, public stares) and at the systemic level (job discrimination, lack of adequate funding for mental health services). Stigma was seen as a response to difference; thus it did not matter if the cause of mental illness was biological or social.

As the Workgroup focused on operationalizing recovery, two perspectives on solution approaches became apparent. The first looked to recovery as a means of reform. Although some of the suggestions offered under this approach were in fact fairly profound shifts—e.g., changing the laws specifying provider liability, promoting consumer choice—they essentially sought to modify the existing system to make it both more effective and more humane. The second perspective, however, called for nothing less than transformation. The solutions offered under this approach—e.g., turning control over to consumers, doing away with the idea of "treatment"—were directed at revolution, at a seismic "mind shift." When superimposed on the problem-level approaches described above, the reform and transformation perspectives revealed very different definitions of recovery.

Individual-level reform solutions had to do with providing improved education, access, and choice to persons diagnosed with mental illness. Recovery occurred when the individual consumer "accepted the illness" and sought treatment, including medication and psychosocial services, with good results in terms of functioning and happiness. As a family member and mental health advocate said, recovery means "in some facet of their lives," those who recover have "improved and feel better about themselves." She went on to expand on what she called "objective standards of recovery":

> The person is not throwing gasoline on a bus and killing or maiming five people. [A reference to an incident that had recently occurred in the city.] The person is not going in stores and shoplifting. The person is taking medication and showing much less depression, showing all kinds of good symptoms. The person is not necessarily working, but shows an interest that eventually that person will try to work in the public area, to get money to live on.[4]

Individual-level transformation solutions, on the other hand, required that the individual be empowered. Recovery was about consumers becoming aware and active, developing "full and productive lives regardless of the diagnosis" and gaining the strength to reduce dependence on (and perhaps eventually sever all connection with) the system. This definition had less to do with symptom abatement and functionality and more with what one Workgroup member, a psychiatrist, called "a *socially defined* change in one's role . . . [that] has nothing to do with whether the underlying disease is cured or not." A mental health advocate, for example, described the way she thinks about recovery:

> I see it as a fairly fundamental shift in the way that mental health providers have thought about consumers and the way consumers have thought about themselves. . . . I think the shift is movement from a notion of maintenance and staying out of the hospital to one of much fuller participation in life. And from the consumer perspective, it's also taking responsibility for one's own . . . life in some ways but also for one's own healing. Because I think so often . . . the expectation has been set up

that the patient is the one who is in the helpless situation and they go to the professional to get fixed. . . . And I think what we're seeing now is that people are wanting to change that.

System-level reform solutions were about providing a greater range of effective services, improving provider training, and getting more (or more flexible) funding into the system. Here, recovery was the outcome of an integrated system of highly rationalized and humane services. The administrator of a community-based mental health program clarified that talking about recovery meant

> individualizing services in a way that enhances [clients'] ability to get their own life in order. . . . [R]ecovery has a real nice ring to it that I like a lot. Individualized services. Individualized service planning or person-centered planning isn't any easier for people to understand. But it might say more directly what we are talking about.

System-level transformation solutions looked to the eventual dissolution of the current system and its replacement by a nonhierarchical network of consumer-run (and government-funded) alternatives. Recovery was the transfer of control from a professionalized (and medicalized) system to a consumer movement with a broader understanding of the causes and effects of mental illness. In this way, a Workgroup member noted, recovery represented a challenge to "what really has been the dominant model in the mental health system for quite a while." She explained:

> Once mental health care got medicalized, then they really glommed onto the medical model thing in a big way. And I guess to me that's the primary thing that's being challenged, and it's consumers saying . . . , "This individual knows a lot about their own life experiences, their illness, what may help them in the healing process." And that data is as valuable as the diagnosis and treatment regimens that people are taught about at medical school or social work school or nursing school or anyplace else. And . . . the consumer is, at the very least, a peer

with the professional in terms of participating in what it is that's going to help them in their life. And some people actually think the consumer should be on top in terms of directing things.

Societal-level reform aimed to increase society's understanding of (and thus tolerance for) mental illness as a biologically based disease. Recovery would become possible as persons suffering mental illness met with such increased understanding and tolerance. An example of this approach is NAMI's campaign to establish mental illnesses as "brain disorders," an effort the organization believes will lead to more resources being allocated for mental health research and services. Some Workgroup members clearly saw recovery as a prompt to—as well as an effect of—such resource allocation. As one member said:

> We have to be able to show the voting and the financially supporting public that people *do* recover. We better jolly well show them because every human service agency and everybody who is doing anything for people is liable to be cut in this extremely materialistic stage we're in in this country. So you'd better be able to show objectively that some people are recovering.

Societal-level transformation solutions, however, called for the elimination of all stigma (defined broadly as any negative attitude, including fear, toward persons labeled as different). The object of recovery was society itself. As one service provider said, "We know that recovery refers to society being messed up." Workgroup members drew on civil rights history to describe this solution approach, noting, for example, that the solution for racism was not to tell African Americans to "recover" from it. As an exemplar of societal recovery, members often cited the disability rights movement and, in particular, the ideology of "accommodation, not rehabilitation" as operationalized by the Americans with Disabilities Act. (A more cynical Workgroup member, however, opined that only "natural law"—"waiting for the bigots to die off"—would solve the problem of stigma.)

The third axis of conflict involved ideas about the most effective strategy for making change. The Workgroup as a whole believed that change (either reform or transformation) was determined both by what people believed and what they did. While some members of the group thought that change in policies and practices could be facilitated by first changing the beliefs of those involved in the system, others were convinced that change was best served by first mandating new policies and programs, arguing that people would adopt new beliefs as they worked in new ways. While the latter position might be described as pragmatic, the former may be categorized as idealistic. A mental health advocate talked about these two approaches:

> I think you have to think about a lot of this stuff very
> strategically. Let it kind of creep up on people. . . . You have
> to have this . . . leadership part, but I've certainly learned
> that you don't create lasting change by beating people over
> the head. . . .You get them more to . . . internalize it by
> experiencing it, thinking about it, coming to it, having it
> be their own idea, their own transformative experience.

My presentation of these problem axes comes with two caveats. First, the definitional types I have described could not be categorized as belonging to specific groups. That is, the provider members of the Workgroup were not necessarily pragmatists who defined the problem as disease and the solution as providing medications. Nor could it be said that consumers were idealists who tended toward societal attributions and transformation ideologies more than other Workgroup members. Instead, definitional positions seemed highly idiosyncratic—a product of a lifetime's worth of personal experiences and philosophical understandings—and situational—subject to shifting under different conditions. (For example, when discussing the historical inequities between the northern part of the state and Madison and Milwaukee, a consumer residing in the north could speak passionately about that region's need for better access to expert psychiatrists and the newest medications. When discussing the implications for identity of receiving a psychiatric diagnosis, however, she could entirely reject the biological basis of mental illness.) Second, these definitional differences were almost never made explicit. Instead, they arose obliquely, in discussions of how to operationalize recovery.

In the exchange recounted above, the discussion ended when a Workgroup member interrupted to ask if there was a definition of recovery. Several people responded by mentioning the definition in the commission's report. Others cited definitions by experts in the field. At this point, however, one of the Workgroup cochairs (fearful, she later told me, that definition was a morass the group would never overcome) cut off the discussion, saying, "We may not know exactly what recovery is, but we can operationalize it anyway."

This statement provided a temporary solution to the Workgroup's apparent impasse—ending the discussion by redirecting the group to other matters at hand. Yet the periodic reemergence of the problem of defining recovery suggested that it was something that had to be dealt with substantively at some point. How, then, did the Workgroup specify recovery when there were so many definitional differences among the members of the group?

By January 1999, the Recovery Workgroup had produced two draft documents that described its recommendation for operationalizing a recovery-oriented system. The first document focused on strategies for promoting recovery in the managed care demonstration projects. In it, the Workgroup presented a collection of what it termed "conceptual" recommendations. The recommendations suggested a number of requirements for the upcoming managed care demonstration projects, including the following: that the managed care organizations (MCOs) provide "training on the concept of recovery" to all MCO staff, consumers, and family members; that "consumer operated services such as peer support groups, drop-in centers, crisis responses, peer connections and help in transitions for consumers in hospitals or other institutions" be included in the list of covered benefits; that MCOs ensure no loss of eligibility for any enrolled consumer; that MCOs work toward integrating recovery principles into all services, policies, and procedures, with special emphasis on "consumer/provider interaction and relationships, use of natural supports and community resources, strengths based planning, individualized services and supports, consumer choice, and other ways to promote consumer recovery"; that MCOs improve access to services; that MCOs institute quality improvement procedures and include consumers and families in all quality improvement efforts; that MCOs ensure consumer and family representation on all governing structures; and that they provide easily accessible complaint and grievance procedures.

The second document listed recommendations to be implemented statewide. The recommendations called upon the state to establish an ongoing recovery advisory group (a successor to the original Workgroup) that would work with the bureau to develop recovery education programming in the state; to promote consumer and family involvement on the state level; to examine risk and liability issues that hindered the implementation of recovery principles and work to change them; to facilitate "partnerships between consumers and professionals" by means such as recovery dialogues, focus groups, and education; to promote self-management of symptoms by consumers; to facilitate the ability of consumers to find and engage in "work and other meaningful activities"; and to recognize and address "the special problems of persons with dual diagnoses."

The definitional problem was resolved in two ways. First, the group capitalized on the structural division of labor described earlier in this chapter, leaving many definitional choices to be made among the smaller subgroup of bureau staff and the cochairs. Second, the Workgroup never did "define" recovery. Rather, the members settled the definitional problem by tacitly agreeing on a set of overarching values—hope, knowledge, collaboration, individualization, choice, and change. These values were seen to represent the "essence" of recovery yet were nonspecific and flexible enough to accommodate the range of positions found in the Workgroup. Choice, for example, encompassed both the reform position that consumers should have a range of service options from which to choose and the transformation position that consumers should be able to exercise their option to leave the system entirely.

The policies that the Workgroup decided to promote in its recommendations shared the same kind of flexibility. These policy solutions were both congruent with its overarching values and potentially effective at resolving many different kinds of problems. For example, one of the group's key policy recommendations, the provision of recovery training and education, was clearly linked to one of its overarching values, knowledge. Because the content that defined knowledge was never fully specified (although the group did delineate some of its aspects, including the idea that recovery is possible and strategies for self-management of symptoms), the content of educational programming remained similarly vague. In this nonspecificity, education, like knowledge, retained its ability to satisfy the requirements of a range of definitions.

Sometimes the Workgroup members settled on a policy first and then backtracked to determine how the policy could be interpreted as promoting recovery. During a meeting in which the Workgroup was starting to formulate the managed care recommendations, the members were getting bogged down in the task of developing contract requirements vis-à-vis support of consumer-run services. One member raised a question about the goal of promoting consumer-run services: "Is it just to be able to say they exist? Is it to provide work for consumers? To serve as a source of consumer role models? To fill a gap in available services?" What the group was able to agree on was that consumer-run services are important to promoting hope. In writing the recommendations, then, the Workgroup deferred specifying (i.e., requiring that a certain proportion of funds be spent on consumer-run services) to emphasize the "conceptual" point that consumer-run services had to be officially supported in order to promote hope.

The ease with which the group moved between policies as by-products of values and values as by-products of policies suggests that the third axis of ideological difference, the conflict between pragmatism and idealism, was resolved in favor of *both* positions. That is, the group looked to situations rather than to a hard and fast rule to find the most effective strategy for making change. Under some circumstances, promoting new values would facilitate change; in others, values change would follow the implementation of new policies.

The differences that arose when the Workgroup interacted with other policy development entities were not resolved as easily, however. In these instances, definitional conflicts became much more explicit, and the Workgroup put a great deal of time and effort into finding ways to have its recommendations accepted. From the point of view of the Workgroup, the main differences between it and the groups with which it interacted (e.g., the BRC-IAC, other work groups) were a resistance to change, in general, and, specifically, a commitment to the status quo that clouded understanding of the true meaning of recovery. The following vignettes show how the Workgroup dealt with these challenges.

LEGITIMIZING

As the Recovery Workgroup was working toward meeting its mandate, so too were many other work groups whose responsibilities encompassed other substantive areas. At times the work done by different groups intersected. One such intersection occurred when a bureau staffer who was working with the System Design Workgroup[5] brought one of its draft work products to the Recovery Workgroup to be vetted. Because the System Design Workgroup was composed mainly of county system administrators and representatives of provider organizations, the staffer worried that they might not have fully internalized a "recovery orientation" and wanted their work to be reviewed to see if it was consistent with recovery principles.

The document in question was meant to guide providers in a comprehensive client assessment protocol. Nine pages long, it included a form asking for general information about the client (e.g., name, demographic data, legal status, and benefits eligibility) and eight more pages listing the domains to be assessed and the information the clinician should collect to make a complete assessment of each domain. The overall domains were mental health and alcohol or other drug abuse/use; vocational and educational functioning; social and community supports; living/residential environment; independent living skills; physical health; legal; and cultural. Specific questions within each domain included things like DSM-IV diagnosis, education and work history, social skills, current living situation, self-care ability, medical history, arrest and commitment histories, and church affiliation.

Members of the Recovery Workgroup reacted very strongly against this assessment protocol, objecting both to the content to be assessed and to the way in which the assessment was to be conducted. Specifically, the Recovery Workgroup saw the protocol as universally pathologizing all aspects of a consumer's life. They perceived it as calling for a provider to "interrogate" the consumer about personal information without first establishing any trust or rapport. Its categories and questions, they argued, reflected only the concerns of providers and system administrators; the consumer's voice was silent. Most importantly, the form of the assessment protocol suggested to the Workgroup that recovery was running a very real risk of becoming just an "addendum" to the status quo, a philosophy that was endorsed in rhetoric but not in practice.

Embedded in the Workgroup's critique of the assessment protocol was an implicit comparison between the values represented by the document and the overarching values that the group was using to define recovery. In this comparison, the assessment protocol fell woefully short, particularly in its failure to endorse the values of collaboration, individualization, and change. Instead of demonstrating these values, the assessment was tainted by the power imbalances and the stigmatizing assumptions that characterized the old system.

The Recovery Workgroup suggested that in a recovery-oriented mental health system, assessment would consist of just three questions: "Tell me your story"; "What do you want?"; and "How can I be useful to you?" Unfortunately, the answers to these three questions would not provide for the data needs built into the new system's accountability requirements. Given this incompatibility, the Workgroup decided to work with the System Design group to come up with a protocol that could both meet the data requirement and reflect a recovery orientation. It was determined that several members of the Recovery Workgroup would first work with the system design staffer to come up with ideas for a new assessment document and then meet with the System Design Workgroup to negotiate a recovery-oriented assessment protocol.

Several weeks later, when the Recovery Workgroup delegation met with the System Design Workgroup, they offered several suggestions. First, they proposed that the assessment procedure be bifurcated, with one assessment document to be completed by the provider and another by the consumer. The delegation had taken several steps toward this bifurcation, reviewing the draft assessment to determine which items the consumer could complete. In the domain of vocational/educational functioning, for example, they suggested that information on educational background and goals, employment history and status, and employment goals should all be completed by the consumer, while information on literacy, previous use of vocational services, and an assessment of vocational strengths and needs could be provided by the provider. They had also drafted a version of the consumer-completed assessment form, which they provided to the System Design Workgroup for review.

The discussion of bifurcating the assessment process highlighted the divergent goals and ideologies of the Recovery Workgroup and the System Design Workgroup. While the Recovery Workgroup was concerned solely with promoting the overarching values of recovery, the System Design Workgroup bore responsibility for fulfilling certain system needs. Thus the discussion reflected conflicts between the importance assigned to values like individualization and choice (on the Recovery Workgroup's side) and the system's need for full, complete, and valid data (on the System Design Workgroup's side). For example, System Design Workgroup members expressed concern that consumers would either refuse to complete the assessment or try to "game" the system by providing inaccurate information. To the former concern, the Recovery Workgroup delegation insisted on complete voluntariness, allowing only that if a consumer refused to provide information that was crucial to providing services might the provider seek their permission to gather it from another source. To the latter concern, they argued that it was the consumer's *perceptions* that were important, not the "reality" as endorsed by the provider and reflected in the idea of "valid data." They rejected the idea that consumers were manipulators who sought to "game" the system but agreed that data needed for fiscal decisions (e.g., eligibility determinations) might be independently verified.

The process of reviewing and revising the draft consumer-completed assessment form demonstrated how recovery values could be operationalized. The Recovery Workgroup's recommendations sought to accommodate diversity (e.g., asking about attendance at "religious services" rather than "church attendance"); to lessen the imposition of provider assumptions and values on consumers (e.g., instead of "infantilizing" consumers by asking about their relationship with their parents, asking about "the people who are most important" to them); to reduce consumer burden and intrusiveness by questioning why each item was necessary (e.g., did the provider really need to know if the consumer had had childhood friends?); to frame the assessment process positively (e.g., asking consumers about their strengths rather than focusing on weaknesses); to allow room for consumers' own self-assessments (e.g., instead of asking, "Do you get enough exercise?" ask, "Do you think you get enough exercise?"); and to demonstrate respect (e.g., making the very first question "How would you like to be addressed?")

The evolution of one set of items shows how negotiations between the Recovery Workgroup and the System Design Workgroup affected the development of the consumer-completed assessment form. In the initial draft, the tool's final section was called "Chief complaint or concern." It contained several questions: "Why are you seeking help from this place?"; "Did someone suggest you get help here?"; "What areas do you want help in the most?"; and "What would you like to change in your life?" The System Design Workgroup perceived these questions as random and unfocused. Its members worried how someone who "lacked insight" would answer them. Drawing on the Recovery Workgroup's principles, they noted that the questions were not framed positively. In the final version of the tool, the section title had been omitted. The questions had been moved to the beginning of the instrument and had been revised to read: "What are the things that are going well in your life?"; " What are the things you do well?"; "What do you do to help yourself?"; "What are the things that are bothering you the most?"; "What areas do you want help in the most?"; and "How can we be most useful to you?"

Negotiations between the Recovery Workgroup and the System Design Workgroup over the issue of consumer assessment sought to balance the concerns of the two groups. That balance was achieved in compromise, where the assessment process was bifurcated, with one process (the provider-completed assessment protocol) reflecting the values of the old system and the other (the consumer-completed assessment tool) reflecting the values of recovery. This compromise ensured that both sides could find reason to claim that their goals and ideologies were being represented. In the process of reaching this resolution, the Recovery Workgroup had served as a resource to the System Design Workgroup, legitimizing its work with the imprimatur of adequate adherence to recovery values.

STRATEGIZING AND PERSUADING

In January 1999, the Workgroup was ready to present its recommendations to the BRC-IAC, the body charged with overseeing the planning for the system redesign. The meeting agenda called for the recommendations to be presented in the morning, followed by reaction and questions, followed by lunch. After lunch, I was scheduled to speak about the ways other states were implementing recovery in their public mental health systems.

The task of presenting the recommendations fell to one of the Workgroup's cochairs, who structured her presentation around a series of overhead transparencies. These transparencies listed the recommendations, giving brief explanations that she then augmented verbally. (The recommendations presented pertained only to the managed care demonstration projects and fell into the categories I have described: education; consumer-run services; recovery-oriented services and supports; recovery/treatment plan; consumer choice; and consumer/family participation.)

The discussion session that followed the presentation was extremely contentious, more so than anything that had occurred within the Workgroup. The members of the BRC-IAC raised objections in two areas: the likely cost of implementing the recommendations (costs they argued would exceed the funds available for the managed care demonstrations), and the perception that the state was being overly prescriptive toward the counties, destroying the flexibility implied in the notion of demonstration projects. In fact, the Recovery Workgroup had rarely if ever discussed cost issues as it worked toward its recommendations. Nor had the tensions between the state and the counties—tensions born of the historical role of the state as both centralized policymaker and regulator—been part of its considerations.

As these omissions demonstrated, there were huge gaps between the concerns of the Workgroup and those of the BRC-IAC. These gaps extended to their understandings of recovery. For example, the Workgroup's recommendation that consumers be represented on the MCO-governing bodies was seen as highly problematic by some BRC-IAC members, who suggested that instead there be separate consumer advisory boards. The consumer advisory board was an idea that had been considered and explicitly rejected by the Workgroup as a form of "tokenism." That the idea was even suggested showed the Workgroup cochairs that the BRC-IAC did not understand recovery in the same way that they did.

In the midst of this discussion, a member of the BRC-IAC asked if there was a definition of recovery. Other members of the committee said no, but then a louder tide of voices around the room said yes, there was a definition in the commission's report. One of the cochairs then spoke up to say that the Recovery Workgroup had defined the most important principles of recovery.

The question about definition suggested that the BRC-IAC saw the Recovery Workgroup's recommendations as arbitrary, unanchored in any sort of conceptual framework. Although the members of the BRC-IAC had certainly read the commission's report, including the section that "defined" recovery, they were not able to see the logic that connected the definition to the Workgroup's operationalizations. I would submit that this was in large part because the Workgroup's overarching values were not made explicit in the recommendations or in the presentation and thus could not be shared by the members of the BRC-IAC.

The presentation to the BRC-IAC was seen as a failure by the bureau staff and Recovery Workgroup cochairs who had orchestrated it. In reviewing the event, the staff and cochairs identified what they felt had been a series of strategic errors. First, they wondered if the presentation would have gone more smoothly if it had been preceded, rather than followed, by my presentation on strategies being used in other states. Their reasoning was that the consistency between the Workgroup's recommendations and these strategies would have legitimized the former, demonstrating to the BRC-IAC that Wisconsin's plans were entirely consistent with what was going on elsewhere in the country. Second, they were concerned that some of the most vociferous objections had come from a woman on the BRC-IAC who had also been a member of the Recovery Workgroup. They thought some of these objections might have been headed off if she had been introduced as having served on the Workgroup. (They did not, however, seem concerned about what this suggested about the "representativeness" of the Workgroup's recommendations.) One bureau staffer thought that the prescriptiveness objections could have been reduced if the Workgroup's statewide recommendations had been presented at the same time. Doing so, she theorized, would have shown that the state was assuming much of the responsibility for the implementation, not simply foisting it off on the counties in the form of the reviled "unfunded mandates."

The dissension of the BRC-IAC meeting had ended with the suggestion that the recommendations be brought to a meeting of the County Planning Partners for their reaction. That meeting was scheduled for spring 1999, several months after the presentation to the BRC-IAC. In the interim, the Workgroup staff and cochairs retooled the recommendations, seeking to forestall the kinds of objections that had arisen during the BRC-IAC meeting.

The same Workgroup cochair who had presented at the BRC-IAC

meeting did so at the gathering of the County Planning Partners. This time, however, her presentation began with a series of "expert" definitions of recovery, culled from the Blue Ribbon Commission's report. She next discussed the "recovery principles" that had guided the Workgroup in formulating its recommendations. These principles mixed the "basic recovery-oriented principles" described in the commission's report (e.g., "Recovery is possible" and "Just start anywhere") with statements that had been developed by the Workgroup and emphasized the overarching values of hope, choice, and collaboration. She continued with a description of the Workgroup's process that emphasized the diversity and representativeness of the Workgroup's membership and the congruence of its recommendations with what was going on around the country. Her presentation ended with the assertion that "it's clear that we do have outlines of what recovery is."

The recommendations document given to the county planning partners also showed some changes since its presentation to the BRC-IAC. The document began with definitions of selected key terms (e.g., "consumer," "individualized recovery/treatment plan," "consumer operated services"). Substantively, the recommendations themselves had been altered. For example, while the January draft had listed eight different specific recommendations under the heading "Meaningful consumer choice," the spring draft included seven, six of which were identified as the responsibility of the MCO. The January document had noted that "the MCO contract must ensure that consumers and/or families have a choice of service providing agencies, individual providers . . . , living arrangements, use of consumer operated services, and use of other agencies/supports in the community. Individuals must also have a choice over level of services to be received, including the right to refuse services unless under a court order." The spring draft directed only that "consumers and/or family members will have a choice of no less than two service providing agencies and no less than two individual providers" and that "individual consumer and family input shall direct the MCO's decision-making about what services the consumer or family receives in order to promote recovery." Additionally, the recommendations document had been visually revised to emphasize the shared responsibility of the MCOs and the state for implementing the recommendations, specifying who was to do what.

The process the Workgroup had used to assign responsibility reflected the group's assessment of the qualities necessary for implementation and the distribution of these qualities among Wisconsin's mental health system stakeholders. This list of qualities might be categorized under the general domains of power, legitimacy, expertise, reach, and effectiveness. The power domain encompassed control over funding as well as the authority and jurisdiction to promote change by making and enforcing decisions. The power players were the state and the counties. Legitimacy and expertise, closely linked, revolved around moral authority, experience, and voice. Consumers and consumer-run organizations were viewed as the most legitimate advocates for recovery, the groups that could be counted upon to have internalized the "right spirit." Reach addressed existing structural networks of influence. In the current situation, reach was primarily a quality of the state, which was able to exert influence through its existing organizational structures (e.g., regulatory bodies). Such structures were in their infancy for existing consumer groups, and thus their reach was limited. Unfortunately, no one entity had the effectiveness to promote recovery implementation: the state was hampered by the resentment of the counties; the counties restricted by their lack of expertise; consumer groups because they did not have the reach. The Workgroup's distribution of responsibility sought to capitalize on the strengths of each entity while shoring up their weaknesses. Thus the state was asked to exert its authority to mandate certain expectations, the specifics of which would be defined by experts like consumers. Counties would be held accountable for meeting these expectations but would also be assured of a place at the table when they were being determined. The proposed recovery advisory group, the successor to the Recovery Workgroup, was to serve as something of a hub in this distribution: a mechanism for vetting expectations and overseeing implementation. (The work of this ongoing body is the subject of Chapter 5.)

The County Planning Partners' discussion of the recommendations was quite different from that which occurred during the BRC-IAC meeting. The planning partners raised questions about the recommendations, but these questions were largely directed at details that had not been adequately specified. There was not the same challenge to the substance of the recommendations, nor did anyone raise the issue of defining recovery. The Workgroup cochairs left the meeting feeling satisfied that the presentation had been a success.

While the Workgroup's presentation to the BRC-IAC represented a failure of definition, legitimization, strategizing, and persuasion, the retooled presentation to the County Planning Partners demonstrated how the Workgroup was able to deploy its diverse resources in order to define, legitimize, strategize, and persuade effectively, drawing upon resources both within and outside the group in its successful presentation. Explicit references to expert definitions of recovery were examples of the latter, while the description of the Workgroup's process, with an emphasis on the representativeness and active participation of its membership, used the former. The revised recommendations showed the Workgroup's willingness to integrate the concerns of other groups in order to increase its powers of persuasion. For example, the Workgroup's attempt to specify responsibility sought to see the redesign from the point of view of the administrators and providers who made up the membership of the County Planning Partners, and to reassure the partners that their interests would not be lost in the process. Finally, the presentation showed how the products of the Workgroup's policy specification activities created the conditions for its ability to promote the recommendations: the overarching values derived by the Recovery Workgroup in its internal negotiations here were used strategically to convince another, more skeptical group of the legitimacy and feasibility of its policy product.

POLICY AS PROCESS

The Workgroup embarked on its charge with joint substantive and processual goals: to devise a recovery policy that reflected the participation of each of the stakeholder groups involved in the process. Over the course of the Workgroup's lifespan, these goals became increasingly intertwined, with potential policy problems being resolved by proposed processual solutions.

For example, as the Workgroup moved toward making specific policy recommendations at the same time that the state's managed care model was being developed, potential barriers to implementation became apparent. These barriers arose at the junction between recovery values and managed care models—practices and ideas like contracting, medical necessity, and accountability.

The contract (that is, the agreement between the state and the county as MCO) was seen to be crucial to the actual implementation of change. Because the contract would define the MCOs' recovery obligations in the new system, and because it was the received wisdom among Workgroup members that the MCOs would do as little toward recovery as they could get away with, the Workgroup's initial impulse was to specify these obligations in great detail. As the reaction to the group's MCO recommendations at the BRC-IAC meeting showed, however, the counties were resentful of and resistant to such attempts at what they perceived as state control. The concept of medical necessity was believed to be an even greater barrier. Members of the Workgroup chafed against the notion, seeing in it an implicit endorsement of the supremacy of the medical model and a thinly veiled mechanism for cost cutting. Their concern was that consumers who defined their problems as something other than biologically based and those who wanted and needed recovery options other than hospitalization, medication, and psychiatric care would be denied. Medical necessity would become the enemy of choice. Accountability, particularly requirements for ongoing assessment of client outcomes, raised other difficulties. Because recovery was seen as multidimensional, the imperative to measure it posed a threat.[6] That is, Workgroup members worried that the process of measurement would tend to reify outcomes and value certain impacts over others. For example, they saw a potential for their emphasis on the importance of "work and other meaningful activities" to be reduced to the binary outcome of employed/unemployed. If programs and service providers were to be assessed on the basis of such specific and limited measures, they would naturally focus their efforts on achieving these outcomes rather than directing their attention to the broader goal of working with a client to achieve that client's particular desires.

The barriers to arise out the clash between these specific recovery values and managed care approaches reflected two deeper, interrelated conflicts: the difficulty of balancing the kind of "thinking outside the box" necessary for developing a recovery-oriented system with the guidelines and restrictions that are implicit in a managed care model, and the tensions between the state and the counties.

In its final version of the managed care recommendations, the Workgroup attempted to manage these conflicts. In general, the recommendations eschewed the kind of detail that might be read as a mandate and kept careful control over the relative number of "wills" (requirements) and "shoulds" (suggestions). While the document included a few imperatives (e.g., consumer-operated services will be a covered service; consumers will have a choice of living arrangements), it emphasized the promise that all stakeholders would work together to create best practices guidelines around issues like developing consumer/provider partnerships, doing strengths-based planning, and promoting opportunities for consumer choice. The threat of medical necessity was neutralized with the recommendation that the concept be explicitly defined "to clearly require that services have a recovery focus and that they reflect consumer choice and input." The document addressed the accountability issue by suggesting that it, too, become a collaborative process. That is, it urged the involvement of consumers and family members in defining and measuring quality.

As I explained earlier in this chapter, the Workgroup addressed the state/county tension by defining the roles of the two levels of government. In particular, it assigned joint responsibility for most of the recommendations, portraying recovery implementation as a goal that would be achieved through the shared efforts of all stakeholders—including the state, the counties, consumers and family members, and an ongoing recovery advisory group—over a period of years.

The Recovery Workgroup served as a model for this kind of processual solution. That is, in its representativeness, its emphasis on participation, and its distribution of responsibility through an effective division of labor, the Workgroup embodied the processes, and thus the policies, it had specified.

Interstice 3
Participant Observer

The quandaries I faced in my relationship with the Workgroup revolved around the question of how to fulfill the participant part of the participant observer role. (The observer part came easily to me.) In general, I didn't talk much during meetings, nor did I take part in the brainstorming exercises set for the members by the cochairs. (I always took notes on these activities, however. My constant scribbling did not go unnoticed: a new member once referred to me as "that woman with the curly hair who's always writing.") The times I wanted to speak were those when I could see the group getting tied up in knots and talking at cross-purposes because they were not recognizing that each member meant something different by *recovery*. Given my interest in how the group was defining *recovery*, those instances were, of course, the very interactions I was most interested in observing. Intervention driven by my own sense of frustration would have been harmful to my goals, so I bit my tongue.

But because my engagement with the Workgroup was an activity tied to my postdoctoral fellowship, and because I felt obliged to make some sort of contribution, I was an active participant in providing research-based information to the Workgroup (the early reports that I wrote about existing recovery strategies). In this way I suspect I had some influence on the Workgroup's eventual products—an influence that research purists might consider a form of contamination, but that I felt was appropriate given the situation. (It is likely the Workgroup would have gotten the information from some other source, at some point, anyway.)

My real uneasiness with participation emerged when the Workgroup tried to use my status as an "expert" in recovery implementation strategies to convince others of the legitimacy of its recommendations (for example, when I was asked to give the presentation on recovery implementation to the BRC-IAC) and when I felt that the Workgroup, or individuals with whom I came into contact, assumed that I was an advocate for a particular definition of *recovery*. I was uncomfortable with the ascription of expertise because my own knowledge of recovery seemed so shallow. I had no personal or professional experience in the matter. At the time, I knew little about existing mental health systems or the broader context of the state's redesign project. I had a dog and pony show, a summary account of nascent recovery implementation strategies. I couldn't say much about what these strategies looked like in practice; I couldn't answer questions about their effectiveness. (What I could do was make the interactive components of these presentations part of my own research, as when I noted that some audiences were concerned about proof of effectiveness, whereas others were willing to take assertions on faith.)

The advocacy assumption was incompatible with what I saw as my own critical, or at least ambivalent, stance toward recovery. That is, I still wasn't sure it was anything different from hype, a new bottle containing all the stale wine of old arguments and reform attempts. I had no investment in that history. The rather nasty truth was that I didn't really care if Wisconsin was able to claim to have a recovery-oriented system or not. (This is more complicated than such a stark statement: certainly I thought that a good system was better than a bad system and I wished the best for all involved, but I wasn't interested in taking sides when "good" or "best" were being debated.) My interest was in elaborating the multidimensionality of recovery, discovering its complexities and paradoxes, not in fixing it as any one particular agenda.

This reluctance to assume the roles of expert and advocate conflicted with my equally strong desire to reciprocate for the privilege of observing the Workgroup in ways that the members could find meaningful. I wanted to be useful to them, but to do so in ways that were consistent with my own interests. So I did presentations and tried to learn from them as much as I could teach, and I advocated for understanding the multiplicity of recovery definitions and their varying implications—that is, if an audience seemed too certain about the meaning of recovery I'd try to throw them a monkey wrench.

Such an equivocal position was a luxury afforded me by my fellowship, a regular source of income that was not linked to any particular activity. When my employment circumstances changed and I wanted (needed) to be paid for the work I was doing, I had to relinquish some of the distance I'd tried to maintain by taking a more active role in some of the projects described in the next chapter.

As an observer I am not a camera loaded with blank film that can be exposed and then processed to unspool an uninflected record of events. Instead, observation is series of acts: decisions taken and interpretations made. The previous chapter and the next are my representations of the acts of the makers of recovery policy in Wisconsin. In a sense, our positions have now shifted and they, if they choose, are now observing me acting. (Perhaps, as readers, they may be biting their own tongues.)

5
FROM BONES TO BRIDGES

The plan for and the promise of the advisory group that would guide Wisconsin's recovery implementation were embedded in the Recovery Workgroup's statewide recommendations, which called upon the state to "[e]stablish an ongoing Recovery Implementation task force to develop training and identify recovery oriented materials, to oversee the implementation of recovery concepts in the managed care demonstration projects, to advise the Department regarding the implementation of the statewide recommendations, and to identify or help create best practice guidelines for recovery implementation." Or, as a Workgroup member said, the task force would "keep the spirit of recovery alive."

In the spring of 1999, during the interim between the Recovery Workgroup's presentation of recommendations and the formation of the task force, several members of the Workgroup and staff from the Bureau of Community Mental Health met with a consultant to discuss priorities for the task force. After a review of the Workgroup's recommendations, the consultant set the group a series of exercises, asking them to select the three most critical steps toward advancing recovery implementation in Wisconsin, the three easiest, the three that could be done with resources that were currently available, and the three that were most important to accomplish within the next year. The group used these criteria of urgency and feasibility to determine two tiers of priorities. In the first tier were formation of the task force, development of educational tools, and increased consumer involvement. In the second were a hodgepodge of priorities, including review of existing policies, development and promulgation of best-practice guidelines, and development of new approaches to managing risk and liability.

Next, the consultant drew a five-year timeline, asking the group to think about where they wanted to be by the end of those five years and what would need to be done in order to get there. This exercise revealed the complexity of implementing recovery, the lack of a clear, linear path. It seemed that every priority had to be accomplished first, because their interdependence was such that each seemed necessary for laying the groundwork for another. For example, the group determined that education should be started in Year One but then realized that much of the content of educational programming would have to be determined by the new best-practice guidelines, which were not slated to be finalized until Year Three.

Recognizing this quandary, and also concerned that the small group in attendance should not be drawing up the agenda for the entire task force, the group reverted to a familiar process, deciding that several people would work together to write a draft list of priorities and a time line, and then present them at the next, and final, meeting of the Recovery Workgroup for reaction.

If clarity had been the expectation of this exercise, it was not the result. Instead, the Workgroup's discussion of the draft priorities and time line provoked a searching examination of the assumptions and implications of each of the priorities. For example, consideration of the risk/liability priority led the Workgroup to a conversation about the link between risk/liability and the quality of consumer/provider relationships. Many members of the group agreed that the stronger these relationships (the closer, the more trusting), the less "risk" (of litigation) would be faced by the provider, and thus the more willing the provider would be to allow the consumer to take the "risk" of recovery. Others, however, opined that liability concerns were a front that providers used to mask their own need for control. This group doubted that changing the liability laws would induce such providers to allow their clients the "dignity of risk."

Prioritizing was complicated by practical questions as well. The group wondered if all of the priority initiatives should be directed at the managed care demonstration sites or spread out across the state. While the more focused strategy would reduce the difficulty of implementation, it also carried risks: any effort would reach a limited number of consumers, leaving out individuals who were not being served in one of the demonstration counties. In addition, restricting the recovery initiatives to the demonstrations meant linking the fate of recovery implementation to the fate of the demonstration projects. If the latter were to fail, so too might recovery.

Money was another concern. The funds to support the task force (mainly staff time and compensation for consumer members) were being provided by the bureau, but it was unclear where support for the implementation activities would be found. The Workgroup thought that it might request a portion of the state's mental health block grant (the federal money provided to states) from the Mental Health Council (the body that made block grant fund distribution decisions) but realized that the initiatives were not yet well-enough defined to be described in a proposal to the council.

In the end, the priorities for the task force's first few years were determined by the funding situation. While the availability of new money was uncertain, the Wisconsin Coalition for Advocacy (WCA) (the state's protection and advocacy agency)[1] had already budgeted for several recovery-focused projects: the production of an educational video; the development of a self-assessment process to be used in mental health agencies; and the compilation and distribution of a packet of written materials about recovery. These three projects became the focus of much of the task force's effort. The WCA's involvement also provided a solution to the question of whether to focus on the demonstration projects or the entire state: because the WCA's mandate was to serve the entire state, the projects, too, were directed at a broader audience.

Meanwhile, the state was moving forward with plans for the managed care demonstration projects. In June 1999, it issued a draft request for consideration (RFC). The goals of the demonstration, as stated in the RFC, were familiar: to implement the principles endorsed by the Blue Ribbon Commission; to make recovery the cornerstone of the system; to emphasize prevention and early intervention; to increase consumer/family involvement in the system; to blend funding streams to allow greater flexibility; to use managed care principles to reduce the rate of growth of system expenditures; to provide coordinated mental health, physical health, and substance abuse services; to improve access to services; and to maintain the role of the counties in the mental health system (the "Wisconsin Plan").

Structurally, the RFC set forth a blueprint for merging the two dominant funding streams in the system: Medicaid and Section 51.42 money. Because counties feared a complete merger would place them under greater financial obligations,[2] the RFC described a compromise, a mixed model in which counties would deliver services under both the traditional fee-for-service structure and a new managed care (capitated) structure. The dual systems would be distinguished by their patient populations, with those individuals needing more intensive ongoing services to be given the option of enrolling in the capitated part of the system. On the managed care side, counties would be expected to devise procedures for improving access, screening, and service coordination and for providing choice to all service recipients. Services reimbursable under the Medicaid rules (e.g., psychiatrist visits or medication) would be provided if they were found "medically necessary," while other services (e.g., vocational programs or housing support) would be judged using the criterion of "clinical necessity"—operationally defined as being part of the client's "treatment and recovery plan." Both arms of the system would be expected to implement the recovery and consumer/family involvement recommendations and to institute new management information systems for tracking and reporting service utilization and cost.

With the June release of the draft RFC, the state embarked upon a process of education and consultation. Seminars aimed both at explaining the RFC to the counties and service providers and at soliciting their comments were held. When this process was completed, and after the state legislature had passed its biennial budget, the final RFC was issued in January 2000. It called for proposals from applicant counties to be delivered to the state in May 2000. Notice of award would be made in June. Four demonstration projects would be selected, with two going forward in July and (for budget reasons) two starting in January 2001. Each demonstration project would receive $160,000 in startup money. Many features of the managed care part of the demonstrations—in particular, rate setting for the capitation component of the project—would be phased in over a period of eighteen months.

THE VIDEO *MOVIN' ON:*
STORIES FROM THE RECOVERY ROAD

The Recovery Implementation task force met for the first time in the fall of 1999. In composition, it resembled the Workgroup, but on a smaller scale, with a total membership of about eighteen. (As with the Workgroup, there soon developed a core group of regular attendees, usually ten to twelve people.) Many of the task force members had also served on the Workgroup. Once again, the group included consumers, providers, administrators, and advocates representing different geographic areas of the state (but with a heavy concentration from Madison and Milwaukee). The group met on a monthly or semimonthly basis for four or five hours at a time to work through an agenda written by the task force chairperson (who had been one of the cochairs of the Workgroup).

The very first item on the agenda at the first task force meeting was planning and production of a recovery video. A Madison production company, one that had worked on the WCA's projects in the past, had already been contracted to produce the video. At this meeting, the videographer posed two questions to the group: What concepts did they wish the video to portray and who was the intended audience?

Quite quickly, the task force members settled on two main messages. They wanted to show what was new about recovery—in particular, how it differed from the idea of maintenance—and they wanted to show how recovery was a process that would be unique for each individual. Initially, the group wanted the video to be directed at every possible audience—consumers, family members, providers, and the general public. When the videographer pointed out the difficulty of addressing each of these possible audiences in a single video, however, the group settled on two primary targets—consumers who would be "inspired" by the video and providers who would be "converted" by it. The group's wish to emphasize the unique nature of recovery and their decision to pitch the video to both consumers and providers led to a suggestion about content: the video should tell the stories of several consumer/provider dyads, showing how each individual provider and consumer had experienced the recovery process.

With these initial decisions made, the task force dug deeper into the issues they wanted the video to engage. There was concern that the video not imply that recovery was the result of an individual's interaction with the mental health system. Rather, the group wanted to emphasize that it was the affective and relational aspect of the consumer/provider partnership that might prove beneficial. Additionally, the group was adamant that the video should portray the power realignment seen to be crucial to recovery—that the camera should capture a moment in which power shifted from the provider to the consumer. Other task force members urged that the video show the "struggle" of recovery—that it not make the process look too easy. Those who saw the main purpose of the video as "converting" professionals to the possibility of recovery warned that the video should not be overly provocative or too radical in its critique of the mental health system. These members argued that the emphasis should be on the positive—that recovery was a "win-win" situation for the consumer and provider, that recovery would allow the provider a greater sense of self-efficacy and accomplishment—rather than on "trashing the system" and thus making providers defensive and hostile.

At a subsequent task force meeting, the videographer returned to solicit suggestions for individuals, or types of individuals, who might be featured in the video. She asked the group to think about what characteristics were important to show. She herself, for example, thought that it was important to focus not just on consumer/provider dyads—a representational strategy that might send the message that recovery was simply a matter of finding a good provider—but also on an individual consumer who was "guiding their own recovery" without resort to the mental health system. In a similar vein, task force members listed a number of qualities they thought should be represented: ethno-racial diversity, geographic diversity, demographic diversity, diagnostic diversity, diversity of illness severity, and diversity in recovery paths. With these criteria in mind, the videographer set off to find participants and produce the video.

Movin' On: Stories from the Recovery Road (WCA 2001) was premiered to the task force in July 2000. The video features the stories of three Wisconsin residents—Pete, Diana, and Mona—each of whom has struggled with mental health issues. The video begins with a map being spread open on a Formica counter strewn with salt and pepper shakers, a coffee cup and saucer. Someone is setting off on a journey.

Pete, a heavyset man in his forties, talks about a past life marked by drug and alcohol abuse, psychotic episodes and blackouts, cross-country journeys by freight train, and the violence of the streets. He describes how his initial interactions with the mental health system left him feeling "pissed off" at providers' lack of respect. Pete's recovery is portrayed as the result of a confluence of factors: meeting Jane—a psychiatric nurse whose attitude and actions differed from those of other providers he had seen—and Pete's decision to change the way he had been living, to stop drinking and drugging and to examine his choices. Now Pete is involved and engaged, working with a number of service organizations and policy-making committees to improve the mental health system in Wisconsin. Pete's story uses the metaphor of a train. As he narrates a description of the chaos of his younger days, he is shown wandering among the tracks and rust of a freight yard. As the story shifts to present day, however, he boards and rides the passenger rail near his home in Milwaukee.

Diana, a Madison artist, is shown in her home studio and teaching a class at Cornucopia, a local consumer organization. Diana alludes to an abusive childhood, hospitalizations, an unhappy marriage. Her lack of self-knowledge and an unwillingness to face the past led to constant anxiety and fear. She reports finding her path to personal discovery, integration, and healing in the creative process—in dark paintings that emerged intuitively and provided her with a visual reckoning and, more recently, in witty sculptures that encourage audience interaction. Her work at Cornucopia, teaching classes of consumer artists, is another sort of reaching out through art. Diana calls her recovery "a work in progress," noting that its key components have included leaving the past behind, telling secrets, and growing into a sense of comfort with herself.

Mona's story begins with a scene of Mona and her teenage daughter laughing together. Mona, an African American woman, describes her own girlhood: several suicide attempts, increasingly intrusive voices, violence. She is first labeled a "troublemaker" and then a "schizophrenic" and sent away to juvenile facilities and hospitals. She enters nursing school, has three children, finds work in a long-term care facility for people with psychiatric disabilities (where she feels superior to her patients, but recognizes the irony that "the person who should have been taking the Thorazine was giving out the Thorazine"). She suffers another breakdown and loses custody of her children. Eventually she moves to Madison, where she becomes involved with Yahara House (a clubhouse fashioned on the Fountain House model) and with Jan, a rehabilitation worker at Yahara. The focus of Mona's life, the key to her recovery, becomes her quest to regain custody of her children, a goal she has repeatedly been told is unrealistic. Mona narrates the story of her attempt to pull her life together and of the legal battle that ends when a judge recognizes her hard work and progress and returns the children to her custody. In the final scene Mona stands before an audience at Yahara House, singing her favorite song, Gershwin's "Summertime":

> One of these mornin's
> You gonna rise up singin'
> You gonna hoist your wings
> And take to the sky.

After the first viewing, the task force sat silent for a few moments, absorbing the impact of the video. In general, the members were pleased. (In the minutes for the meeting, the reaction was recorded simply as "It was great!") The video portrayed three very different individuals with three very different stories. It seemed to have been successful in identifying professionals as a part of recovery, though not the key to it. Its take on the power shift was subtle but might be perceived in Pete and Jane's descriptions of their equalitarian relationship and in Mona's eventual triumph in regaining custody of her children. The video had not achieved the aim of geographic diversity (all three stories were set in Madison or Milwaukee), and the central figures were all close in age. No one in the task force complained about these omissions, however.

The criticism that was voiced revolved around the issue of the apparently high level of functioning and achievement of each of the three figures portrayed. Several members of the task force were concerned that the severity of the consumers' illnesses, past and present, had been glossed over or elided. One member later said:

> My biggest concern with the video . . . was that it made it
> seem like folks weren't still struggling with mental illness.
> And that really concerns me. Because I think that [recovery]
> then becomes about not having symptoms, rather than
> going through a personal journey and a personal process of
> . . . working on yourself. . . . [Instead] it becomes about . . .

not having symptoms . . . [and that] seems unattainable to individuals who are really struggling with symptoms.

As this woman articulated it, one perceived danger of the video's failure to focus on symptoms and illness was the possibility that consumers would be discouraged rather than inspired, feeling that they could never live up to the high standard set by the three individuals featured. The other danger was the "exceptionalism" argument—that providers would dismiss the three individuals and their recovery experiences as exceptions made possible by the relative mildness of their illnesses. Recovery was a possibility for people like this, providers might conclude, but not for "our" consumers, who are really sick.

Among the task force members, there was a range of reactions to this criticism. Several people noted the practical difficulties of portraying someone at the height of illness—for example, the impossibility of receiving informed consent to film from a person who is experiencing psychosis. Others thought that showing a highly symptomatic person would obscure the point of the video. Viewers would focus on the horror of the suffering rather than on the inspirational message of hope. The members who approved of the decision not to focus on symptoms noted that there were other videos that served that purpose and that this video was meant to be positive in its outlook. Several task force members disagreed with the premise of the criticism: they thought that the past severity of Pete's, Diana's, and Mona's illnesses was apparent in the ways they had told their stories. It was not necessary to show the bad times.

For the videographer, the decision not to focus on symptoms and illness severity had been deliberate but had not been made for practical reasons nor with the intent of affecting the credibility of recovery. Rather, she had a strong belief that the central problem facing persons with psychiatric diagnoses was the "us and them" mentality that "normal" people used to distinguish themselves from "crazy" people. In her view, if the video had emphasized illness it would have perpetuated this divide. Her aim was to portray the universality of recovery, to argue against the idea that recovery is something only people with mental illness do.

THE SELF-ASSESSMENT: "GUIDED REFLECTION"

The champion of the self-assessment (a member of the task force) conceptualized it an intervention in consciousness raising, a process that agencies could use to examine the organizational status of recovery implementation. She envisioned a two stages in the development of the self-assessment: the identification and explication of "key recovery concepts" and the formulation of an interactive process that would facilitate examination of these concepts.

Initially, members of the task force expressed some hesitation. Their worries centered on a perception that assessment would "objectify" the subjective process of recovery. That is, if agencies were asked to evaluate themselves according to how well their clients were "recovering," there was a possibility that recovery would come to be defined by only a narrow set of outcomes. Some members of the group thought that an assessment process might risk imposing standardized recovery implementation strategies on agencies, ignoring their particularities. Others, however, were leery of the possibility that the self-assessment would encourage each agency to reinvent the wheel. Together, these worries pointed to a central dilemma: the potential conflict between rigidity and creativity as recovery was implemented at the organizational level.

In the spring of 2000, the WCA hired me to develop a discussion paper on "key recovery concepts." I began by cataloging the values and principles that had emerged, both implicitly and explicitly, as the Recovery Workgroup had devised its recovery recommendations—concepts like knowledge, choice, hope, "recovery is possible," and "just start anywhere." I took this initial inventory to the task force and received more suggestions—empowerment, voice, responsibility. I then did a review of the literature on recovery, seeking to abstract from it any concepts that I might not have identified. When I believed that I had "saturated"[3] the list of key concepts, I began to look for ways to categorize them. My initial categories, for example, included things like "concepts that describe recovery" and "concepts that name strategies for promoting recovery." I continued to play with my categories, trying to find a model that would be parsimonious yet express the complexity of all that was subsumed under the term *recovery.* One morning I wrote each concept on an index card and began a "pile sort,"[4] seeking to find the underlying structure I thought was there, but had as yet eluded me. Soon, the floor of my bedroom was strewn with paper, and I was scrambling to add cards to one pile, remove them from another. The pile sort brought me to a kind of breakthrough: a model that integrated the key concepts while maintaining their distinctness.

I drew diagrams that showed the key concepts and their relationships to one another, and then I wrote some twenty pages of text to try to explain it all. I took the model to the task force for its reactions and showed it to other people to get their comments. I modified, revised, and clarified.

The final model is described in detail elsewhere (Jacobson 2000; Jacobson and Greenley 2001), but, briefly, it conceptualizes recovery as a multidimensional process that is "linked to two kinds of factors: *internal* conditions, or attitudes, processes, and experiences that go on inside recovering individuals, and *external* conditions, or the environmental states, events, and practices that when present can facilitate recovery in individuals" (Jacobson 2000, 3, emphasis in the original). The internal conditions are hope, healing, empowerment, and connection, while the external conditions are human rights, "a positive culture of healing," and recovery-oriented services. Each condition is further described by some of its characteristics. The process of recovery is a result of the interaction between internal and external conditions. In a circle of influence, recovery then feeds back to interact with the internal and the external.

For example, one of the external conditions describes the characteristics of what Daniel Fisher (1993) has called "a positive culture of healing." In a mental health agency, the four elements of such a culture are climate (an environment characterized by tolerance, empathy and compassion, respect, trust, diversity, etc.), empowered professionals (staff who are engaged in their work and believe that they can make a difference), collaborative relationships (consumers and providers who relate to each other on a human level and work together around issues of choice, participation, and risk), and a human rights orientation (an agency-wide emphasis on consumer rights, including full information and meaningful consent).

With this conceptual model in hand, the development of the self-assessment process began in earnest. The plan was to design a series of assessment exercises based on the material in the model. These exercises would be developed by a small group—composed of several members of the task force along with several nonmembers—that would report to the task force. Once the process was finalized, it would be piloted in one or two agencies, refined, and then taken to the managed care demonstration sites, which would be contractually obligated to engage in some sort of assessment. The possibility existed that the process might then be made more widely available.

The development process took place over the course of a year, from summer 2000 until summer 2001. In one of the planning group's first discussions, the rather modest purposes for which the process had been conceived were further elaborated. In addition to its assessment function, it was decided that the process should educate, serve as a mechanism for planning and continuous monitoring, provide an infusion of enthusiasm for the participating agencies, build recovery leadership within the agencies, and help to develop practical knowledge of the linkages between specific strategies and recovery outcomes.

Other discussions dealt with questions of focus (Should the exercises examine the internal or external conditions of the model—that is, should it focus on the experience of recovery among agency clients, or should it look at the environment being created by the agency?), of format (Should the assessment be conducted by the agency itself? by a team external to the agency? Should focus groups be used? structured interviews?), of participation (Who should be included in the process? consumers? staff? administrators? family members? members of the agency's board?), of constraint (How much time would agencies be willing to devote? Would agencies be honest in their self-assessments or would they try to make themselves look good?), of philosophy (Was the self-assessment process intended to be an individual-level recovery intervention in and of itself?), and of evaluation(How should the self-assessment process be evaluated? How should the participating agencies evaluate the extent to which they were successful in making and following through with plans for improvement?).

The result of these discussions was a plan for a day-and-a-half-long workshop to be taken to community mental health agencies by a team of external facilitators—initially, members of the group that had developed the process. On the first day, volunteers drawn from agency administrators, staff, and consumers would watch *Movin' On: Stories from the Recovery Road* and then be briefed on the internal conditions of the conceptual model. A facilitator would lead the group in a discussion of the experience of recovery, then ask them to consider how providers and agencies might be useful in supporting or encouraging the experience. In the afternoon, the group would have a briefing on the external conditions of the model, followed by small group discussions focused on a "positive culture of healing" and how the subject agency was or was not creating such a culture. The discussion would lead each group to a list of what was or what was not working in the agency. At the end of the day, the small groups would reconvene to share the content of their discussions. On day two, a subset of volunteers who had attended day one would meet to acknowledge their successes—the things the agency was doing well—and to determine priorities for action from the list of things that the agency needed to improve. After identifying priorities, this "recovery action team" would develop a plan for making change. In recognition of its focus on interaction and facilitated self-examination, the self-assessment process was renamed the "Guided Reflection" (Jacobson et al. 2003).

Throughout the year, the small group that was developing the Guided Reflection would periodically report to the task force, which would raise issues and questions. For example, the task force was particularly worried about how the facilitators would create an environment in which consumers—who were likely to be receiving services from people in the room—would feel safe and free to speak. One strategy, holding separate discussion groups for consumers, was endorsed by some members of the task force but rejected by others as a form of segregation that ran counter to the integrative, participatory principles of recovery. A second strategy suggested was to create a sense of safety in numbers by requiring that the participants for each guided reflection include a certain percentage of consumers (between 25 and 50 percent of participants). The issue would then become how to induce consumers to attend. If compensation were to be offered, how much would be effective without being coercive? Who would pay?

Development issues often devolved into subtle distinctions of language. A first draft of some of the discussion questions, for example, asked participants to consider the role of the agency and its providers in "supporting" clients as they made the kinds of changes associated with the internal conditions of the model. This phrasing implicitly endorsed a helper and helped model of service provision and implied that recovery was a matter of individual change. The questions were rewritten to read, "How do you create an environment in which . . . ?" with the implication that it was not only the clients who were undergoing change.

Eventually, the small group that was planning the Guided Reflection developed a template for structuring the discussion questions. This template sought to make concrete the abstract concepts of the model through explanation, example, and the solicitation of experience. For example, the set of questions about collaborative relationships began by describing what was meant by collaboration ("consumers and staff share power, rather than staff having power over consumers"), proceeded to several examples ("consumers are part of the team that does their case planning"; "consumers have a say in their medication, including what has worked well for them and what side effects they are unwilling to tolerate"; "consumers take an increasing amount of responsibility for their own lives and staff relinquish their control"), and then sought to prompt participants to talk about their own experiences ("What does collaboration mean to you?" "What scares you about collaboration?" "What are the advantages and disadvantages of collaboration for consumers and for providers?"). The final set of questions asked participants to consider the specific rules and policies of the agency that either promoted or hindered collaborative relationships.

The issue of evaluation encompassed the two interrelated endeavors that were under scrutiny: the ability of the participating agency to identify its shortcomings and work effectively to remedy them, and the effectiveness of the Guided Reflection at aiding these processes. Thus the evaluation plan developed by the group had four levels: a debriefing session of the planning group/facilitation team at the end of each day that explored how well the various components of the guided reflection were received; a brief written evaluation form to be filled out by participants immediately following day one of the workshop—what participants like/disliked, what they learned, etc.; a follow-up with members of the recovery action team some months after the end of the workshop to determine if plans were being implemented and change was occurring; and finally, a determination of whether the recovery action team had devised a plan that included an evaluation component.

In June 2001, the planning group conducted the first pilot test of the Guided Reflection. The agency that had volunteered to participate was located in a small city in northeastern Wisconsin. This county-run organization had two community support teams, with some 20 direct care staff providing services to about 220 clients in the area. The agency director was active in statewide recovery planning efforts and was a member of the task force. Staff and consumers from the agency had been involved in a variety of recovery education and implementation-focused efforts long before the arrival of the Guided Reflection team.

Approximately thirty people, about half of whom were consumers, attended all or part of the first day of the workshop. (The WCA had agreed to compensate consumers at the rate of fifty dollars a day for their participation. The agency was providing lunch and refreshments.) The morning discussion of the experience of recovery—sparked by the video and a briefing on the model's internal conditions—was dominated by consumers, who spoke about issues like the violence in their own lives, the need to find a balance between accepting an illness and defining oneself by a diagnosis, and the roles of creativity and spirituality in healing. The member of the planning team who was acting as the main facilitator then asked the group to share the words that came to mind for them when thinking about the qualities of a recovery-oriented agency. Responses included "individualized services," "respect," "honesty," "goal oriented," "flexible," "dignity of risk," "nonjudgmental," "empathetic," and "up-to-date."

After lunch, on the basis of preferences attendees had earlier indicated, individuals were assigned to a consumers-only group, a providers-only group, or a mixed group. A member of the planning team facilitated each group, with the consumers-only group being led by a consumer member of the team. Over the course of the afternoon, every group addressed the same set of questions about agency culture.

There were some marked differences between the groups. The providers-only group was the most confrontational, with the facilitator often challenging participants' statements. The consumers-only group became quite emotional at points and needed to take breaks more frequently than had been scheduled. The mixed group spent a great deal of time teasing one another and laughing. (These differences may be attributed both to the self-selection of the participants and to the differing styles of the facilitators.) The issues discussed by the three groups showed some variation as well. The staff-only group devoted a lot of time to talking about the difficulty of balancing power and trust, with participants noting that they often felt obligated to respond to consumers' breaches of trust (e.g., lies, failures to follow through) with shows of power. Another topic of discussion was the group's perception that some "boundary" rules newly instituted by the agency were detrimental to their ability to establish trusting relationships with the clients. For example, rules against making small loans or accepting gifts seemed to reinforce the status differences between staff and clients. The consumers-only group also expressed negative opinions of these rules. From their point of view, the rules were designed to prevent "real" friendships between clients and staff, a barrier that served to increase the consumers' loneliness and isolation. The consumers also described their hesitance to speak openly to their case managers, their fear that any revelations might be shared with others and used against them. The mixed group talked about the need for more consumer-run services and for increased flexibility in traditional services. They also explored the lack of training in consumer rights and the resulting ignorance of rights among both staff and consumers.

Four priority issues were identified and carried over to day two discussions. The first was that of climate and the differing perspectives of consumers and staff. For example, consumers often felt that their trust had been betrayed if they learned that an issue revealed to their case manager had been discussed in a provider team meeting. From the providers' point of view, however, such sharing of information was essential to the effective functioning of the team. The second issue was the lack of any sort of formal structure for peer support within the agency. The third was the dearth of rights training, which was seen to have adverse consequences both within the agency and for interactions between agency staff and consumers and external entities like the local hospitals and the courts. A final issue was the new rules relating to staff/client boundaries and the perception that these rules would hinder the development of collaborative relationships.

In day two discussions it became apparent that each of these issues had a long history and that some of them—the boundary guidelines, in particular—had polarized the agency. While the recovery action team was able to make some specific plans—to institute a new regime of rights training for both staff and clients, to explore the possibility of building a new peer support program—the more difficult issues could only be examined, not resolved. The members of the recovery action team had a frank, and at times difficult, discussion of boundaries and consumers' and providers' differing perceptions of friendship, for example, but no action was planned.

Evaluations of the Guided Reflection process itself were quite positive. In particular, attendees were enthusiastic about the high level of consumer participation and the successful creation of an atmosphere in which people felt they were able to voice their opinions and be heard by others. Most negative comments related to the length of the day, especially the marathon small group discussions in the afternoon. There seemed to be some confidence that the Guided Reflection would result in change. People thought, for example, that the agency probably would do something about rights education. However, most of that confidence related to the change process that the agency had already embarked on, of which the decision to engage in the Guided Reflection was a sign.

Many consumers reported that they had been empowered by their participation. In the section of the evaluation form that asked what the participant had learned, consumers wrote things like "that I have rights," "that I can be a functioning person and contribute to society," and "that you should be treated with respect." On the second day, one consumer sent a message to the facilitators reporting that she had been "so excited about my recovery potential that I couldn't sleep!" Many staff also reported feeling gratified to learn of consumers' fondness for them and by the overall message that they were doing their jobs well. In these ways, then, the Guided Reflection had turned out to be a personal intervention as well as an organizational one.

Certain aspects of the process were problematic, however. While some issues—like the length of day and the need for more breaks—could be addressed easily, others did not present ready solutions. The first pilot test revealed some of the disadvantages of bringing in outsiders to act as facilitators. Among these was a lack of historical and political context in which to situate the issues raised. A second, related issue was the difficulty of distinguishing between personal grievances and issues that were having a more general impact on the agency. Additionally, despite the positive comments about feeling free to speak, some threats to safety remained. In the pilot agency, for example, even an issue that, in an attempt to maintain one consumer's confidentiality, was framed abstractly became immediately identifiable to the administrators and staff.

THE RECOVERY PACKET

The project of compiling and distributing a packet of written materials about recovery was initiated with three purposes: to provide a resource for use in a future recovery education/training curriculum (as specified in the statewide recommendations); to make information about recovery available to individuals who were just entering the mental health system; and to form a basis for empowerment and advocacy by individuals already in the system. The task force thought that the recovery packet might be used in staff training, in peer counseling groups, or in the context of a first meeting between a case manager and a new client. Thus the main target audiences, once again, were consumers and providers. Physically, the packet was envisioned as a group of articles and other texts collected in either a spiral binding or a loose-leaf notebook. Philosophically, it was seen as important that the packet be "local" in flavor—that it express the particularities of recovery as defined and lived in Wisconsin.

Developing the packet necessitated two kinds of decisions: decisions about content and decisions about presentation. The diversity of desired purposes and audiences complicated both of these decisions. Would consumers and providers respond to the same articles, or should separate packets be compiled for each audience? Should the packet be pitched at an introductory level or should it contain more difficult or technical information? Should there be "beginner" and "advanced" versions? Would the packets be obsolete as soon as they were printed? Should there be a mechanism for updating the material? Planning for the packets began at the task force's first meeting, in the fall of 1999, but the packets themselves did not appear until December 2001, more than two years later.

Much of the organizational work was assigned to a graduate student who was doing an internship with the WCA. This student, under the general direction of the task force and its chairperson, would work independently on certain developmental chores, report her findings to the task force, and take on new assignments in response to the task force's reactions. At various times, subcommittees and individuals were recruited to work on the packets. Near the end of the process, the production company that had made the video was contracted to do the graphic design and printing work.

The process of determining the packet's contents began with a survey of the materials already in the possession of the task force, the WCA, and the state Bureau of Community Mental Health. The student reviewed all of this material, categorized it by topic or approach (e.g., personal journey, research, state-level strategies for implementation) and brought these categories to the task force to ask what important topics were missing and should be sought out for inclusion in the packet. The task force members suggested finding and adding materials on subjects like culturally specific conceptions of recovery, medication and recovery, dual diagnosis, "hopeful" research, and spirituality and recovery. At times, the student was able to locate relevant materials. Other suggestions, however, fell by the wayside either because nothing had been written (e.g., culturally specific conceptions of recovery) or because available material was seen to be inconsistent with the message of recovery the task force wanted to convey (e.g., dual diagnosis material that suggested that recovery could not occur until individuals acknowledged an intrinsic "defect").

Despite these limitations, however, the written materials accumulated rapidly. Recognizing the need to winnow, the task force sought volunteers for a subcommittee that would review the articles to determine which were the "best" for inclusion in various categories. Unfortunately, this exercise resulted in little consensus. In one particularly sharp disagreement, several reviewers very much liked a short piece called "The ABC's of Mental Health: One Client's Guide to Recovery" (Keil 1994) that gave a pithy definition of the concept using the "A is for . . . B is for" structure of a children's book. However, the very first line—A is for Appropriate—enraged many of the reviewers, who saw in the word "appropriate," as applied to consumers' behavior, a vestige of some of the worst of the old system.

The volume of available material suggested that the working conception of the packet as a bound collection of written materials might be too narrow. At various times, the task force's discussions raised the possibility of reconceiving the packet as a kind of index or guide to resources (rather than presenting materials, it would direct readers to where they might find or purchase the material), as an ever-evolving distribution center, or perhaps as a table of materials that would be set up at meetings and conferences, or as a Web site. The expansion of categories and the large number of articles also meant that less of the material was specific to Wisconsin. The task force saw this as problematic because it feared that Wisconsin consumers would not be able to identify with material that was not local. There was also a sense that the particular definition and operationalization of recovery in Wisconsin was something special, a source of pride, and should be emphasized. Several practical issues also needed to be taken into consideration. The difficulty and expense of securing copyright permissions to reprint previously published work militated toward reducing the number of such articles contained in the packet. Similarly, the cost of printing reinforced the decision that the packet be kept relatively short, aiming for quality rather than comprehensiveness.

By the summer of 2000, the task force was overwhelmed. The question of purpose was engaged once again, resulting in more modest hopes: that the packet serve an educational function by providing information about resources and that it give consumers some idea about "Where do I go from here?" This decision led to several others. The packet would open with several recovery "classics," but in the main would be made up of the "personal journey" stories of Wisconsin consumers. (Some of these accounts would be taken from existing publications; others would be solicited for the specific purpose of inclusion in the packet.) The back of the book would be devoted to a "resource guide" with summary and contact information for a variety of organizations and materials. The articles would be spiral bound—to lie flat for photocopying—with tabs indicating the various sections. To signal the importance of recovery, however, money would not be stinted: the packet would be produced using quality materials.

The task force made its final design and content decisions after completion of the recovery video and the conceptual model of recovery. The packet showed the influence of the choices made in each of these projects. Visually, it replicated the metaphors of maps and travel used in the video. Conceptually, the packet drew on the model, using many of the internal and external conditions as subject headings.

Recovery and the Mental Health Consumer Movement in Wisconsin (2001) is described in its preface:

This resource guide lays out internal and external conditions that are critical components of consumer pathways toward recovery. It provides testimony to the fact that recovery from mental disorders is possible and generates the sense of hope that all mental health consumers can and will get better. The guide provides assistance and direction to people who impact an individual recovering from the effects of being diagnosed with a mental disorder and the effects of living with the disorder.

The cover shows stills of Mona and Pete taken from the recovery video, superimposed over a map of Wisconsin, a motif that is also used for the various section headings. The packet opens with a several diagrams taken from the conceptual model of recovery, then, in a section entitled "General Information" reprints the text of the model, Kathleen Crowley's discussion of recovery excerpted from the Blue Ribbon Commission's final report, and a piece by Laurie Curtis called "Moving Beyond Disability: Recovery from Psychiatric Disorders." The sections that follow are labeled "hope," "healing," "empowerment," "connection," and "human rights" and include research or practice-oriented articles, "classics" by authors like Pat Deegan, Rae Unzicker, and Judi Chamberlin, and short essays or poems by Wisconsin consumers. The resources section provides contact information for organizations like the National Empowerment Center, NAMI, and the WCA.

THE RECOVERY RFP: PROVINCIAL BUT TERRITORIAL

From the beginning, the Recovery Task Force had ambitions for projects beyond the three I have described. In particular, the group was eager to develop a recovery education curriculum and to plan and execute a statewide recovery conference. During the first year of its existence, much of the task force's time was devoted to brainstorming about these endeavors. As with the video, the Guided Reflection, and the recovery packet, these discussions revolved around the interconnected issues of purpose, audience, substantive content, and format.

The task force determined that the goals of training should be first to introduce recovery concepts and then to provide some direction for how these concepts could be implemented in provider practice and agency policy.[5] As discussions progressed, the task force's initial intention to do training sessions about the mechanics of implementation was supplanted by a decision to focus on the desired outcomes of implementation. These outcomes were understood to be two processes: a redefinition of the relationship between providers and consumers (i.e., moving toward relationships characterized by partnership and power-sharing) and, for consumers, a redefinition of the individual's relationship to the self (i.e., promotion of increased self-determination and self-esteem leading to increased self-efficacy). These decisions about substance were mirrored in decisions about presentation. The task force agreed that partnership was best modeled by holding training sessions for mixed audiences of consumers and providers and by making a policy that a mixed team should conduct all training sessions.

Similarly, the task force envisioned the recovery conference as a large gathering of consumers and providers from across the state. In addition to a keynote address by a nationally renowned recovery expert (suggestions included Pat Deegan, Judi Chamberlin, and William Anthony), conference attendees would be offered a series of workshops focused on the key processes of redefining relationships and redefining the self.

Although the task force spent a lot of time discussing recovery training and the recovery conference, the lack of dedicated funds for these projects meant that little could be done beyond such brainstorming. Then, in the spring of 2000, the state decided to allocate a portion of its federal mental health block grant money to promoting recovery and issued a request for proposals (RFP).

The RFP offered $95,000 a year for three years for the purposes of "develop[ing] and [implementing] a recovery-focused mental health system" in Wisconsin. Specifically, the RFP called for projects that would

- Educate and increase awareness among state and county administrators, mental health providers, consumers and family members of the principles of recovery, and how these principles can be applied in day-to-day practice,
- Increase consumer and family involvement at all levels of service delivery and system change efforts,
- Create and implement best practice guidelines for providing recovery-focused services, and

- Promote the development of *partnerships* between consumers and service providers to promote recovery. [emphasis in the original]

Proposals were invited from nonprofit corporations, public agencies, and tribal governments. All proposals were to be evaluated by a review panel (including several task force members) using a system that allotted a fixed number of points for criteria such as organizational experience, project goals, statement of outcome expectations, collaboration with community partners, a clear plan for evaluation, and budget.

Six proposals were submitted. Half were from county mental health departments, the others from nonprofit community agencies. Although each prospective grantee proposed to do some form of recovery education and best-practices development, the submissions varied in comprehensiveness, sophistication, and quality. Some proposals were clearly too local in focus—proposing to provide services within a single county or setting. Others came from organizations that appeared to lack the infrastructure and skills to accomplish what they said they were going to do. Several proposed using best-practice models that were based on work done in other places or implementation strategies that were ideologically suspect—for example, the widespread dissemination of a recovery education curriculum that emphasized the biological basis of mental illness.

The winning proposal came from a consortium composed of two Madison-based consumer-run organizations and two out-of-state consultants (one of whom had already worked with the Recovery Workgroup and the task force and was well known to the staff at the bureau).[6] The proposal described a wide range of activities directed at education and information dissemination—regional training sessions, a statewide conference, videos, written "recovery briefs," and a Web site. Perhaps most importantly, the consortium proposed a ground-up, Wisconsin-based process for developing recovery best practices, a process that would involve an advisory committee, the demonstration site counties, and a network of "Participatory Development Partners" from across the state. Additionally, the proposal included a plan for pre- and post-evaluation with both quantitative and qualitative components.

Announcement of the award was made in August 2000. At its meeting in September, the task force received a detailed work plan for the activities of the new recovery initiative, soon named Recovery-in-Action. Immediately, members of the task force became concerned with a number of issues. First, the work plan seemed to indicate a greater focus on the demonstration sites than had been intended in the RFP. Second, there was confusion about the overlap between some Recovery-in-Action activities and those that were being planned by the task force: Was the "best practices conference" mentioned in the work plan the same as the "recovery conference" the task force had been discussing? Was the "self-assessment" process described as part of Recovery-in-Action's evaluation plan the same as the self-assessment (Guided Reflection) the task force/WCA team was developing? Third, the lack of specificity about Recovery-in-Action's "advisory committee" left the task force wondering if it would be that committee (an impression that had been given to the members unofficially) or if the Recovery-in-Action team would select a new group of advisors. At bottom, each of these concerns revolved around a core issue: would the shape of recovery implementation in Wisconsin be controlled locally, in concordance with the work already done by the Workgroup and the task force, or would authority be ceded to outsiders?

The task force's concerns prompted the bureau to call a meeting between state staffers, several representatives of the task force, and the out-of-state consultant who was the chief architect of Recovery-in-Action. The mood of the discussion was captured by one state staffer, who commented, "We may be provincial, but we're territorial." That is, while the task force recognized and admired the expertise of the consultant, it didn't want an "imported" model of recovery imposed in Wisconsin.

Resolution came through clarification—for example, an explication of Recovery-in-Action's "self-assessment" that showed how it was distinct from, yet complementary to, the task force's Guided Reflection—and through a commitment to improved communication. The task force would become the official advisory body to the Recovery-in-Action team. In that capacity, the task force would receive regular updates from the team, and a team member would be invited to sit on the task force. In addition, the consultant assuaged the tension by asserting that while she was an outsider, she had no intention of imposing anything. Rather, she said, her hope was to use Wisconsin as "a laboratory" to develop a model of recovery best practices that could be exported to other locales. (She also noted one way in which outsider status could be an advantage: her lack of formal association with the state would make it easier to work with counties that bore a great deal of resentment toward Madison.)

Over the first year of its funding, the Recovery-in-Action team made regular reports to the task force, giving progress updates and seeking advice when plans proved infeasible. As the project developed, some of the initiative's activities changed—for example, the original qualitative evaluation strategy was revised, and the team devoted more time than it had proposed to doing technical assistance with the demonstration counties. While Recovery-in-Action remained committed to developing a best-practices model, the team reported that because there was a "continuum of understanding" on the ground, it was proving very difficult to "actualize" the "simple language" of the recovery principles.

Implementing Recovery

Just as the morphology of the Recovery Workgroup was altered when it became the Recovery Task Force, so too were the group's purposes and the processes it used to achieve its aims. While the Workgroup was largely concerned with conceptualizing recovery and making recommendations for its operationalization, the task force was much more involved with inciting change—both reform and transformation. As it worked through the process of determining its priorities and projects, it was also addressing the question of the best strategy for making change. What emerged in the task force was an implicit theory of behavior change, one that saw such change as the result of changed attitudes.[7] Thus, the task force focused on developing products that intervened at the level of attitude. These products sought to make recovery something tangible and accessible to a broad audience of consumers, providers, administrators, and policy makers.

The work of production necessitated the deployment of a number of subprocesses. First, the task force had to identify and prioritize its goals. Then, it had to find ways to concretize the abstract concepts whose promotion was the aim of implementation. Most of these concepts were variants of the overarching values that had allowed the Workgroup to make policy recommendations. The very flexibility of these values became problematic once they were to be applied by the task force, however.

For example, the nonspecificity of the value "knowledge" had to be pinned down when the task force was faced with developing a recovery education curriculum. Sometimes concretizing meant continuing the definitional work—the task force's description of recovery as a dual process of redefining consumer/provider relationships and redefining the relationship with the self. At other times it meant determining the desired characteristics of its planned interventions—the need to promote diversity and participation. Decisions about content and presentation format were key to concretizing.

Contracting became an important element of the implementation process. The task force used contracting as a strategy for completing the video, the Guided Reflection, and the recovery packet. In each of these projects, the task force maintained a strong hand—setting agendas and time lines, vetting ideas, and contributing to or approving decisions about content and presentation. Although these projects were often delayed or accomplished with less than stellar efficiency, they proceeded fairly smoothly, in large part because the contractors were cognizant of, and generally accepted, the authority of the task force. (In most cases, the contractors either were, or became, de facto members of the task force.) However, in the fourth project described in this chapter, Recovery-in-Action, which was largely designed by an individual unconnected to the task force, issues of authority engendered overt (if polite) conflict. As I have indicated, this conflict had two facets: the task force's wish that its own work be acknowledged and its standards followed, and the strong belief—which extended beyond the task force—that Wisconsin implementation strategies should be based on homegrown values. While the "outsider" status of Recovery-in-Action's leader, and the fact that she was directly accountable to the state and not the task force, might have provoked this conflict, these factors may have allowed the project to be carried out with somewhat greater efficiency than much of the work over which the task force had direct authority.

The notion of product development carries with it an explicit focus on market, or audience. While the Recovery Workgroup's attention to its audiences (the BRC-IAC and the County Planning Partners) had been intermittent (and often occasioned only by actual or anticipated resistance to its ideas), the task force kept a sharp eye on its audiences throughout the planning for each of the products described in this chapter. For the video and the packet, efforts were made both to identify target audiences and to design products that would meet the needs and preferences of these markets. The Guided Reflection included an evaluation component so that audience reaction might be judged with evidence beyond that available to the subjective eyes of the Guided Reflection's creators. The task force often found itself using the language of advertising or public relations, for example seeking ways in which to sell recovery implementation as a "win-win" situation for target audiences that might be wary or resistant.

Much of the explicit attention to audience came about because of the changing context of the overall system redesign. The managed care RFC included many of the recommendations that the Workgroup had made, including requirements for recovery training, increased consumer involvement, and provision of consumer choice. In this way, the Workgroup had defined the product needs of the managed care demonstration sites, needs that the task force then could set about meeting. When, in the summer of 2000, announcement was made of the counties selected to be managed care demonstration sites—Dane County (home of Madison), Milwaukee County, Kenosha County (a blue-collar, industrial area south of Milwaukee), and Forest/Vilas/Oneida (a consortium of counties in the rural north)—the task force could use its knowledge of the strengths and weaknesses of each of these sites to further tailor its products.

The goal of the task force, and, more broadly, of a number of the activities that were taking place throughout Wisconsin during the period 1999–2001,[8] was to make the vision of a recovery-oriented mental health system something real—to move from the bones of the ideas contained in the Blue Ribbon Commission's final report and the Workgroup's recommendations to the bridges necessary for successful implementation at the individual, organizational, and system levels. The video and the recovery packet explored the processes of individual change, with the explicit goal of inspiring such change in viewers and readers. The Guided Reflection sought to prompt organizational change in mental health agencies, one agency at a time. Recovery-in-Action, with its wide variety of activities and its broad reach across the state, was aimed at facilitating the changes necessary for the developing a recovery-oriented system. It was the hope of the task force, too, that as change occurred in individuals, organizations, and in the system, the impact would affect the larger society, eventually ending stigma and discrimination.

As this chapter has suggested, however, the actual process of implementation was less smoothly choreographed than the symbolic transformation of a dinosaur into a bridge—the performance art enacted by the Bones to Bridges Collective during the 1999 recovery conference in Madison. In practice, implementing recovery was more improvisational and contingent. It meant prioritizing when everything seemed equally important. It meant finding ways to concretize and package the abstract. It meant negotiating with and asserting authority over contractors who might have had their own ideas. It meant working within historical and political contexts to change individual behavior and institutional procedure. It meant balancing standardization and uniqueness, rigidity and creativity, outsiders' frameworks and Wisconsin ideas.

Interstice 4
MAKING IT PUBLIC

My first book, called *Cleavage,* was a sociological analysis of the history of silicone breast implants, including, and especially, the controversy over their safety that took place in the early 1990s. Breast implants were, and remain, a touchy issue. There have been large sums of money involved—for the implant manufacturers, for the plastic surgeons, and for the women who claim to have been harmed by the devices. Stakeholders have had other kinds of investments in implants as well: ideological investments in the theory and practice of government regulation; professional investments in the legitimacy of an oft-maligned or mocked surgical specialty; personal investments in promoting enhanced self-esteem or winning recognition for betrayal and suffering. *Cleavage* examined the "public problem" of silicone breast implants from many perspectives, but I did not look for or take any public position on the "truth" about safety or harm.

These days, writing a book allows a whole new guilty pleasure: using an internet search engine to look for hits on the book's title. Searching for *Cleavage* turns up much of the usual—syllabi for courses in which the book is assigned, on-line bookstores that stock it, reviews in scholarly journals (not to mention the X-rated sites one finds if one doesn't include the subtitle). I have also found mentions of *Cleavage* in the archived e-chats of two support groups for women who identify as victims or survivors of silicone implants. In one posting, the writer, who had just received the book and read the introduction, calls it "excellent" and "a must read for our people." In the other, a woman who has read a recent review of the book focuses on a short excerpt from my discussion of the social construction of silicone disease and decides that I am a shill for the implant manufacturers. She comments, "More scholars for dollars—where do they get these people?"

In an interview on CBC radio, novelist and poet Margaret Atwood talked about the autonomy of text in the world: its status not as a direct link between author and reader but as an entity with which author and reader have entirely separate interactive experiences.

I had many reasons for wanting to develop the conceptual model of recovery. I wanted to fulfill the terms of my contract with the WCA. I was no longer being supported by my postdoctoral fellowship and needed to bring in money. I wanted to integrate my experience of participant observation with the Recovery Workgroup—to produce something that would reflect back to them the multidimensionality of their discussions as I had understood them. (In a way, their response to the model would provide a validation check of my perceptions.) I thought it was an interesting challenge and wanted to see if I could do it. I wanted to stake my own claim on the recovery landscape. The decision to publish a (much truncated) version of the model in *Psychiatric Services* (Jacobson and Greenley 2001) certainly was driven by this last.

Since making the model public, here are some of the things that have happened:

- A psychometrician, a jobseeker, and several eccentrics have contacted me by e-mail, expecting that we have shared interests and joint aims.
- A friend of mine, a consumer, showed me how she had used highlighters and colored tabs to mark up her copy of the conceptual model. She thumbed through the document and said, rather ruefully, "I just stumbled into my own recovery." I joked back, "You didn't have a guidebook."
- I have made presentations about the conceptual model to students, researchers, prospective employers, policymakers, and service providers.[1]
- In a commentary appended to the *Psychiatric Services* article, a psychiatrist attacked the model for being unscientific and naïve (Peyser 2001). My coauthor and I responded in a letter

to the editor. The psychiatrist was then allowed to respond to our response. Thankfully, the editors ended it there.

- At the "provincial but territorial" meeting between the bureau, the task force, and the Recovery Initiative, the conceptual model was held out as the "local" (Wisconsin) definition of recovery that the Recovery Initiative should follow.

Making it public has meant confronting two key contradictions: the intellectual contradiction between the fluidity and complexity of meaning that the model is trying to capture and the tendency of presentation (and audiences) to fix those meanings in static form on one hand, and the personal contradiction between needing to use recovery as currency toward building professional capital and my continuing reluctance to claim expert status or to advocate for recovery.

The text exists apart from me—people read into it what they wish—yet somehow I remain responsible for the text. I must discourage people who seize upon it as an instruction manual, yet I must encourage people to understand and use the model. I am not an advocate, yet when the model is attacked, I feel attacked and must defend it. I am pleased to have achieved "local" status, yet worried that this means I have not been critical enough, or that I have been duplicitous in hiding my criticism. I am not the expert, yet I have been very careful to maintain first or sole authorship on everything public.

6
THE STATE OF RECOVERY

One set of questions with which I began this examination of recovery had to do with its consequences: What does a recovery-oriented system look like? Who benefits under such a system? In what ways is recovery compatible with other system changes? How will success or failure be evaluated and by whom? What are the implications of recovery for all of the mental health system's stakeholders? In this chapter I address as many of these questions as I can. (The answers to some of them still cannot be known.) I begin by updating the status of recovery implementation in Wisconsin. This update, by necessity, is more summary than analysis, but I hope it provides the reader with some new information and ties up some loose ends. I then look at "the recovery scene" that is burgeoning both nationally and internationally. (Again, this section is but an overview of a vast amount of material.) Lastly, I attempt to grapple with some of the tough questions that recovery is raising in its implementation—the manifestations of recovery-as-politics.

BACK TO WISCONSIN

I went back to Wisconsin early in the summer of 2003, hoping to learn what had happened since I'd been gone. Several task force members readily agreed to speak with me about the current status of recovery implementation in the state. (I thank them, again, for their generosity.) This account is based on our conversations and on the documents they provided me.

In general, the work of implementation has proceeded according to the plans laid out by the task force early in its existence. Members of the task force, together with the Recovery-in-Action team, have focused on education, on further exploration of the elements of a recovery-oriented mental health system, on the promotion of advocacy among consumers and family members, and on information dissemination. These efforts have been directed either at the demonstration sites or, more broadly, at the state as a whole. (In theory, the Recovery-in-Action team has indeed been designated responsibility for the demonstration counties and the task force for the rest of the state. In practice, however, there appears to have been a great deal of overlap, with task force members and Recovery-in-Action team members working cooperatively on many projects.) While the task force's implicit theory of changing behavior through changing attitudes seems still to dominate its work, particularly its educational interventions, the group is realizing the need to understand and promote the specific behaviors that together will characterize a transformed system.

Perhaps the intervention that, to date, has had the greatest reach has been a series of recovery awareness training sessions (dubbed "Recovery 101") held in seven locations around the state in September of 2002. In these one-day workshops, task force members and trained local consumers and/or providers used the recovery video and the reading packet (both of which are described in Chapter 5) to present information about basic recovery concepts and began to discuss the ways in which these concepts could be used to change providers' practices and clients' lives. State staff report that more than three hundred consumers and providers from around the state attended these workshops and that some twenty-five individuals have been trained as recovery awareness presenters. Feedback has been positive, though some attendees have indicated that the material was too basic and that they want more context and depth.

The effort to develop a second level of training that provides such context and depth ("Recovery 202") has been one of the main objectives of the Recovery-in-Action team. As the team had indicated in its application and initial discussions with the task force, they hoped to use the experiences of the Wisconsin demonstration sites to draw up guidelines for recovery-oriented practice. In 2002, the team held a series of focus groups with consumers and providers in the demonstration counties, seeking to learn from them "the kinds of mental health service practices and practitioner competencies that . . . would be necessary to promote and support . . . recovery" (Practitioner Competencies in a Recovery-Oriented Mental Health System 2002, 2). The resulting compendium of competencies is organized around nine domains: core clinical knowledge, positive culture of healing, hope, healing, empowerment, connection, human rights, recovery-oriented services, and worker attributes. Each domain contains a list of key competencies, along with some of the behaviors that should be demonstrated in acting out the competency. For example, in the "recovery-oriented services" domain, a key competency is described as "ensures that service plans and interventions are individualized and personally meaningful to the consumer." The specific behaviors are "mutually determines definitions of success—the best ways to achieve goals; negotiates flexible ways to meet requirements, perform tasks, share responsibilities; encourages consumers to *not* sign anything they do not help develop, fully understand or agree with" (Practitioner Competencies in a Recovery-Oriented Mental Health System 2002, 7, emphasis in the original). A parallel effort to develop best-practice guidelines, a companion list of standards for programs and agencies, is underway (Practitioner Competencies in a Recovery-Oriented Mental Health System 2002, 2).

The ultimate aim, also in process as I write, is to use these core competencies to develop a training curriculum. One of the challenges in this undertaking, as perceived by a task force member I spoke with about it, is to find ways to be specific without being overly directive. That is, the task force is wary of producing a kind of "cookbook" of provider behaviors. Rather, the members want the training to teach the concepts underlying the behaviors—to be demonstrative, to show rather than to tell. Another challenge is, in the task force member's words, learning to "make this something more than words." The work of developing guidelines is difficult: many recovery concepts seem to slip away under the microscope of efforts at behavioral specification. When there is no way but language to describe a changed reality, it becomes easy for cynics to dismiss the change as insubstantial, nothing but words, while even those eager to change can be frustrated by the disjunction between the promise of recovery and the prosaic nature of recommendations for its practice.

One of the areas in which it is most important that recovery become something "more than words" is that of consumer choice. Members of the task force and the Recovery-in-Action team, together with an outside consultant, are exploring the implications of choice for the issues of risk and provider liability that, from the beginning, have been pegged as a likely barrier to implementation of a recovery-oriented system. Similarly, there is a growing recognition of the possible structural barriers to recovery implementation in the existing state-level regulations for Wisconsin's community support programs (CSPs). The risk and liability committee is due to report its findings and recommendations later this year; the hope is that these, too, may be turned into material for training curricula. In 2002, a member of the task force and several staff from the Bureau of Community Mental Health (which has recently been renamed, yet again, the Bureau of Mental Health and Substance Abuse Services) held a series of "listening sessions" with Wisconsin consumers "to gather consumer feedback regarding the quality of the services they are receiving in CSP programs across the state" (Community Support Programs Consumer Listening Sessions Final Report, undated document, 1). As I write this, however, the review of CSP practices and policies seems to have stalled.

Included in the initial charge to the Recovery Workgroup was a request that the group examine ways to promote consumer and family involvement in all facets of the public mental health system. While the Workgroup, and then the task force, embodied this ideal, it spent relatively little time on the topic in its deliberations. The Recovery-in-Action team, however, has made a major commitment to the issue of system-level participation. In 2001 and 2002, the team conducted a statewide survey seeking to ascertain the degree of consumer or family involvement on county boards and mental health or substance-abuse-related councils and committees (Curtis 2002). Results of the survey showed that such participation was relatively rare, despite an apparent recognition among respondents that involvement did have real benefits. In order to increase participation, and to ensure that it is more than tokenism, the Grassroots Empowerment Project, a state-funded umbrella organization for consumer-run programs across Wisconsin and one of the members of the Recovery-in-Action team, has developed a "leadership academy" for consumers, a training workshop that includes information about public policy and advocacy and promotes leadership and communication skills.

The volume of material about recovery has grown enormously and, as it was in its initial discussions about the recovery packet, the task force has been eager to find ways to make information available to consumers and providers across the state. In the summer of 2002, the task force hired a consultant to investigate the attractiveness and feasibility of various models for statewide information dissemination. She traveled throughout Wisconsin, speaking to consumers and providers in many small agencies about their information needs and preferences. The report she wrote recommended the development of a "recovery clearinghouse" that would organize training programs, maintain a Web site and an 800 number, and act as distributor for written materials produced both in Wisconsin and outside the state (Recovery Clearinghouse Study Project, undated document). The task force has endorsed this recommendation, and its realization will be central to the next phase of recovery implementation.

In several months, the three-year contract with the Recovery-in-Action team will be over. As I have noted, the team's work will have had a number of tangible results—training material and curricula, information about the current situation, and recommendations for the future. The task force has continued to play the role it settled into early on: it has served as an advisory body to the team, providing oversight and ensuring a consistency of message (and adherence to the Wisconsin model of recovery) across projects and products. Additionally, the task force and the Recovery-in-Action team have become collaborators in many ways, taking advantage of their joint strengths and shoring up individual weaknesses. My sense is that the relationship has not always been easy, but that it has been fruitful.

Just a week ago, the bureau issued an RFP for the next three-year recovery implementation contract. It focuses, as I have indicated, on the development of a clearinghouse to coordinate recovery training (including the Guided Reflection and the leadership academy) and to disseminate information about recovery.[1] The task force will continue to exist, but it is not yet clear what role it will have.

An irony of the last six years has been the fate of the managed care component of Wisconsin's system redesign. Originally, as I discussed in Chapter 1, the apparent inevitability of managed care in public mental health systems was the driver of the state's reform effort. Recovery was the humanitarian component of this larger project—highly valued by many stakeholders, but a relatively small part of the entire redesign. Workgroups devoted huge amounts of time and resources to sorting out the particulars of implementing a managed care model in the demonstration projects. In practice, however, the state and the demonstration counties have never been able to determine a capitation rate. Thus managed mental health care has been indefinitely postponed.[2] As one person told me recently, the foundering of managed care has meant that the demonstration projects have been able to focus almost entirely on recovery.

The big question is whether all of this activity has made any difference. Have providers changed their practices? Have consumers' lives changed for the better? Are they, in fact, recovering? To this point, relatively little attention has been paid to evaluation. (In my conversation with the task force chair, it seemed that this might be the logical next focus for the work of the task force.) The Guided Reflection allows a kind of assessment, but it is limited to individual agencies that are, almost by virtue of having sought out the Reflection process, already much more likely to have changed. One of the Recovery-in-Action team's final products will be a narrative evaluation of organizational culture change in several of the demonstration sites, based on the stories of consumers receiving services in these organizations, but the lack of a comparison group will make it difficult to draw any conclusions about the effectiveness of demonstration-specific interventions. The state has finally settled on an evaluation instrument to be used in the demonstration sites,[3] but that decision has taken years and the delay has meant that no pre-/post-demonstration comparison will be possible.

Anecdotally, reports of findings from the various focus groups and listening sessions held around the state during 2002—some five years after the Blue Ribbon Commission had begun talking about promoting recovery in Wisconsin—suggested that not too much had changed in many places. Consumers still lacked basic information about their diagnoses and medications, and some reported being threatened with hospitalization or loss of their children if they didn't comply with treatment plans. Providers in certain programs expressed surprise at the idea that people could recover. However, there is a growing group of consumers who are doing systems advocacy work—for example, lobbying the state legislature over recent budget cuts. Individual agencies have made changes—increasing the level of consumer involvement in organizational decision-making and placing greater emphasis on client rights. It seems that change is happening but that most of it is still dependent on the work of committed individuals. It is less clear that recovery has become institutionalized, part of the warp and woof of everyday practice and policy.

In Chapter 4 I discussed the qualities that appeared to be necessary for recovery to be implemented in Wisconsin—qualities of power, legitimacy, expertise, reach, and effectiveness—and the distribution of these qualities among the various stakeholders in the state's mental health system. In part, the work of the last three years of recovery implementation may be seen as a process of equalizing and transforming these qualities across stakeholder groups—a way of laying the groundwork for greater change. While the state and counties have maintained much of their traditional power, initiatives like the leadership academy have made inroads toward allowing the traditionally less powerful—consumers and families, in particular—to have a voice. At the meso and micro levels of organizational and provider behavior, much effort has gone into beginning to find ways for the ideal of power-sharing with consumers to become a practical reality. In the face of potential threats from outsiders to a "Wisconsin Idea," the task force has maintained the power of its local model of recovery. The many focus groups and listening sessions with consumers and providers, techniques used in nearly every implementation project, have served to legitimize their expertise. The various training programs and educational interventions, including information dissemination, have also transferred expertise of many different types. Several implementation initiatives—including the Recovery 101 training sessions and the clearinghouse model—have developed with a subtext of building statewide networks to expand reach. The train-the-trainers approach used in many projects has an explicit goal of creating a cadre of experts whose influence can extend across the state. However, as I have noted, the fact that there has been little sustained attention to evaluation means that the effectiveness of these interventions—on attitude and on behavior—remains in question.

THE RECOVERY SCENE

Since the late 1990s, there has been a proliferation of all things recovery. A 2000 review and synthesis of the recovery literature (Ralph 2000) included some eighty citations, characterized as only "a sample" of the material available. Recovery has been the thematic focus of many conferences, as well as countless continuing education or training sessions. A cadre of consultants and researchers has formed, ready to lend expertise and advice to individuals, organizations, and mental health systems seeking their own recovery orientations. Each of the meanings of recovery explored in this book is represented in this proliferation.

Recovery-as-experience may be seen in the continuing attention to the first-person narratives of individuals who identify themselves as recovering. Such individuals are in great demand as speakers at conferences and other educational events. Their stories are frequently published in professional journals, often in special issues devoted to consumer/survivor voices (e.g., Bassman 2000; Lynch 2000; Tenney 2000). As recovery has gained currency, these narratives have grown more broadly reflective, focusing on the implications of individual experiences of recovery for policy and practice (e.g., Mead and Copeland 2000) and on the recovery value of the act of storytelling itself (Lunt 2000; Weingarten 2002).

Another highly prolific area has been research that uses first-person narratives to model recovery (e.g., Adams and Partee 1998; Fisher and Ahern 1999; Young and Ensing 1999; Williams and Collins 1999; Recovery Advisory Group 1999; Smith 2000; Marsh 2000; Jacobson 2001; Ridgway 2001.) These models portray recovery as a series of overlapping processes or phases—for example, "overcoming 'stuckness,' discovering and fostering self-empowerment, learning and self-redefinition, returning to basic functioning, and improving quality of life" (Young and Ensing 1999) or "anguish, awakening, insight, action plan, determined commitment to become well, and well-being/empowerment" (Recovery Advisory Group 1999)—that describe how individuals move from illness and pain to healing and wellness. These qualitative studies have been complemented by research that seeks to construct recovery as a quantitative phenomenon—something that can be counted or causally modeled (e.g., Corrigan et al. 1999; Markowitz 2001).

Measuring recovery is the focus of the contemporary incarnation of recovery-as-evidence: that is, the drive to find evidence of recovery. Many researchers have sought to develop and refine qualitative, quantitative, or mixed methods tools for assessing the presence or absence of recovery, its stage or phase, and provider or consumer attitudes toward its possibility or likelihood. A compilation of recovery and recovery-related measures (Ralph, Kidder, and Phillips 2000) includes instruments like the Recovery Assessment Scale (Giffort et al. 1995), the Rochester Recovery Inquiry

(Hopper et al. 1996), the Recovery Interview (Heil and Johnson 1998), the Recovery Attitudes Questionnaire (Borkin et al. 1998), the Mental Health Recovery Measure (Young, Ensing, and Bullock 1999), the Well-Being Scale (Campbell and Schraiber 1989), the Hope Scale (Snyder et al. 1991), and the Making Decisions Empowerment Scale (Rogers et al. 1997). Typically, these instruments build on models of recovery-as-experience, using open-ended or, more commonly, scaled (e.g., agree/disagree) items to assess individuals and their recovery status. (I take up some of the problems of measurement later in this chapter.)

The need to measure recovery has arisen as mental health practitioners and programs have embraced recovery-as-ideology and as mental health systems have sought to implement recovery-as-policy. A third area of proliferation has come in efforts to formalize these commitments through the development of recovery-oriented "best practices" and system-level standards. In Wisconsin, as I have described, the Recovery-in-Action team and the task force have devoted much effort to develop practitioner competencies and best-practice guidelines. The published literature now includes a number of similar discussions of recovery best practices in treatment programs and mental health organizations (e.g., Ohio Department of Mental Health 1999; Curtis 2000; Torrey and Wyzik 2000; Ahern and Fisher 2001). In general, these guidelines describe how programs and organizations can create environments that nurture recovery by focusing on provider/client interactions, consumer skill development and confidence building, natural supports and community integration, and the promotion of collaboration, shared responsibility, and empowerment. William Anthony (2000) has explored the implications of his own vision of recovery for system-level standards, suggesting that in order to be truly recovery-oriented, mental health systems must integrate recovery principles into every component of their design and function, including leadership, management, advocacy, training, and funding.

Recovery also has been adopted by the mainstream organizations that make up the mental health establishment in Washington, D.C. In 1999, the Surgeon General's Report on Mental Health included a chapter on recovery that described the concept and noted its "substantial impact on consumers and families, mental health research, and service delivery" (Department of Health and Human Services 1999). The same year, NAMI made recovery the centerpiece of its legislative agenda (NAMI

1999). In a press release, the director of the organization's policy institute was quoted as saying, "Promoting recovery . . . must be the cornerstone of an enlightened public policy" (NAMI 2002). The National Mental Health Association (which originated in Clifford Beers' mental hygiene movement) has noted the recovery promotion value of tools like advance directives (NMHA 2002a) and has launched its own program of recovery education (NMHA 2002b). A recent "model law" written by the Bazelon Center (a D.C.-based mental health law and advocacy organization) seeks to codify "a right to recovery-oriented mental health services and supports" in legislation at both the state and federal levels (Bazelon Center for Mental Health Law 2002). The final report of the President's New Freedom Commission on Mental Health, a group appointed by George W. Bush in 2002, envisions "a future when everyone with a mental illness will recover" (President's New Freedom Commission on Mental Health 2003), while the consumer issues subcommittee of the commission has called for "a National Recovery Initiative" that will promote the values of self-determination and empowerment and work toward the elimination of stigma and discrimination in the nation's mental health systems (Report of the Subcommittee on Consumer Issues 2003). Recovery is attracting attention from "behavioral health" (the term used to encompass mental health and substance abuse treatment) managed care organizations as well, with one company, ValueOptions, appointing a corporate vice president for "recovery, rehabilitation and mutual support" (National Mental Health Consumers' Self-Help Clearinghouse 2001).

Outside of the United States, one sees a similar emphasis. Research in Australia and the United Kingdom has examined the experience of recovery (e.g., Tooth, Kalyanansundaram, and Glover 1997; Baker and Strong 2001). In England, recovery is being promoted by a variety of consumer/survivor[4] initiatives and by local organizations and foundations (Baker and Strong 2001; Turner-Crowson and Wallcraft 2002). New Zealand has embraced recovery and has done much work to promote its implementation in policy and practice. One such effort has been the development of ten categories of culturally-specific "recovery competencies" for mental health workers (O'Hagan 2001).

In Canada, where I have lived since 2001, "the recovery model" has been identified as a philosophical basis for mental health system reform in the province of Ontario (Toronto-Peel Mental Health Reform Implementation Task Force 2002). While the language of recovery is new to the province, two models developed over the last decade speak to similar ideas. "A New Framework for Support" (Trainor, Pomeroy, and Pape 1993), developed in conjunction with the Canadian Mental Health Association, envisions a "community process paradigm" in which the individual is at the center of a web of support offered by four sectors—family and friends, consumer groups and organizations, generic community services and groups, and mental health services—and is assured access to adequate housing and income with opportunities for education and work. In this model, "the person must be an active participant in the community, in decision-making about mental health services, and in choosing which of the supports . . . are most important at any given point in time." The framework's service paradigm is complemented by a new "knowledge resource base" that seeks "a balanced understanding of mental illness" through the integration of medical/clinical, social science, traditional (i.e., culturally specific), and experiential knowledge. Another model, the "Empowerment-Community Integration Paradigm" (Nelson, Lord, and Ochocka 2001), is built around four key values: consumer/survivor empowerment, community integration, access to valued resources (e.g., income and housing), and holistic health care (e.g., treatment and support). In this framework, too, "all interventions should be based on power sharing and participation" (249). Like recovery, both of these models have implications for individuals, for organizations and systems, and for communities and society.

NASH's MIND

When I was midway through the writing of this book, the release of the movie *A Beautiful Mind* brought the story of mathematician John Forbes Nash to public attention. Born in West Virginia in 1928 and educated at the Carnegie Institute of Technology and Princeton University, Nash was, by most accounts, a brilliant, arrogant, and isolated young man driven to achieve the recognition he believed he deserved. His dissertation, a reconceptualization of game theory, earned him a Ph.D. at age twenty-one but did not at the time make the splash he had anticipated.

Nash took research positions at Princeton and with the RAND Corporation and, later, an academic post at MIT. In his late twenties, Nash's behavior grew increasingly erratic, and in 1959 his wife had him committed to McLean Hospital, a private psychiatric facility in the suburbs of Boston, where he was given a diagnosis of paranoid schizophrenia.

Over the next thirty years, Nash's life included short periods of relative calm, but more common were lengthy episodes of disorganization and paranoia, punctuated by hospitalizations in both public and private institutions, where he received most of the treatments popular at the time (an exception being electroconvulsive therapy, which his wife refused to allow because she feared it would damage his mind). After the early 1960s, as his mathematical interests tended more and more toward bizarre numerological schema full of encoded messages, he was unable to hold a job. He and his wife divorced and lived apart for several years—although later, when there was no one else to care for him, she once again took him into her home. A residual respect and affection among his former colleagues in the Princeton math department allowed him to continue to use the university's facilities, and he was familiar to generations of Princeton students as a liminal personage who haunted the department's building.

In the late 1980s and early 1990s, people who had known Nash for years noted that he seemed to be reemerging: his mathematical work began to make sense again, and for the first time in years he was initiating conversations and demonstrating an interest in events and people around him. In 1994, his dissertation work on game theory was honored with a Nobel Prize. In 1998, he was the subject of an award-winning and critically acclaimed biography (Nasar 1998). The movie version of *A Beautiful Mind*, although criticized for distorting the events of Nash's life by ignoring some of its less sympathetic episodes (an arrest for indecent exposure in a public men's room that led to loss of his government security clearance and his job at RAND, an abandoned illegitimate child, a kind of anti-Semitism born of snobbery), went on to win a number of Academy Awards, including best picture of 2001.

In each of the public renderings of Nash's life story (the book, the movie, and, most recently, a *60 Minutes* segment and a PBS documentary), his mental illness and "miraculous" recovery have been central themes. Nasar speculates at some length about the exact nature and likely causes of this recovery, entertaining, but finally dismissing, the possibility that his original diagnosis may have been in error. The movie's explanation comes during its denouement, Nash's Nobel acceptance speech, when he gazes adoringly at his long-suffering and ever-patient wife (in the movie they are never divorced) and says, "It is only in the mystery of love that logic and reason can be found." In televised interviews and conversations with his biographer, Nash himself attributes his recovery to the physiological changes of aging and his ability to overcome the intrusiveness of symptoms through the discipline of rational thought.

For the recovery community, *A Beautiful Mind* and Nash's celebrity status were heaven-sent opportunities to promote one idea: recovery is possible. In feature articles and their own editorials, recovery advocates sought to capitalize on the perceived exceptionalism of the Nash case to argue that, in fact, there was nothing at all exceptional about it:

> mental health experts say that while Nash's life is undeniably remarkable, his gradual recovery from schizophrenia is not. . . . Psychiatric researchers . . . as well as a growing number of recovered patients who have banded together to form a mental health consumer movement, contend that recovery of the kind Nash experienced is not rare. (Boodman 2002)

> The film . . . portrays [Nash's] recovery from schizophrenia as hard-won, awe-inspiring and unusual. What most Americans and even many psychiatrists do not realize is that many people with schizophrenia—perhaps more than half—do significantly improve or recover. That is, they can function socially, work, relate well to others and live in the larger community. Many can be symptom-free without medication. They improve without fanfare and frequently without much help from the mental health system. (Harding 2002)

Like Clifford Beers in an earlier era, Nash has become a poster child, a public figure whose public story has become a public symbol. Like recovery itself, the meaning of Nash's story has been constructed by the gestures of a wide range of social entities—writers, actors, directors, advertisers, journalists, audiences, advocates. It is differently interpretable by each of those entities and can be used for a variety of purposes: Nash's story has something for everyone. In the popular media, as well as at recent lectures and professional meetings, I have heard it cited as a justification for funding mental health services, alluded to while considering the origins of schizophrenia as a neurodevelopmental disorder, and referenced as part of the argument for paying more attention to the stories of patients (although Nash's own narrative has been only a small part of the "Beautiful Mind" phenomenon). Survivors and those of an antipsychiatry bent delight in revealing the "big lie" of the movie, a casual line (reportedly inserted at the behest of a psychiatrist who was a relative of the screenwriter) about the movie Nash's use of the newer antipsychotic medications, when in fact the real Nash has refused all psychiatric drugs for the last thirty years.

INTERROGATING RECOVERY

The range of definitions I found among the members of Wisconsin's Recovery Workgroup persists when one examines the broader trends described in this chapter: while recovery is certainly powerful, it is by no means simple. That is, in the current context of widespread attention to developing recovery-as-policy it is clear that recovery still has many meanings. As in the Recovery Workgroup, these definitions construe recovery as the solution to many different problems, the fulfillment of many different agendas. Elements of recovery-as-evidence, recovery-as-experience, and recovery-as-ideology are embedded in recovery-as-policy. These meanings are shaping the ways in which recovery-oriented systems are being developed; their consequences are being played out in the emerging conundrums and conflicts of recovery-as-policy—What counts as evidence? Whose experience? Which ideology?—the domain of recovery-as-politics to which I now turn.

As described in Chapter 1 and Chapter 3, in the U.S., recovery-as-policy emerged during a period of restructuring in public mental health systems. At the federal level, the government was phasing in plans to tie mental health block grant money to "performance contracting," a procedure by which receipt of funds would be tied to demonstration of certain standardized outcomes. At the state level, many state systems (including Wisconsin) were obtaining federal waivers to shift their Medicaid populations into managed care models of care delivery. Such models have emphasized the cost-efficiencies to be gained through the monitoring and analysis of outcomes data. At the same time, psychiatry—like other medical specialties—was becoming increasingly committed to the development of evidence-based practices, a process that also depends on the collection of outcomes data. Together, these philosophical, structural, and financing changes set the stage for the current interest in evaluating the effectiveness of strategies to implement recovery-as-policy—an undertaking that involves devising ways to measure recovery.

The task of developing measurement tools raises weighty conceptual and technical issues. Reflecting on the work of the Vermont Study, Courtenay Harding (1986) elegantly addressed many of these issues, noting the arbitrariness of fixing "outcome" at a point in time, the difficulty of seeking to understand longitudinal processes using cross-sectional measures, and the sociocultural assumptions built in to standardized measures of functioning. Harding's essay predated the emergence of recovery-as-policy, however—a circumstance that has raised another set of issues.

Attempts to measure recovery are statements about the expected consequences of the phenomenon and thus about its definition. Different definitions of recovery locate the process at different levels: the individual, the organization, the system, or the society. Many of the extant tools, such as those cited earlier in this chapter, focus on the individual level, looking for evidence of recovery in the attitudes and behaviors of persons. Implicitly, then, such tools are based on models of recovery that construe it as an individual-level process. Although one might make an argument that these tools are also effective at evaluating the organizational and systemic levels—by logical extrapolation, an organization or system in which many individuals are recovering is necessarily recovery-oriented—they do little to assess the status of the specific organizational or systemic changes that have been the focus of much policy development. The more recent effort to conceptualize and develop organization-/system-level tools would seem to be an area waiting for creative endeavor. (One challenge of such an endeavor will be to find nontautological ways to assess organizational and systemic outcomes—instruments to measure concepts like flexibility and equity. It seems that the processes that define best practices are often also conceptualized as outcomes.) As yet, there has been little attention to assessing societal-level change—looking for evidence that "society has recovered."

Extant instruments for measuring recovery at the individual level are rife with assumptions about the nature of the process. Taken as a whole, the range of tools currently available seems to encompass the range of ideas about what recovery is: some tools assume that recovery means "real" recovery and look for evidence of symptom reduction and improved functioning; others tend more toward definitions of "practical" recovery and look for indicators of hope and empowerment. It seems likely, however, that in the future, standardization will become more important, and one tool will be used more than the others.

Outcomes constitute one form of evidence-of-recovery. Historically, we have seen that such attempts at measurement are often pressed into service as recovery-as-evidence. That is, data gathered by use of recovery tools are likely to be used to garner political support for particular types of services or systems. The historical confluence of recovery implementation and the shift into managed care models for the provision of publicly funded services suggests that managed care is the service approach that is most likely to be subject to such evidentiary debate. This possibility raises fears that recovery outcomes will be operationalized as a simplistic form of cost-effectiveness—a reduced need for services resulting in monetary savings. For this reason, many recovery advocates state with certainty that recovery and managed care are incompatible, conceptually and financially irreconcilable. Others, however, disagree. In Wisconsin, the state staff who wrote the RFC for the managed care demonstrations believed that this threat could be controlled by including specific language calling for managed care organizations to maintain a full array of services for all eligible individuals and specifically barring them from disenrolling individuals who were not currently using services. A report from executives of a "recovery-oriented" behavioral health managed care organization argued that the structure of managed care provides incentives and cost savings that can be applied to the development of recovery-based innovations in care and service delivery (Forquer and Knight 2001).

An important function of measurement is to make things real. Having a tool (or tools) to measure recovery validates its existence as a phenomenon: If you can measure it, it must exist. If we devote resources to measuring it, it must be important. If services and systems know that recovery is the yardstick by which they will be assessed, it will be taken seriously. There are dangers inherent in these observations, however. The first is the possibility that recovery will be reified as one thing—as symptom reduction *or* empowerment, but not both. Such rigidity in the definition of recovery may reduce the number of people who are seen to recover, in this way perhaps inciting a cycle of pessimism like that which followed Pliny Earle's exposure of the statistics of the "cult of curability." Ossification of recovery as a score on any one set of items (or several sets of similar items) may lead to a phenomenon of "teaching to the test," where providers and service organizations focus on meeting the expectations implicit in those items, with little or no attention to the big picture of the client's life. In the drive to assess outcomes, the quest for valid and reliable data, what will become of the "self pole" of recovery-as-experience (Deegan 1988)?

One of the most powerful effects of recovery-as-experience has been the recognition of a new kind of expertise. In contrast to traditional notions of expertise, which are often based on formal education or professional accomplishment, this expertise is seen to reside in the experience of having been diagnosed and treated in the mental health system. Such experience, the reasoning goes, imbues the individual with insights and knowledge unattainable through any other means. To return to one of the frameworks that structured my analysis of the material in this book, personal experience with the mental health system brings with it the ability to identify the problems that recovery is meant to solve. (Such problem-identification expertise is integral to the Wisconsin idea of "a leadership of the competent"—the practice of conferring responsibility and authority for public policy on individuals made select by their knowledge and ability.)

Perhaps the most important consequence of the recognition of this new kind of expertise has been the subsequent shifts in ideas about power. For individuals, both those with diagnoses and those without, the discovery of an expertise grounded in personal experience, and public recognition of the experts who gave voice to that experience, expanded expectations for what was possible for people who had been diagnosed with severe mental illness. For organizations, particularly programs of service provision, this new expertise challenged traditional ideas about roles and decision-making, leading to a reconceptualization of power—from "power over" to power-sharing—that was tantalizing for some and threatening for others. These individual- and organizational-level consequences implied parallel changes for the larger society—a new acceptance of and accommodation for people with psychiatric diagnoses and tangible support for the new expertise through a redistribution of public funds.

Because expertise is in itself a kind of power, the policy development process risks becoming vulnerable to the claims of those who want the power but lack the experience that would grant them expertise. Thus one of the early problems of recovery-as-policy was that of determining authenticity: Whose experience counts? For example, members of the Recovery Workgroup worried that their recommendation requiring consumer representation on the governing bodies of managed care entities would be distorted by organizations assigning those spots to "HMO vice presidents who were once in marriage counseling." To forestall that eventuality, the Workgroup developed a definition of "consumer" that included references to the "direct impact" of "serious mental illness." The same need for authenticity dogged the new recovery experts, who sought to make their names in the growth industry of research and consulting for recovery policy development. Such experts made frequent references to their own mental illness/recovery experiences, with severity of diagnosis (i.e., schizophrenia over bipolar disorder over major depression) granting extra bona fides.[5]

The conundrums of expertise are those of both exclusivity and diversity. All experts have their own interests, which they promote along with their special knowledge. Making consumer expertise the key driver of system reform may mean not soliciting or even actively discounting other ideas—those of families, of people who work as service providers, and of the general public. While one could argue that the recent attention to consumer expertise is simply providing corrective—a balance to the hundreds of years in which consumer voices were silenced—families, workers, and the general public also have interests in the mental health system. The perception that policy is being developed based solely on the implications of consumers' experiences runs the risk of alienating potential allies within these groups and of provoking a backlash against consumer involvement in mental health policy planning—a backlash that is already apparent in politically conservative health policy sectors (Satel 2002).

Diversity among consumers may be seen as a solution to the exclusivity problem, but it causes other difficulties. When equally expert consumers have differing perspectives, which view should be reflected in policy? A particular flashpoint may be seen in the conflicts between consumers and survivors[6] or, more generally, between those who subscribe to the biomedical model of mental illness and those who reject it. In the Recovery Workgroup, for example, there was often tension between those members who wanted a "recovery-oriented" system to emphasize the importance to recovery of medication and competent psychiatric care and those who sought to minimize the profile of clinical approaches in favor of self-help or empowerment. (While each side might have thought the other was naïve, or misguided, these conflicts were usually resolved by resort to the uniqueness of the recovery process—the idea that recovery would be different for each individual—a solution that assuaged the discomfort of interpersonal conflict, but one that was difficult to operationalize in policy.)

Calls for consumer participation reflect the imperative to make their expertise central to the development of recovery-as-policy. Participation means representation on the decision-making bodies involved in the policy process as well as involvement in service planning and evaluation through mechanisms like consumer satisfaction teams. A common complaint about consumer participation, particularly from service providers, is that the consumers who serve on committees or become involved in governing bodies do not represent the rank and file of clients served—"our consumers."[7] They are smarter, more organized, more articulate, not as ill—the "beautiful consumers" (Lefley 1994). This charge often necessitates refutation—usually by the consumers in question revealing anecdotes from their pasts which demonstrate that they were not always so "beautiful": these anecdotes recount time spent living on the streets or incarceration in the isolation rooms of state hospitals—just like "our consumers."

A possible pitfall of participation is the development of "professional consumers," individuals who end up filling the consumer slots on committee after committee, always being asked to trade on that particular portion of their lives that has to do with mental illness. In addition to being vulnerable to charges of unrepresentativeness, these consumers may end up carrying a large burden, feeling that they are unable to say no. In Wisconsin, there was a group of about half a dozen consumers who were constantly being asked to speak at conferences or to serve on new workgroups or task forces. While some individuals clearly enjoyed this work, others found that if they did not set limits the requests could become overwhelming.

One variation on the participation theme is the idea that in addition to promoting recovery for system users, such activity also promotes recovery for the individual who is participating. As one consumer member of Wisconsin's Recovery Workgroup described it, this assumption makes

> an equation between getting involved in public policy making and recovery. . . . If someone becomes engaged in making political changes which concern mental health services, then the services being improved . . . will help facilitate recovery on the part of consumers who are . . . the recipients of these new services, . . . [and] if someone gets involved in public policymaking and is a consumer, then that act in and of itself is empowering, and becoming an advocate is a step in recovery too.

The corollary to this assumption is an expectation that recovering consumers have an obligation to participate, either to "give something back" or in the interests of their own self-improvement. When this belief was voiced at a Recovery Workgroup meeting, the consumer quoted above reacted with great frustration, noting that, in her mind, recovery was what happened when one gave up always thinking about mental illness in favor of engaging other activities or interests.

Perhaps the greatest danger of the current call for consumer participation is tokenism—the appearance of representation without any real power. In my experience, tokenism is less a problem within any one planning body and more a structural matter. That is, consumers tend to be well represented, and very vocal, on those committees dealing with issues like recovery or stigma, but fewer in number, or even absent, when the issues at hand are fiscal ones. In part, this is a problem of capacity: few lay people—consumers or not—are trained to deal with highly technical processes like rate setting or risk adjustment. The context in which recovery-as-policy has emerged in the United States, however, means that these committees will have a huge influence on the shape of future mental health systems. The distribution of consumer representation is worrisome because it suggests an invidious, and perhaps perpetual, division between the "hard" fiscal issues and the "soft" philosophical ones (although, as the postponement of the managed care component of the Wisconsin redesign suggests, for a variety of reasons the fiscal issues may not always prevail).

As it develops, recovery-as-policy shows the influences of many ideologies. For example, when mainstream organizations like NAMI speak about "recovery," they mean something different than do most consumer/survivor activists. To such organizations recovery is a phenomenon of clinical improvement and functional normalization made possible by ensuring access to new medications and cutting-edge service delivery models—the "best practices" of elite professionals.[8] Individuals may be encouraged to engage in autonomous decision-making, but only after their symptoms are deemed to have been reduced to a level where those decisions are trustworthy (Frese et al. 2001). To many consumer/ survivor activists, however, recovery is a political experience, one with the potential to transform the world through its practice of linking consciousness-raising and social action. Because of this potential, recovery is being appropriated—and distorted—by the mainstream.[9] Both of these conceptions of recovery are profound (as are many others), but they are likely to appeal to very different constituencies, and to be used for different purposes. While the former definition may be seen to strengthen the existing power structures (e.g., the psychiatric profession and pharmaceutical manufacturers), and thus to be something those in power are likely to endorse and promote, the latter calls those structures (and the very nature of power) into question and seems more likely to grow from the ground up. Conceptually and organizationally, then, systems that remake themselves according to the assumptions and implications of one or the other ideology are going to look very different.

Ideologies of recovery vary in the extent to which they emphasize individual or social transformation. The first of the two polarized views I have described above, for example, the "mainstream" view of recovery as a process of symptom reduction and normalization, attends to the systemic and structural requirements necessary to promote recovery, but conceptualizes the process itself as one of individual change. By contrast, the more "radical" perspective on recovery perceives it as almost entirely a matter of social change. As I noted in Chapter 3, "other recoveries" show a similar variability in emphasis and have garnered criticism based upon those emphases. Extant critiques of the AA-influenced recovery movement accuse it of pathologizing, and thereby depoliticizing, behavior by looking to individuals rather than social structures for the causes of, and solutions to, dysfunction (e.g., Haaken 1993; Rapping 1996). Conversely, critiques of the social model of disability that serves as the ideology for much of the disability rights movement charge it with eliding individual differences in lived experience (such as those linked to gender and race) and with forcing individuals to claim a "disabled" identity if they are to speak authoritatively about disability (e.g., Barnes, Mercer, and Shakespeare 1999; Marks 1999; Lee 2002).

These critiques imply that recovery-as-policy must take account of several kinds of dangers: Policies that conceptualize recovery as individual transformation must not lose sight of broader contextual issues—or risk limiting the extent to which real change occurs. (For example, focusing on symptom reduction without attending to stigma reduction may help individuals to "pass," but it won't end discrimination.) Policies that conceptualize recovery as social transformation must be wary of generalized interventions that may not be particularly useful to individuals (e.g., focusing exclusively on promoting employment accommodation when many people find work oppressive for other reasons) or of trapping people in certain social roles—and thus in the disabled identities they no longer wish to stress (such as those of the "professional consumers" who feel pressured to continue participating in policy development or advocacy activities even when they want to move on to other interests).

Implicit in the ideology of policy development is a process of problem identification, including the assignment of responsibility for the problem—in the dual sense of both locating blame and fixing the obligation to remedy what is wrong. Although the problems that recovery is meant to solve have been variously located at the levels of mentally ill individuals, mental health services, systems, or the broader society, remedies to these problems have tended to focus on changes in the mode and manner of service provision. Thus, the responsibility for implementing recovery—as individual transformation and as social transformation—may be perceived to rest primarily with providers and administrators in service delivery organizations. Indeed, the recent attention to developing practitioner competencies and best-practices guidelines for recovery-oriented services reinforces the argument that service organizations are the key point of intervention in the work of building a systemic recovery orientation.

What, exactly, are service delivery organizations to be responsible for? Extant best-practices guidelines suggest that the most important organizational innovations are those that change the nature of the relationship between providers and consumers. These guidelines address the need for providers to subscribe to hope and to demonstrate optimism in their dealings with clients. They call for flexibility and individualization in treatment (recovery) planning. They direct organizations in ways in which services may strengthen consumer autonomy rather than promoting increased dependence. Finally, emerging best practices seek to demonstrate how the abstraction of power-sharing may be made manifest.

These new responsibilities risk clashing with the old responsibilities: existing organizational and system-level policies and professional practice guidelines that emphasize the role of providers in maintaining safety. What families fear in recovery is, in part, a scenario in which recovery is used as justification for honoring individual "choices" up to and including self-harm. What rouses the general public is that nightly news stereotype—the "schizophrenic" or "mental patient" who commits murder after being prematurely discharged from the hospital. In turn, what providers can envision, and dread, is a double bind in which they are held responsible both for encouraging clients to make their own choices *and* for any adverse effects of these choices. (I believe that much of what is labeled "resistance" on the part of providers is a response to this dread.) The key to implementing recovery-as-policy may be finding a model for responsibility-sharing that mirrors that being developed for power-sharing.[10]

A related issue of responsibility and structural consistency is the debate over the compatibility of recovery and various forms of coercion. Some recovery advocates argue that no system can be recovery-oriented as long as it wields the power to threaten involuntary commitment or forced treatment. Others are exploring how mediation and alternative dispute resolution can be used to promote recovery by reducing the need for coercion in mental health settings (e.g., Blanch and Prescott 2002). Many providers working in coercive contexts (prisons or forensic units) or under conditions of coercion (court-ordered outpatient treatment) are eager to find strategies for promoting recovery in these situations by working with clients in ways that emphasize matters that the incarcerated or court-ordered individual *can* control (e.g., Everett 2001).

More general questioning of the idea of responsibility raises other issues. As we have seen, the historical shift from institutional care to community-based services extended the range of life dimensions (e.g., work, interpersonal relationships) that mental health services were expected to affect. (These dimensions thus came to define what counted as recovery.) The social justice/human rights rhetoric of recovery-as-policy may presage a similar expansion—one that moves into areas of equality and equity. But is a mental health system being set up for failure when it is expected to address the sociostructural inequities suffered by the people it serves?

THE RECOVERY STATE

As this question suggestions, recovery-as-politics has a broader domain as well. One might begin to explore this domain by following Warner (1994) and examining the political economy of recovery. In his dissection of the history of recovery from schizophrenia, Warner argues that recovery rates have been reflections of socioeconomic conditions. In good times, when labor markets are expanding and jobs are plentiful, more patients are able to "recover"—that is, to rejoin society and become productive members of the community. Conversely, when times are bad and unemployment rates are high, individuals are more likely to stagnate or deteriorate in institutions or in treatment. These patterns hold true despite changes in treatment approach or service delivery. Thus, cycles of optimism and pessimism about recovery from mental illness would seem to be driven by underlying economic cycles. (Warner's argument suggests that the "attitudes" that make recovery a reality may be more akin to those that drive the stock market up and down than to values like choice and collaboration that have been the focus of many recovery interventions!)

The current attention to recovery-as-policy began during the recession of the early 1990s, but it peaked in the boom years of the late

1990s and 2000 (when Madison was profiled in the *New York Times* magazine as being the city with "0% unemployment" [Brooks 2000]). The economic good times certainly made the contraction in human services more palatable—for example, the fact that jobs were available made sense of the "work not welfare" emphasis of welfare reform efforts (in Wisconsin and elsewhere)—and the surpluses in many state budgets allowed investment in reform rather than the indiscriminant slashing of programs that had been common in the bust years of the 1980s. (It was still necessary, however, to sell these investments as "good" ones—i.e., as expenditures that would pay off later in greater economic efficiencies.)

Of course, lately the economic bubble has burst. Though the attention to recovery-as-policy has continued, it is unclear to what extent that enthusiasm is a matter of momentum that may be slowed. It seems likely that government investments in recovery may be reduced or ended and that recovery-as-policy will become another area for arguments over the distribution of scarce resources in the nation's public mental health systems.

Many of those arguments about resources are likely to take place over services and programs that are nonmedical in their orientation. As I have noted, recovery-as-policy has followed other mental health reform movements in expanding the number and type of life dimensions for which the mental health system bears responsibility. Many visions of recovery-oriented systems call for programs or providers to play a role in assisting clients with a long list of requirements—from eating a healthy diet to finding decent housing to securing a living wage. What are the implications of conceptualizing access to food, shelter, work, and income security as "mental health needs"? Should mental health dollars be used to buy cars for system clients whose "recovery plans" include a need for transportation while citizens who live in poverty but lack mental illness diagnoses are left to manage with inadequate public transportation?

Since deinstitutionalization, the economic underpinnings of the nation's public mental health systems have been the federal and state mechanisms for income support—programs like SSI and SSDI. These mechanisms are based on what Deborah Stone (1984) has described as the use of disability as an administrative category. Eligibility for payments is dependent on the individual proving his or her incapacity for work to the proper authorities and on a societal determination that certain kinds of incapacities (but not others) are "deserving" of aid. Recovery advocates have criticized income support programs on many grounds: that the process of application (proving incapacity) is demeaning; that the payment amounts keep recipients in dire poverty; that program-mandated limits on the amount of wage income that may be earned serve as disincentives to work; that the process of claiming disability affirms the disabled identity. Proposals for reforming the income support system have been part of recovery-as-policy, but there has been little will to confront the challenge posed to the system by the idea of recovery. What would "recovery" look like as an administrative category? How would it be assessed or validated in an eligibility determination? Should "recovering" lead to lower payments? At what stage will society become unwilling to continue to support "recovered" individuals?

Finally, like disability (Albrecht 1992), recovery is also a private sector commodity. (The old joke about "the insurance cure" would have it that for-profit corporations have always promoted recovery.) As I have noted, behavioral health care organizations have taken an increasing interest in recovery-as-policy. While some of this interest is probably driven by cost-containment concerns shared with the public sector, it is also true that recovery is an ideal marketing device. Indeed, a proprietary vitamin and mineral supplement that claims to reduce the symptoms of mental illness is being sold under the name "Empowerplus" (Laucius 2003).

RECOVERY AS . . .

The history of recovery, as explored in this book, may be read as a case study of the uses of definition. Definition has served many purposes—strategy, authority, and vision. Definitions of recovery have been used to settle values and to quell dissent, to reveal and to obscure. These uses have been shown to be rooted in context—a palimpsest of evidence, experience, and ideology accreted over time—and to have consequences—policy and politics—for other definitions. The dinosaur was inscribed with the past, then converted into a bridge to the future. It seems certain that the meaning of recovery will continue to be transformed and thus also to have transformative effects.

Notes

Introduction

1. As I explain in Chapter 3, the terms used to describe individuals who have been diagnosed with serious mental illness and received mental health services are fraught with political significance. I chose to use the word "consumer" here because it is term most Wisconsin consumers applied to themselves.

1
On Wisconsin

1. Despite the rhetoric of deinstitutionalization and structural change, in some counties individuals with mental illness were left to languish in these nursing homes for years (Dianne Greenley, lecture to the Mental Health Services Research Training Program weekly seminar, October 1997).
2. In fact, as early as 1987 legislation had been passed requiring the development of a plan for implementing a managed care program for mental health and substance abuse treatment in the state. Although such a plan was formulated, it never took effect (Wisconsin Department of Health and Social Services 1990).

2
Four Scenes from the History of Recovery

1. Similarly, the administrators at the York Retreat used their statistics to solicit "subscriptions" (donations) from members of the Society of Friends. Subscribers whose contributions reached certain financial thresholds were able to reserve one or more places at the retreat for their own families or friends. High rates of recovery thus could be expected to appeal to both the altruism and self-interest of potential donors.
2. Recovery was embedded even in the terminology applied to institutions.

An asylum was where people with mental illness received custodial care in perpetuity, while the more prestigious "hospital" was the site for treatment leading to eventual discharge.

3. In his study of concepts of mental illness in eighteenth- and nineteenth-century America, Norman Dain (1964) disputes the accuracy of Earle's reanalysis. Dain suggests that although the rates were probably not as high as 90 or 100 percent, they likely exceeded 50 percent.

4. One of the earliest such groups used the name "Recovery Incorporated." Recovery, Inc., as it is now known, was founded in 1937 by an Illinois psychiatrist named Abraham Low, who developed a system of symptom management techniques ("will-training") to be practiced by patients meeting regularly in groups (Low 1950).

5. Kraepelin apparently reversed himself several times around this issue. At one point, Bleuler reports, he "considered the many cases which . . . could be cured permanently or arrested for very long periods as also belonging to the dementia praecox group" (Bleuler 1950 [1911], 7), but later reverted to his original, exclusionary, classification.

6. Phenomenological examinations of recovery required different methods than those used to build dimensional and categorical models. The qualitative methods advocated by Strauss and others (see Strauss, Bartko, and Carpenter 1981) ran counter to the trend toward quantification and biological reductionism that psychiatry had adopted in order to increase its legitimacy within the larger medical community.

7. I have been accused of perpetuating the same privileging of expert voices. Following a public presentation of some of the material in this chapter, a member of the audience berated me for telling the story of recovery through the eyes of professionals, rather than from the perspective of the individuals who, throughout history, have recovered from mental illness. I have several responses to this criticism: First, my intention in this analysis has not been to write a comprehensive history of recovery, but instead to examine its social construction over time—in particular, in the context of several major mental health reform movements. The sad fact is that the "social construction of reality" is, in large measure, the privilege of the powerful over the powerless. Second, my lack of attention to the voices of consumers in this chapter is in part an artifact of the way I have organized my material. I do take up those voices in Chapter 3, which deals with the consumer/survivor movements and the power of individuals' collectivized voices to make change. Although I discuss them separately, the consumer/survivor movements were coincident with the deinstitutionalization and community support events mentioned in this chapter and in Chapter 1. Third, I recommend that interested readers take a look at the burgeoning field of consumer/survivor history—scholarship aimed at developing a "people's" history of mental illness and mental

health services. (See, for example, Reaume 2000 and the Consumer/Survivor History Project being conducted at the National Empowerment Center, which can be accessed at www.power2u.org.) Such work requires an almost archaeological commitment to unearthing primary sources that are not readily available. I did not have the resources to devote to such an effort for something that is a relatively small part of this book. Finally, as became quite apparent when the audience member and I had some further conversation about the matter, his criticism was as much political as it was intellectual. That is, he wanted me to tell the story in a particular way in order to promote a particular agenda (one that is not necessarily my own).

Interstice 2

1. In an article I wrote (Jacobson 2001), I argued that a key subprocess in the overall experience of recovery is that of recognizing and naming the problem, or making sense of the "what happened."

2. I passed the second, smaller kidney stone uneventfully, then saw the stone man for follow-up over a period of six months or so—the only woman in a urology department waiting room full of middle-aged and elderly men—until he lost interest in me and the very ordinary chemical composition of my stones. I eventually had surgery for endometriosis and then started taking medication, reducing the chronic pain I'd suffered immeasurably. (All this only after taking the hospital's gynecology department to task for using cotton booties advertising Zoloft to pad the stirrups in their examination rooms.) Any apparent blood abnormalities have come to naught.

3
A SIMPLE YET POWERFUL VISION

1. Bleuler's book contains many references to his influential father. In one anecdote, the younger Bleuler recounts how his father, after leaving the clinic where he had worked for many years, occasionally would visit on the weekends. He would return home discouraged, disappointed at seeing once again the same patients who remained resident in the facility, with no apparent improvement, for years and years after his departure. The more optimistic son, however, pointed out the bias inherent in his father's perspective: he "did not know how many improved patients were out for their Sunday walks during his visits, and certainly not how many had been released and were living at home, recovered" (Bleuler 1978 [1972], 413).

2. Bleuler used several criteria to define recovery: full employment in "gainful work"; resumption of the patient's "former role in society"; the patient's family no longer considering the person mentally ill; and relief from psychotic symptoms (Bleuler 1978 [1972], 191). "Improved" patients remained

somewhat symptomatic but were able to live outside the hospital and to work.

3. Although some psychiatrists (including John Wing, H. Richard Lamb, and Robert Paul Liberman) were at the forefront of conceptualizing psychiatric rehabilitation and have been vocal advocates for it, most psychiatric rehabilitation practitioners are trained in nonmedical disciplines (e.g., psychology, social work). As psychiatric rehabilitation grew in prominence, tensions emerged between its proponents and some members of the psychiatric profession (Bachrach 1992).

4. Following William Anthony's publication of several articles on recovery as a new "vision" for mental health services provision, psychiatric rehabilitation as promoted by his home institution, the Center for Psychiatric Rehabilitation at Boston University, became essentially indistinguishable from some conceptualizations of recovery in its structure, goals, and rhetoric.

5. Sociologists who have studied the activities and structures of consumer/survivor organizations have classified them as belonging to a social movement (Brown 1981; Everett 1994). Citing several social movement theorists, Everett (1994; 2000) points to the following characteristics of consumer/survivor groups as being constitutive of a social movement designation: they are united around a common set of ideas; they develop an "us" and "them" view of the world; they seek to promote specific changes; they consist of active leaders and followers; and they draw an equivalence between individual and social change.

6. SAMHSA is the federal agency with responsibility for mental health and substance abuse services in the United States. It is composed of the Center for Mental Health Services, the Center for Substance Abuse Prevention, and the Center for Substance Abuse Treatment. Federal appropriations for block grants to the states flow through SAMHSA. The agency also provides technical assistance to the states and funds grants for research and demonstration projects. The responsibilities of the Center for Mental Health Services originally resided in the NIMH but were moved out of the research agency when SAMHSA was formed.

7. Similar notions of consumer expertise have become prominent in many other arenas as well, including health-related public policymaking (Ard and Natowicz 2001) and health care for persons with physical disabilities (Bowers et al. 2003).

8. Barbara Everett (2000) notes that this equivalence is a characteristic of "new" social movements that "don't separate individual change from social action. Instead, members see their own transformation as integral to wider societal change" (56).

9. Deegan's article appeared in *Psychosocial Rehabilitation Journal*, part of a

trend in which professional journals solicited first-person accounts from "patients."

10. Although I have not included this in the text for simplicity's sake, readers concerned with the compatibility (or lack thereof) between recovery from mental illness and the recovery movement will be interested in the following: Some time after the Blue Ribbon Commission's report appeared, a decision was taken by the State to integrate state-funded substance abuse treatment programming into the system redesign. Bringing the two service systems together to plan for this integration proved to be somewhat problematic, in large part because of a history of mental health and substance abuse services having had to compete for scarce resources. In the context of the Recovery Workgroup, definitional and ideological differences between the two groups often became manifest. While the substance abuse world has its own concept of "recovery" this concept is not entirely the same thing as the notions of recovery to emerge in the mental health arena. For example, AA requires an admission of character defects and attention to making amends for harms committed by the recovering individual, while recovery from mental illness is much more concerned with building self-esteem and with seeking restitution for wrongs committed *against* the recovering individual. AA promotes the realization of powerlessness and the submission to a "higher power," while mental health recovery principles focus on getting individuals recognize and act upon their own power and autonomy. Tensions also became apparent during discussions of specific implementation strategies (see Chapter Four). Consumers and substance abuse treatment providers accustomed to a tradition of voluntary self-help groups strongly objected to the idea that consumers should be paid for providing such peer support services. For Workgroup members coming from the mental health arena, however, ensuring that consumer-run services be eligible for reimbursement and that consumers be paid for their time were central to promoting the legitimacy of these services.

11. The early strength of recovery in the northeastern region of the United States may have been due to the presence in the area of several organizations that championed the concept. Anthony's Center for Psychiatric Rehabilitation and the National Empowerment Center (a technical assistance center funded by the federal Center for Mental Health Services), where Pat Deegan, Judi Chamberlin, and Daniel Fisher were affiliated, were both in the Boston area. Burlington, Vermont, was home to Paul Carling's Center for Community Change, an organization that came to mental health services issues from a community development perspective and promoted recovery as consistent with its aim of promoting full citizenship for individuals with psychiatric diagnoses.

12. Crowley prefers, and has attempted to promote, the term "procovery" instead of recovery. She argues that recovery, defined as "to regain a former state of health" implies that one is moving backward. Procovery, on the other hand, means "attaining a productive and fulfilling life *regardless* of the level of health assumed attainable" and implies that one is moving forward (Crowley 1996, emphasis in the original).

13. Interestingly, both sides of this issue used diabetes as a recovery trope. For those who endorsed biological explanations, the example of diabetes was presented as a hopeful model: mental illness could be managed, like other serious chronic diseases. A person might always have to deal with diabetes, but he or she need not allow being "a diabetic" to become the sole determinant of identity. Conversely, for those who rejected biological explanations, diabetes was used as an example of regressive thinking, one that implied that an individual diagnosed with mental illness would always be dependent on medication, always needing to be wary, always under threat.

4
SPECIFYING RECOVERY

1. The data that form the basis for the analysis reported here were gathered from Workgroup documents (agendas, minutes and work products) and from field notes recorded at the Workgroup's meetings. I was a regular observer at these meetings, where I took detailed notes on the substance and process of the group's work. In addition, I had informal conversations with members of the Workgroup and was witness to many such conversations between members. I also conducted seven in-depth, semistructured interviews with members of the Workgroup (and the Recovery Task Force, the successor body to the Workgroup). Each interview was tape-recorded and transcribed.

   Approval for the interview component of the project was obtained from the Health Sciences Human Subjects Committee at the University of Wisconsin. All interview participants provided written consent. The Recovery Workgroup was a quasi-public body whose members were appointed by the state's Bureau of Community Mental Health. I did not obtain written consent from Workgroup members to observe, but at the beginning of each meeting I identified myself as a researcher who was interested in recovery and in studying the Workgroup. Workgroup members may recognize themselves and each other in this chapter, but I have extended the anonymity promised interview participants to all individuals involved in the Workgroup.

   A different version of this chapter was published as a paper in the journal *Qualitative Health Research*. Before I began working on that paper, I sought approval from Workgroup members, sketching for them its general content and objectives. The only question they asked was whether I would portray the group in a "favorable" light. When I responded that my approach would be descriptive and analytical, not evaluative, they readily agreed that I could write about them. I made a draft of the paper available to Workgroup members. Those who read it commented that they found it interesting and did not raise any objections to how I had portrayed the group.

2. These frameworks were the social worlds/arenas approach (Strauss 1978a, 1982, 1984, 1993; Clarke 1991, 1997; Garrety 1997), the transformation of intentions approach (Strauss 1978b; Estes and Edmonds 1981; Hall and McGinty 1997), and the social construction of public problems approach (Gusfield 1981; Spector and Kitsuse 1987; Hilgartner and Bosk 1988).

Social worlds have been defined as "groups with shared commitments to certain activities, sharing resources of many kinds to achieve their goals, and building shared ideologies about how to go about their business" (Clarke 1991, 131). Social worlds mediate structural conditions and individual action. They are themselves subject to great flux, constantly shifting and reforming with changes in conditions and action. These shifts and reformations take place through processes of conflict, competition, negotiation, co-optation, and exchange both within and between social worlds (Strauss 1982, 1984, 1993; Clarke 1991). Social worlds are defined and bounded by shared resources, goals, and ideologies, all of which reflect the structural context in which they exist. The notion of arenas encompasses social worlds as a collectivity, the collective action of social worlds, and the interactions between and among social worlds over substantive matters (Strauss 1993).

The transformation of intentions approach shares many of the interactionist assumptions of the social worlds/arenas approach in that it sees policy as a social product that is "emergent and continuously being negotiated through reaffirmation or resistance" (Estes and Edmonds 1981, 76)—an idea summed up by the phrase "policy is the process" (Estes and Edmonds 1981, 81). As the use of the term "resistance" suggests, however, this approach pays close attention to power, particularly to the competitions that take place over meaning and who prevails in the struggle to "define the situation." Hall and McGinty (1997) apply and expand the transformation of intentions approach by cataloging a number of the "processes of meta-power" that are manifest in policy development. Attention to these processes reveals the ways in which the emergence of policy is not haphazard but shaped by those with the power to control the policy development arena.

The final piece of my theoretical scaffolding was the social construction of public problems approach, which is based on Blumer's observation that "social problems are fundamentally products of a process of collective definition" (Blumer 1971, 298). Sociologists working in this tradition seek to understand the processes through which putative situations become public problems (Gusfield 1981) and how definition is used as a tool by those concerned with claims-making and claims-staking (Spector and Kitsuse 1987; Hilgarnter and Bosk 1988).

Each of these frameworks provided sensitizing categories and questions I used to analyze my data. The social worlds/arenas analysis of health policy development, for example, focused my attention on the Workgroup as a social world composed of many smaller subworlds and on the fluid and emergent nature of policy as process or action. It prompted me to ask questions about how the resources, ideologies, and goals of the Workgroup (and its subworlds) were embedded in its processes of conflict and negotiation. The transformation of intentions approach led me to ask questions about power—especially in the content of members' definitions of recovery and in the relative legitimacy granted different definitions. The social construction of public problems approach supplied me with the insight that recovery was the solution to a problem—spoken or unspoken—and that the key to understanding members' definitions of recovery lay in understanding the problems they were attempting to promote.

3. The following incident suggests that the Recovery Workgroup was equally prone to such difficulties, and that it was only through discipline and good sense that it, too, did not get bogged down: At one extremely busy meeting it became apparent that the usual one-hour lunch break would need to be sacrificed in order to get through the planned agenda. The subject of what to do about lunch became an agenda item in and of itself, with Workgroup members suggesting that there be a lunch break but that it be shorter than usual or that the entire group place a take-out order (an idea that occasioned another lengthy discussion of what take-out options were available and acceptable) and continue to work while eating. The group eventually made a decision, but when the time came to break for lunch, everyone did what he or she had been accustomed to doing at past meetings, with no regard for the putative decision or for the discussion that led up to it!

4. Oral quotations have been edited for readability but have not been altered in substance.

5. The System Design Workgroup was made up of members of the Fiscal Issues and Benefits Design work groups. It was formed when these two work groups found many areas of overlap in their assigned tasks and decided it would be more efficient to combine their efforts. In general, the charge to the System Design Workgroup was to specify the component parts of the redesigned system, including eligibility, enrollment, and assessment procedures, service array, and funding structure (e.g., capitation rate).

6. Some Workgroup members also saw measurement as a potentially positive process for consumers, viewing it as a kind of intervention. For example, one member talked about how pleased she would have been to fill out some kind

of survey during her hospitalization—it would have given her the feeling her opinion mattered to someone and broken the monotony of inpatient life. Similarly, she thought a tool meant to assess how well facilities were protecting the rights of clients could serve an educational function. That is, clients might not be aware that they had any rights until they were asked if these rights had been respected.

5
FROM BONES TO BRIDGES

1. As a condition for receiving mental health block grant money, the federal government requires each state to contract with an organization charged with protecting and advocating for individuals served by the mental health system. Protection and advocacy agencies monitor conditions in mental health facilities; work to ensure access to treatment, rehabilitation services, and income support programs; and provide legal representation to disabled individuals.

2. Medicaid is an entitlement program that requires services be provided to any individual who meets eligibility criteria. In the Section 51.42 system, however, counties' financial expenditures are limited to ceilings set by the amount of funds provided by the state and locality. Counties must provide services to all Medicaid-eligible residents (and may bill Medicaid for the elements of their care that are reimbursable under Medicaid rules) but may set limits on the number of non-Medicaid-eligible individuals served. Had the RFC required the counties to move into a "pure" managed care system, where eligibility would be determined by population-based enrollment, the Medicaid-associated entitlement might reasonably have been assumed to extend to all county residents, creating a situation that the counties believed would be financially untenable.

3. Saturation is a concept that refers to the stage of qualitative data analysis in which no new findings are emerging. Rather, the data are simply replicating what the analyst has already discerned.

4. The pile sort is one of a number of so-called systematic data collection techniques used in qualitative research, particularly in those traditions that focus on some form of domain analysis (Weller and Romney 1988). In a typical pile sort, the researcher writes down single concepts on a series of cards, then asks an informant to sort the cards into piles that "go together." After all the cards have been sorted, the researcher engages the informant in a discussion of the logic that guided the categorization. The process is then repeated with a number of informants from the same group. In this way, the researcher hopes to understand the underlying structures, or domains, through which the group understands its world.

5. Occasionally, the task force would discuss incidents that reminded everyone of the necessity for such training. Once, for example, a task force member described her experience doing a presentation about recovery to a group of community support program case managers: after she had finished her talk, the case managers expressed agreement with everything she had said and asserted that they were already putting many of the ideas into practice. At that point, however, one case manager said she had a difficult client and would like to get the group's advice. The client was a new mother who wished to breast-feed and thus would have to go off her psychiatric medication for a time. The case managers responded with statements like "She's just being manipulative" and "You can outmanipulate her—just take the baby away."

6. I was officially listed as a paid consultant for this proposal. However, because I moved away soon after work began, my participation was limited to several telephone calls during the planning stages and I never received any payment.

7. This theory represents a refinement of the "idealistic" approach to change-making described in Chapter 4. One might speculate that the task force had the luxury of focusing on this approach because other elements of the system redesign effort (e.g., the guidelines for the managed care demonstrations) were implementing the more directive "pragmatic" approach.

8. Throughout the state, many efforts at recovery implementation were proceeding independently of the task force. For example, there was the Next Step conference, a new training program for consumers being run by the local NAMI chapter, and individual agency-based activities like workshops and speakers.

Interstice 4

1. I have, at times, received money for making these presentations. The money goes to my employer, where it is held in account for my use in defraying research expenses. For example, presentation money paid for the index to this book.

6

THE STATE OF RECOVERY

1. Full disclosure: I have recently agreed to serve on the review panel that will select the winning proposal.

2. That postponement may have ended, but the end has come in an unexpected way: recently, the state has announced its intention to put all SSI recipients into managed care programs. This policy shift has emerged entirely separate from the mental health redesign effort, and it has not drawn on any of the planning work done by the BRC-IAC or its work groups.

3. The tool, called the Recovery-Oriented System Assessment (ROSA), is a vari-

ant of a similar instrument that Wisconsin has been using in its long-term care system. It seeks to draw inferences about the quality of services by assessing the "personal outcomes" of clients in the domains of self-determination, connection, health, and human rights (Recovery-Oriented System Assessment 2003). The instrument is used as a guideline for separate interviews with both clients and their case managers. Interviewers work in teams, with all teams including a consumer.

4. In the United Kingdom, as in many countries outside of North America, the term preferred over "consumer" or "survivor" is "user."

5. In these cases, authenticity may be a more nuanced matter than I have indicated here. Many recovery consultants rely on their own experience not only as a credential but also as an exemplar. That is, their models of how recovery works often are grounded in their own experience. This factor makes it important that the individual has both experienced the problem and recovered from it. Challenges to expertise might rely on attacks to either of these; that is, the individual's recovery or the true nature of the problem he or she has experienced may be questioned. This is one reason so many recovery experts, even those who reject the biological explanation for mental illness, react so strongly against the charge that they have managed to recover because they had been misdiagnosed originally.

6. When I was working as a health policy fellow for the Health Subcommittee of the U.S. Senate Labor Committee, I spoke to a prominent psychiatric survivor who was angry that a prominent consumer had been invited to testify before the subcommittee. His attack on the consumer included ad hominem references to the man's emotional instability and unpredictability but clearly was grounded in the wish that the consumer not be perceived as a public expert when he was likely to say things that were contrary to the survivor's own views.

7. Barbara Everett (2000) argues that the charge to an individual consumer that "you don't speak for the people who are really sick" is often based on a circular argument which assumes that because mentally ill people can't speak for themselves, anyone who does cannot be mentally ill (167–68). She notes that this argument is predicated on a belief that people with mental illness cannot recover—that mental illness is a static (or deteriorating) condition. Beresford and Campbell (1994) examine the "unrepresentative" epithet and locate its origins in divergent meanings of representation—typical of individuals vs. representative of collectivities—which in turn are linked to "competing models and cultures of democracy" (323).

8. In a speech at the 2001 annual meeting of the American Public Health Association, Howard Goldman suggested that systems grounded in evidence-based best practices would be the fifth cycle of mental health reform in the United States (Goldman 2001).

9. As early as 1998, I spoke with a consumer/researcher who was concerned that the rush to build "recovery-oriented" mental health systems constituted a co-optation of an idea that had begun with consumers. State-level efforts to implement recovery were willfully oblivious, she said, to the existence of people who had "really" recovered—those who no longer used or needed services. Instead, recovery had become a way to "validate the concept of chronicity," that is, to justify an expectation of lifelong dependence on the system.

10. In Wisconsin, part of the work of developing a model for responsibility-sharing has been delegated to the risk and liability committee I described earlier in this chapter. Additionally, the WCA has been involved in developing a training seminar for social workers that explores issues of boundaries and ethics in a recovery framework. The emphasis of this training is on assessing the nature and extent of risk (e.g., risk of what to whom?) and on disentangling the emotional and power dynamics that may be in play when choices become controversial (Dianne Greenley, personal communication, June 2003).

REFERENCES

Adams, S. M., and Partee, D. J. (1998). "Hope: The Critical Factor in Recovery." *Journal of Psychosocial Nursing* 36 (4): 29–32.

Ahern, L., and Fisher, D. (1999). *Personal Assistance in Community Existence.* Lawrence, MA: National Empowerment Center.

——— (2001). "Recovery at Your Own PACE (Personal Assistance in Community Existence)." *Journal of Psychosocial Nursing* 39 (4): 22–32.

Al-Anon Family Groups (1994). *From Survival to Recovery: Growing Up in an Alcoholic Home.* New York: Al-Anon Family Group Headquarters.

Albrecht, G. L. (1992). *The Disability Business: Rehabilitation in America.* Newbury Park, CA: Sage.

Alcoff, L., and Gray, L. (1993). "Survivor Discourse: Transgression or Recuperation?" *Signs* 18 (2): 260–90.

Anspach, R. R. (1979). "From Stigma to Identity Politics: Political Activism among the Physically Disabled and Former Mental Patients." *Social Science and Medicine* 13A: 765–73.

Anthony, W. A. (1991). "Recovery from Mental Illness: The New Vision of Services Researchers." *Innovations and Research* 1 (1): 13–14.

——— (1993). "Recovery from Mental Illness: The Guiding Vision of the Mental Health System in the 1990s" *Psychosocial Rehabilitation Journal* 16 (4): 11–23.

——— (2000). "A Recovery-Oriented Service System: Setting Some System-Level Standards." *Psychiatric Rehabilitation Journal* 24 (2): 159–68.

Anthony, W. A., Cohen, M., and Farkas, M. (1990). *Psychiatric Rehabilitation.* Boston: Center for Psychiatric Rehabilitation.

Anthony, W. A., and Liberman, R. P. (1986). "The Practice of Psychiatric Rehabilitation: Historical, Conceptual, and Research Base." *Schizophrenia Bulletin* 12 (4): 542–59.

Ard, C. F., and Natowicz, M. R. (2001). "A Seat at the Table: Membership in

Federal Advisory Committees Evaluating Public Policy in Genetics." *American Journal of Public Health* 91 (5): 787–90.

Bachrach, L. L. (1992). "Psychosocial Rehabilitation and Psychiatry in the Care of Long-Term Patients." *American Journal of Psychiatry* 149 (11): 1455–63.

Baker, S., and Strong, S. (2001). *Roads to Recovery: How People with Mental Health Problems Recover and Find Ways of Coping.* London: Mind, The Mental Health Charity.

Barnes, C., Mercer, G., and Shakespeare, T. (1999). *Exploring Disability: A Sociological Introduction.* Cambridge: Polity.

Barnes, C., Oliver, M., and Barton, L., eds. (2002). *Disability Studies Today.* Cambridge: Polity.

Bassman, R. (2000). "Agents, Not Objects: Our Fights to Be." *JCLP/In Session: Psychotherapy in Practice* 56 (11): 1395–411.

Bazelon Center for Mental Health Law (2002). "An Act Providing a Right to Mental Health Services and Supports: A Model Law." At www.bazelon. org/newvisionofpublicmentalhealth.html.

Beale, V., and Lambric, T. (1995). *The Recovery Concept: Implementation in the Mental Health System.* Ohio Department of Mental Health.

Beers, C. W. (1960 [1908]). *A Mind That Found Itself: An Autobiography.* New York: Doubleday.

Beresford, P., and Campbell, J. (1994). "Disabled People, Service Users, User Involvement and Representation." *Disability and Society 9* (3): 315–25.

Berger, P. L., and Luckman, T. (1966). *The Social Construction of Reality: A Treatise in the Sociology of Knowledge.* New York: Anchor Books.

Blanch, A., and Prescott, L. (2002). *Managing Conflict Cooperatively: Making a Commitment to Nonviolence and Recovery in Mental Health Treatment Settings.* National Association for State Mental Health Program Directors and the National Technical Assistance Center for State Mental Health Planning.

Bleuler, E. (1950 [1911]). *Dementia Praecox or the Group of Schizophrenias.* Translated by Joseph Zinkin. New York: International Universities Press.

Bleuler, M. (1978 [1972]). *The Schizophrenic Disorders: Long-Term Patient and Family Studies.* Translated by Siegfried M. Clemens. New Haven: Yale University Press.

Blue Ribbon Commission on Mental Health (1997). *Final Report.* Madison, Wisconsin.

Blumer, H. (1969). *Symbolic Interactionism: Perspective and Method.* Berkeley: University of California Press.

——— (1971). "Social Problems as Collective Behavior." *Social Problems* 18: 298–306.

Boodman, S. G. (2002). "Beautiful—but Not Rare—Recovery." *Washington Post.* February 12, 2002.

Borkin, J. R., et al. (1998). "Recovery Attitudes Questionnaire." Ohio Department of Mental Health.

Bowers, B., et al. (2003). "Improving Primary Care for Persons with Disability: The Nature of Expertise." *Disability and Society* 18 (4): 443–55.

Boym, S. (2001). *The Future of Nostalgia*. New York: Basic Books.

Breier, A., and Strauss, J. S. (1984). "The Role of Social Relationships in the Recovery from Psychotic Disorders." *American Journal of Psychiatry* 141 (8): 949–55.

Brooks, D. (2000). "0% Unemployment." *New York Times Magazine*. March 5, 2000.

Brown, C., and Jasper, K., eds. (1993). *Consuming Passions: Feminist Approaches to Weight Preoccupation and Eating Disorders*. Toronto: Second Story.

Brown, P. (1981). "The Mental Patients' Rights Movement and Mental Health Institutional Change." *International Journal of Health Services* 11 (4): 523–40.

Buenker, J. D. (1998). *The History of Wisconsin*. Vol. 4, *The Progressive Era, 1893–1914*. W. F. Thompson, general ed. Madison: State Historical Society of Wisconsin.

Campbell, J., and Schraiber, R. (1989). *The Well-Being Project: Mental Health Clients Speak for Themselves*. Sacramento: California Department of Mental Health.

Caplan, R. (1969). *Psychiatry and the Community in Nineteenth-Century America*. New York: Basic Books.

Caron, C. D., and Bowers, B. J. (2000). "Methods and Application of Dimensional Analysis: A Contribution to Concept and Knowledge Development in Nursing." In *Concept Development in Nursing: Foundations, Techniques, and Applications*, 2nd ed., ed. B. L. Rodgers and K. A. Knafl. Philadelphia: W. B. Saunders.

Carr, V. J. (1983). "Recovery from Schizophrenia: A Review of Patterns of Psychosis." *Schizophrenia Bulletin* 9 (1): 95–121.

Chamberlin, J. (1978). *On Our Own: Patient-Controlled Alternatives to the Mental Health System*. New York: McGraw-Hill.

——— (1984). "Speaking for Ourselves: An Overview of the Ex-Psychiatric Inmates' Movement." *Psychosocial Rehabilitation Journal* 8 (2): 57–65.

——— (1990). "The Ex-Patients' Movement: Where We've Been and Where We're Going." *Journal of Mind and Behavior* 11 (3 and 4): 323–36.

Charon, J. M. (1995). *Symbolic Interactionism: An Introduction, an Interpretation, an Integration*. 5th ed. Englewood Cliffs, NJ: Prentice Hall.

Clarke, A. E. (1991). "Social Worlds/Arenas Theory as Organizational Theory." In *Social Organization and Social Process: Essays in Honor of Anselm Strauss*, ed. David R. Maines. Hawthorne, NY: Aldine De Gruyter.

———— (1997). "A Social Worlds Research Adventure: The Case of Reproductive Science." In *Grounded Theory in Practice*, ed. Anselm Strauss and Juliet Corbin. Thousand Oaks, CA: Sage.

Community Support Programs Consumer Listening Sessions Final Report. Undated, unpublished document. Wisconsin Bureau of Community Mental Health.

Corrigan, P. W., et al. (1999). "Recovery as a Psychological Construct." *Community Mental Health Journal* 35 (3): 231–39.

Crowley, K. (1996). "The Vision of Procovery." Health Action Letter.

———— (2000). *The Power of Procovery in Healing Mental Illness.* San Francisco: Kennedy Carlisle Publishing for Health Action Network.

Curtis, L. C. (2000). "Practice Guidance for Recovery-Oriented Behavioral Healthcare for Adults with Serious Mental Illnesses." In *Personal Outcome Measures in Consumer-Directed Behavioral Health*. Towson, MD: Council on Quality and Leadership in Supports for People with Disabilities.

Curtis, L. C. (2002). Wisconsin Consumer and Family Participation Inventory 2001/2002 Findings Report. Unpublished document. Wisconsin Bureau of Community Mental Health.

Dain, N. (1964). *Concepts of Insanity in the United States, 1789–1865*. New Brunswick, NJ: Rutgers University Press.

———— (1980). *Clifford W. Beers: Advocate for the Insane.* Pittsburgh: University of Pittsburgh Press.

Davidson, L., and Strauss, J. S. (1992). "Sense of Self in Recovery from Severe Mental Illness." *British Journal of Medical Psychology* 65: 131–45.

Deegan, P. E. (1988). "Recovery: The Lived Experience of Rehabilitation." *Psychosocial Rehabilitation Journal* 11 (4): 11–19.

———— (1992). "The Independent Living Movement and People with Psychiatric Disabilities: Taking Back Control over Our Own Lives." *Psychosocial Rehabilitation Journal* 15 (3): 3–19.

DeJong, G. (1993). "Defining and Implementing the Independent Living Concept." In *Independent Living for Physically Disabled People*, ed. N. M. Crewe, I. K. Zola, and Associates. San Francisco: Jossey-Bass.

Department of Health and Human Services (1999). *Mental Health: A Report of the Surgeon General*. Rockville, MD: U.S. Public Health Service.

Deutsch, A. (1949). *The Mentally Ill in America*. New York: Columbia University Press.

Donlon, P. T., and Blacker, K. H. (1973). "Stages of Schizophrenic Decompensation and Reintegration." *Journal of Nervous and Mental Disease* 157 (3): 200–209.

Earle, P. (1972 [1887]). *The Curability of Insanity: A Series of Studies*. New York: Arno Press and New York Times.

Eastland, L. S. (1995). "Recovery as an Interactive Process: Explanation and

Empowerment in Twelve-Step Programs." *Qualitative Health Research* 5 (3): 292–314.

Ebert, T., and Trattner, W. I. (1990). "The County Mental Institution: Did It Do What It Was Designed to Do?" *Social Science Quarterly* 71 (4): 835–47.

Estes, C. L., and Edmonds, B. C. (1981). "Symbolic Interaction and Social Policy Analysis." *Symbolic Interaction* 4: 75–86.

Estroff, S. E. (1981). *Making It Crazy: An Ethnography of Psychiatric Clients in an American Community.* Berkeley: University of California Press.

Everett, B. (1994). "Something Is Happening: The Contemporary Consumer and Psychiatric Survivor Movement in Historical Context." *Journal of Mind and Behavior* 15 (1 and 2): 55–70.

——— (2000). *A Fragile Revolution: Consumers and Psychiatric Survivors Confront the Power of the Mental Health System.* Waterloo, ON: Wilfrid Laurier University Press.

——— (2001). "Community Treatment Orders: Ethical Practice in an Era of Magical Thinking." *Canadian Journal of Community Mental Health* 20 (1): 5–20.

Farrow, J. (1973). *Winnebago State Hospital, 1873–1973.* Winnebago, WI.

Fisher, D. B. (1993). "Towards a Positive Culture of Healing." In *The Department of Mental Health Core Curriculum: Consumer Empowerment and Recovery,* part I. Boston, MA.

——— (1994). "Health Care Reform Based on an Empowerment Model of Recovery by People With Psychiatric Disabilities." *Hospital and Community Psychiatry* 45 (9): 913–15.

Fisher, D. B., and Ahern, L. (1999). "Empowerment Model of Recovery from Mental Illness." In *Personal Assistance in Community Existence,* ed. L. Ahern and D. Fisher (1999). Lawrence, MA: National Empowerment Center.

Forquer, S., and Knight, E. (2001). "Managed Care: Recovery Enhancer or Inhibitor?" *Psychiatric Services* 52 (1): 25–26.

Frese, F. J. (1998). "Advocacy, Recovery, and the Challenges of Consumerism for Schizophrenia." *Psychiatric Clinics of North America* 21 (1): 233–49.

Frese, F. J., et al. (2001). "Integrating Evidence-Based Practices and the Recovery Model." *Psychiatric Services* 52 (11): 1462–68.

Garrett, C. J. (1997). "Recovery from Anorexia Nervosa: A Sociological Perspective" *International Journal of Eating Disorders* 21: 261–72.

Garrety, K. (1997). "Social Worlds, Actor-Networks, and Controversy: The Case of Cholesterol, Dietary Fat, and Heart Disease." *Social Studies of Science* 27: 727–73.

Giffort, D., et al. (1995). "Recovery Assessment Scale." Chicago: Illinois Department of Mental Health.

Glaser, B. G., and Strauss, A. L. (1967). *The Discovery of Grounded Theory: Strategies for Qualitative Research.* New York: Aldine.

Goldman, H. (2001). "Mental Health Policy at the Crossroads: Looking Forward and Back over Forty Years." Annual Meeting of the American Public Health Association. Atlanta, GA.

Goodrick, D. (1989). "State and Local Collaboration in the Development of Wisconsin's Mental Health System." *Journal of Mental Health Administration* 16 (1): 37–43.

Greenley, D. (1985). "Impact of a Model Program on State Mental Health Policy Development." In *The Training in Community Living Model: A Decade of Experience,* ed. L. I. Stein and M. A. Test. New Directions for Mental Health Services 26. San Francisco: Jossey-Bass.

Greenley, J. R. (1995). "Madison, Wisconsin, United States: Creation and Implementation of the Program of Assertive Community Treatment (PACT)." In *Innovating in Community Mental Health: International Perspectives,* ed. R. Schultz and J. R. Greenley. Westport, CT: Praeger.

Grob, G. N. (1983). *Mental Illness and American Society, 1875–1940.* Princeton, NJ: Princeton University Press.

——— (1991). *From Asylum to Community: Mental Health Policy in Modern America.* Princeton, NJ: Princeton University Press.

——— (1994a). "Mad, Homeless, and Unwanted: A History of the Care of the Chronic Mentally Ill in America." *Psychiatric Clinics of North America* 17 (3): 541–558.

——— (1994b). *The Mad Among Us: A History of the Care of America's Mentally Ill.* New York: Free Press.

Grob, S. (1983). "Psychosocial Rehabilitation Centers: Old Wine in a New Bottle." In *The Chronic Psychiatric Patient in the Community: Principles of Treatment,* ed. I. Barofsky and R. P. Budson. New York: Spectrum.

Gusfield, J. R. (1981). *The Culture of Public Problems: Drinking-Driving and the Symbolic Order.* Chicago: University of Chicago Press.

Haaken, J. (1993). "From Al-Anon to ACoA: Codependence and the Reconstruction of Caregiving." *Signs* 18 (2): 321–45.

Hall, P. M., and McGinty, P. J. W. (1997). "Policy as the Transformation of Intentions: Producing Program from Statute." *Sociological Quarterly* 38 (3): 439–67.

Harding, C. M. (1986). "Speculations on the Measurement of Recovery from Severe Psychiatric Disorder and the Human Condition." *Psychiatric Journal of the University of Ottawa* 11(4): 199–204.

——— (2002). "Beautiful Minds Can Be Reclaimed." *New York Times* Op-Ed section. March 10, 2002.

Harding, C. M., and Brooks, G. W. (1980). "Longitudinal Assessment for a Cohort of Chronic Schizophrenics Discharged Twenty Years Ago." *Psychiatric Journal of the University of Ottawa* 5: 274–78.

Harding, C. M., Zubin, J., and Strauss, J. S. (1987). "Chronicity in Schizophrenia: Fact, Partial Fact, or Artifact?" *Hospital and Community Psychiatry* 38 (5): 477–86.

Harding, C. M., et al. (1987a). "The Vermont Longitudinal Study of Persons with Severe Mental Illness, I: Methodology, Study Sample, and Overall Status Thirty-Two Years Later." *American Journal of Psychiatry* 144 (9): 718–26.

———— (1987b). "The Vermont Longitudinal Study of Persons with Severe Mental Illness, II: Long-Term Outcome of Subjects Who Retrospectively Met DSM-III Criteria for Schizophrenia." *American Journal of Psychiatry* 144 (9): 727–35.

Heil, J., and Johnson, L. K. (1998). "Recovery Interview." Athens, OH: Institute for Local Government Administration and Rural Development.

Herman, J. L. (1992). *Trauma and Recovery.* New York: Basic Books.

Herzog, D. B., et al. (1999). "Recovery and Relapse in Anorexia and Bulimia Nervosa: A 7.5-Year Follow-Up Study." *Journal of the American Academy of Child and Adolescent Psychiatry* 38 (7): 829–37.

Hilgartner, S., and Bosk, C. L. (1988). "The Rise and Fall of Social Problems: A Public Arenas Model." *American Journal of Sociology* 94 (1): 53–78.

Hopper, K., et al. (1996). "Rochester Recovery Inquiry." Orangeburg, NY: Center for the Study of Public Issues in Mental Health.

Jacobson, N. (1998a). "Recovery: A Compendium of Resources." A report prepared for the Wisconsin Blue Ribbon Commission Recovery and Consumer-Family Involvement Workgroup.

———— (1998b). "Policy and Programming: How States Are Implementing the Recovery Model." A report prepared for the Wisconsin Blue Ribbon Commission Recovery and Consumer-Family Involvement Workgroup.

———— (1998c). "Strategies for Promoting Recovery." A report prepared for the Wisconsin Blue Ribbon Commission Recovery and Consumer-Family Involvement Workgroup.

———— (2000). "A Conceptual Model of Recovery." Developed under a contract with the Wisconsin Coalition for Advocacy. Madison, Wisconsin.

———— (2001). "Experiencing Recovery: A Dimensional Analysis of Recovery Narratives." *Psychiatric Rehabilitation Journal* 24 (3): 248–56.

———— (2003). "Defining Recovery: An Interactionist Analysis of Health Policy Development, Wisconsin, 1996–1999." *Qualitative Health Research 13* (3): 378–393.

Jacobson, N. and Altenberg, J. (in process). "Exploring Recovery with Alternatives."

Jacobson, N., and Curtis, L. (2000). "Recovery as Policy in Mental Health Services: Strategies Emerging from the States." *Psychiatric Rehabilitation Journal* 23 (4): 333–41.

Jacobson, N., and Greenley, D. (2001). "What Is Recovery? A Conceptual Model and Explication." *Psychiatric Services* 52 (4): 482–85.

Jacobson, N., et al. (2003). "Guided Reflection: A Participatory Evaluation and Planning Process to Promote Recovery in Mental Health Service Agencies." *Psychiatric Rehabilitation Journal* 27 (1): 69–71.

Johnson, H., and Broder, D. S. (1996). *The System: The American Way of Politics at the Breaking Point.* New York: Little, Brown and Co.

Joint Commission on Accreditation of Healthcare Organizations. *Principles for Biopsychosocial Rehabilitation.* Undated document.

Kaminer, W. (1992). *I'm Dysfunctional, You're Dysfunctional: The Recovery Movement and Other Self-Help Fashions.* Reading, MA: Addison-Wesley.

Keil, J. (1994). "The ABC's of Mental Health: One Client's Guide to Recovery." *Journal of the California Alliance for the Mentally Ill* 5 (3): 34.

Kraepelin, E. (1919 [1896]). *Dementia Praecox and Paraphrenia.* Trans. R. M. Barclay. Edinburgh: E and S Livingstone.

Kritsberg, W. (1985). *The Adult Children of Alcoholics Syndrome: From Discovery to Recovery.* Pompano Beach, FL: Health Communications.

Lamb, H. R. (1994). "A Century and a Half of Psychiatric Rehabilitation in the United States." *Hospital and Community Psychiatry* 45 (10): 1015–20.

Laucius, J. (2003). "The Lure of a Miracle Pill for Mental Illness." *Ottawa Citizen.* July 21, 2003.

Lee, P. (2002). "Shooting for the Moon: Politics and Disability at the Beginning of the Twenty-First Century." In *Disability Studies Today*, ed. C. Barnes, M. Oliver, and L. Barton. Cambridge: Polity.

Lefley, H. (1994). "Thinking about Recovery: Paradigms and Pitfalls." *Innovations and Research* 3 (4): 19–23.

Levine, R., and Weiss, P. (1967). *The Origins of the Wisconsin County Hospital System.* Madison: Wisconsin Psychiatric Institute.

Lord, J., et al. (1998). "Analysis of Change within a Mental Health Organization: A Participatory Process." *Psychiatric Rehabilitation Journal* 21 (4): 327–39.

Lovejoy, M. (1984). "Recovery from Schizophrenia: A Personal Odyssey." *Hospital and Community Psychiatry* 35 (8): 809–12.

Low, A. A. (1950). *Mental Health through Will-Training: A System of Self-Help in Psychotherapy as Practiced by Recovery, Incorporated.* Boston: Christopher.

Lunt, A. (2000). "Storytelling: How Nonconsumer Professionals Can Promote Recovery." *Journal of Psychosocial Nursing* 38 (11): 44–45.

Lynch, K. (2000). "The Long Road Back." *JCLP/In Session: Psychotherapy in Practice* 56 (11): 1427–32.

Markowitz, F. E. (2001). "Modeling Processes in Recovery from Mental Illness: Relationships between Symptoms, Life Satisfaction, and Self-Concept." *Journal of Health and Social Behavior* 42: 64–79.

Marks, D. (1999). *Disability: Controversial Debates and Psychosocial Perspectives.* London: Routledge.

Marsh, D. (2000). "Personal Accounts of Consumer/Survivors: Insights and Implications." *JCLP/In Session: Psychotherapy in Practice* 56 (11): 1447–57.

Massachusetts Department of Mental Health (1993). "The DMH Core Curriculum: Consumer Empowerment and Recovery." Office of Clinical and Professional Services.

McCarthy, C. (1912). *The Wisconsin Idea.* New York: Macmillan.

McGlashan, T. H. (1988). "A Selective Review of Recent North American Long-Term Follow-Up Studies of Schizophrenia." *Schizophrenia Bulletin* 14 (4): 515–42.

Mead, G. H. (1982 [1909]). "Social Consciousness and the Consciousness of Meaning." In *Pragmatism: The Classic Writings,* ed. H. S. Thayer. Indianapolis: Hackett. Originally published in *Psychological Bulletin* 6.

——— (1982 [1913]). "The Social Self." In *Pragmatism: The Classic Writings,* ed. H. S. Thayer. Indianapolis: Hackett. Originally published in *Journal of Philosophy, Psychology, and Scientific Methods* 10.)

Mead, S., and Copeland, M. E. (2000). "What Recovery Means to Us: Consumers' Perspectives." *Community Mental Health Journal* 36 (3): 315–28.

Mechanic, D. (1998). "Emerging Trends in Mental Health Policy and Practice." *Health Affairs* 17 (6): 82–98.

Morrissey, J. P., and Goldman, H. H. (1986). "Care and Treatment of the Mentally Ill in the United States: Historical Developments and Reforms." *Annals of the American Academy of Political and Social Sciences* 484: 12–27.

NAMI (1999). "Omnibus Mental Illness Recovery Act (OMIRA)." At *www. nami.org.*

NAMI (2002). "NAMI Establishes Policy Institute to 'Drive National Debate on Mental Illness.' " Press release. At www.nami.org.

Nasar, S. (1998). *A Beautiful Mind: A Biography of John Forbes Nash, Jr., Winner of the Nobel Prize in Economics, 1994.* New York: Simon and Schuster.

National Mental Health Consumers' Self-Help Clearinghouse. "National Consumer Leader, Ed Knight, Becomes VP at Value Options." At *www. mhselfhelp.org.*

Nelson, G., Lord, J., and Ochocka, J. (2001). *Shifting the Paradigm in Community Mental Health: Towards Empowerment and Community.* Toronto: University of Toronto Press.

Nightingale, D. S., and Mikelson, K. S. (2000): *An Overview of Research Related to Wisconsin Works (W-2).* Washington, DC: Urban Institute.

NMHA (2002a). "Advance Directives Help Prevent Psychiatric Crises and Promote Recovery." Press release. At *www.nmha.org.*

——— (2002b). "New Program Will Support Recovery for People with Mental Illness." Press release. At *www.nmha.org.*

Odegard, B. O., and Keith, G. M. (1940). *A History of the State Board of Control of Wisconsin and the State Institutions, 1849–1939.* Madison: State Board of Control.

O'Hagan, M. (2001). *Recovery Competencies for New Zealand Mental Health Workers.* Wellington, NZ: Mental Health Commission.

Ohio Department of Mental Health (1999). "Emerging Best Practices."

Oliver, M. (1990). *The Politics of Disablement: A Sociological Approach.* London: Macmillan.

Peters, L., and Fallon, P. (1994). "The Journey of Recovery." In *Feminist Perspectives on Eating Disorders,* ed. P. Fallon, M. A. Katzman, and S. C. Wooley. New York: Guilford.

Peyser, H. (2001). "What Is Recovery: A Commentary." *Psychiatric Services* 52 (4): 486–87.

Porter, R. (1987). *A Social History of Madness: The World through the Eyes of the Insane.* New York: Weidenfeld and Nicolson.

Practitioner Competencies in a Recovery-Oriented Mental Health System (2002). Unpublished document. Developed by the Recovery Implementation Task Force and Recovery in Action. Wisconsin: Wisconsin Bureau of Community Mental Health.

President's New Freedom Commission on Mental Health (2003). *Achieving the Promise: Transforming Mental Health Care in America.* Rockville, MD: President's New Freedom Commission on Mental Health.

Ralph, R. O. (2000). "Review of Recovery Literature: A Synthesis of a Sample of Recovery Literature 2000." National Technical Assistance Center for State Mental Health Planning, National Association for State Mental Health Program Directors.

Ralph, R. O., Kidder, K., and Phillips, D. (2000). "Can We Measure Recovery?: A Compendium of Recovery and Recovery-Related Instruments." Evaluation Center at HSRI. Center for Mental Health Services.

Rapping, E. (1996). *The Culture of Recovery: Making Sense of the Self-Help Movement in Women's Lives.* Boston: Beacon.

Ratey, J. J., Sands, S., and O'Driscoll, G. (1986). "The Phenomenology of Recovery in a Chronic Schizophrenic." *Psychiatry* 44: 277–89.

Reaume, G. (2000). *Remembrance of Patients Past: Patient Life at the Toronto Hospital for the Insane, 1870–1940.* Don Mills, ON: Oxford University Press Canada.

Recovery Advisory Group (1999). "Recovery Model: A Work in Process." At *www.mhsip.org.*

Recovery and the Mental Health Consumer Movement in Wisconsin (2001). Bureau of Community Mental Health. Wisconsin Department of Health and Family Services. Madison, WI.

Recovery Clearinghouse Study Project: Proposal for Developing a Wisconsin Clearinghouse on Recovery (undated). The Grassroots Empowerment Project, Wisconsin Bureau of Community Mental Health, and Recovery Task Force. Madison, WI.

Recovery-Oriented System Assessment (2003). Unpublished document.

Report of the Subcommittee on Consumer Issues: Shifting to a Recovery-Based Continuum of Community Care (2003). New Freedom Commission on Mental Health. Accessed at *www.mentalhealthcommission.gov.*

Rhode Island Department of Mental Health, Retardation, and Hospitals. *RI*Cover. Undated document.

Ridgway, P. (2001). "ReStorying Psychiatric Disability: Learning from First-Person Recovery Narratives." *Psychiatric Rehabilitation Journal* 24 (4): 335–43.

Robison, D. W. (1980). *Wisconsin and the Mentally Ill: A History of the "Wisconsin Plan" of State and County Care, 1860–1915.* New York: Arno.

Rochefort, D. A. (1993). *From Poorhouses to Homelessness: Policy Analysis and Mental Health Care.* Westport, CT: Auburn House.

Rodgers, D. T. (1982). "In Search of Progressivism." *Reviews in American History* 10 (4): 113–32.

Rogers, E. S., et al. (1997). "A Consumer-Constructed Scale to Measure Empowerment Among Users of Mental Health Services." *Psychiatric Services* 48 (8): 1042–47.

Roschke, R. (2000). *History, Principles, and Historical Themes of the Consumer/ Survivor Movement.* Report to the Bureau of Community Mental Health. Madison, WI.

Saenger, G. (1970). "Factors in Recovery of Untreated Psychiatric Patients." *Psychiatric Quarterly* 44 (1): 13–25.

Satel, S. (2002). *PC, M.D.: How Political Correctness Is Corrupting Medicine.* New York: Basic Books.

Schatzman, L. (1991). "Dimensional Analysis: Notes on an Alternative Approach to the Grounding of a Theory in Qualitative Research." In *Social Organization and Social Process: Essays in Honor of Anselm Strauss,* ed. D. R. Maines. New York: Aldine De Gruyter.

Scull, A. (1977). *Decarceration: Community Treatment and the Deviant: A Radical View.* Englewood Cliffs, NJ: Prentice-Hall.

——— (1979). *Museums of Madness: The Social Organization of Insanity in Nineteenth-Century England.* London: Allen Lane.

Sicherman, B. (1980). *The Quest for Mental Health in America, 1880–1917.* New York: Arno.

Smith, M. K. (2000). "Recovery from a Severe Psychiatric Disability: Findings of a Qualitative Study." *Psychiatric Rehabilitation Journal* 24 (2): 149–58.

Snyder, C. R., et al. (1991). "The Will and the Ways: Development and Validation of an Individual-Differences Measure of Hope." *Journal of Personality and Social Psychology* 60 (4): 570–85.

Spector, M., and Kitsuse, J. I. (1987). *Constructing Social Problems*. New York: Aldine De Gruyter.

Stein, L. I., and Ganser, L. J. (1983). "Wisconsin's System for Funding Mental Health Services." In *Unified Mental Health Systems: Utopia Unrealized*, ed. J. A. Talbott. New Directions for Mental Health Services 18. San Francisco: Jossey-Bass.

Stone, D. (1984). *The Disabled State*. Philadelphia: Temple University Press.

Strauss, A. (1978a). "A Social World Perspective." *Studies in Symbolic Interaction* 1: 119–28.

———— (1978b). *Negotiations: Varieties, Contexts, Processes, and Social Order*. San Francisco: Jossey-Bass.

———— (1982). "Social Worlds and Legitimation Processes." *Studies in Symbolic Interaction* 4: 171–90.

———— (1984). "Social Worlds and Their Segmentation Processes." *Studies in Symbolic Interaction* 5: 123–39.

———— (1987). *Qualitative Analysis for Social Scientists*. Cambridge: Cambridge University Press.

———— (1993). *Continual Permutations of Action*. New York: Aldine De Gruyter.

Strauss, J. S., Bartko, J. J., and Carpenter, W. (1981). "New Directions in Diagnosis: The Longitudinal Processes of Schizophrenia." *American Journal of Psychiatry* 138 (7): 954–58.

Street, P. (1997). *Only Work Should Pay: The Recent History and Future of Welfare Reform in Six Midwestern States*. Northern Illinois University, Office for Social Policy Research.

Tenney, L. J. (2000). "It Has to Be about Choice." *JCLP/In Session: Psychotherapy in Practice* 56 (11): 1433–45.

Thompson, K. S., Griffith, E. E. H., and Leaf, P. J. (1990). "A Historical Review of the Madison Model of Community Care." *Hospital and Community Psychiatry* 41 (6): 625–33.

Thwaites, R. G. (1900). *The University of Wisconsin: Its History and Its Alumni*. Madison: J. N. Purcell.

Tooth, B. A., Kalyanansundaram, V., and Glover, H. (1997). *Recovery from Schizophrenia: A Consumer Perspective*. Final Report to the Health and Human Services Research and Development Grants Program. Centre for Mental Health Nursing Research. Queensland University of Technology, Red Hill, Australia.

Toronto-Peel Mental Health Reform Implementation Task Force. *On the Way to "Making It Happen": Phase 1 Consultation Document*. March 2002.

Torrey, W. C., and Wyzik, P. (2000). "The Recovery Vision as a Service Improvement Guide for Community Mental Health Center Providers." *Community Mental Health Journal* 36 (2): 209–16.

Trainor, J., Pomeroy, E., and Pape, B. (1993). "A New Framework for Support." Canadian Mental Health Association.

Tuke, S. (1813). *Description of the Retreat, An Institution Near York for Insane Persons of the Society of Friends*. York: W. Alexander.

Turner-Crowson, J., and Wallcraft, J. (2002). "The Recovery Vision for Mental Health Services and Research: A British Perspective." *Psychiatric Rehabilitation Journal* 25 (3): 245–54.

Van Tosh, L., and del Vecchio, P. (2000). *Consumer-Operated Self-Help Programs: A Technical Report*. Rockville, MD: Center for Mental Health Services.

Vermont Legislative Summer Study Committee (1996). "A Position Paper on Recovery and Psychiatric Disability."

Warner, R. (1994). *Recovery from Schizophrenia: Psychiatry and Political Economy*. London: Routledge.

WCA (Wisconsin Coalition for Advocacy) (2001). *Movin' On: Stories from the Recovery Road*. Madison: Advocate Media.

Weller, S. C., and Romney, A. K. (1988). *Systematic Data Collection*. Newbury Park, CA: Sage.

Weingarten, R. (2002). "Writing about Our Lives: Stories of Work and Recovery." Presented at the IAPSRS Annual Meeting. Toronto, ON. June 2002.

Williams, C. C., and Collins, A. A. (1999). "Defining New Frameworks for Psychosocial Intervention." *Psychiatry* 62: 61–78.

Wing, J. K., and Morris, B. (1981). "Clinical Basis of Rehabilitation." In *Handbook of Psychiatric Rehabilitation Practice*, ed. J. K. Wing and B. Morris. Oxford: Oxford University Press.

Wisconsin Department of Health and Family Services (1996a). *Designing Managed Care Models for Persons with Mental Illness and Substance Abuse: A Concept Paper*. Madison.

——— (1996b). *Wisconsin Community Service Programs Clients and Expenditures for 1995*. Human Services Reporting System. Madison.

Wisconsin Department of Health and Social Services (1990). *Act 339 Managed Care Plan for Alcohol and Other Drug Abuse and Mental Health*. Madison.

——— (1994). *1994 State Plan, Section II "Wisconsin Mental Health System."* Madison.

Wisconsin Department of Public Welfare (1952). *Institutional Care of Psychiatric Patients in Wisconsin*. Madison.

——— (1958). *Report of the Division of Mental Hygiene 1950–1957*. Madison.

Wisconsin Office of the Governor (1996). Executive Order 282, "Relating to the Creation of the Governor's Blue Ribbon Commission on Mental Health Care." May 13.

Wood, M. (1989). "Early Leaders in Mental Health Reform." *Milwaukee History* 12 (2): 42–49.

Young, S. L., and Ensing, D. S. (1999). "Exploring Recovery from the Perspective of People with Psychiatric Disabilities." *Psychiatric Rehabilitation Journal* 22 (3): 219–31.

Young, S. L., Ensing, D. S., and Bullock, W. A. (1999). "The Mental Health Recovery Measure." Toledo, OH: University of Toledo, Department of Psychology.

Zola, I. K. (1982). *Missing Pieces: A Chronicle of Living with a Disability*. Philadelphia: Temple University Press.

INDEX